SAADIA GAON • YEHUDAH HALEVI •

LURIA • BAAL SHEM TOV • MOSES ME

AM • HERMANN COHEN • FRANZ ROSE

ABRAHAM ISAAC KOOK • ABRAHAM HE

ON • YEHUDAH HALEVI • MAIMONIDES

SHEM TOV • MOSES MENDELSSOHN • T

COHEN • FRANZ ROSENZWEIG • MART

KOOK • ABRAHAM HESCHEL • MORDEC

EVI • MAIMONIDES • MOSES DE LEON

MENDELSSOHN • THEODOR HERZL • A

OSENZWEIG • MARTIN BUBER • LEO BA

HESCHEL • MORDECAI KAPLAN • SAA

DES • MOSES DE LEON • ISAAC LURIA

I • THEODOR HERZL • AHAD HAAM • H

ARTIN BUBER • LEO BAECK • ABRAHA

RDECAI KAPLAN • SAADIA GAON • YEH

LEON • ISAAC LURIA • BAAL SHEM T

L • AHAD HAAM • HERMANN COHEN • F

O BAECK • ABRAHAM ISAAC KOOK • A

AADIA GAON • YEHUDAH HALEVI • M

GREAT JEWISH THINKERS
THEIR LIVES AND WORK

Naomi Pasachoff

BEHRMAN HOUSE, INC.
WEST ORANGE, NEW JERSEY

Project Editor: William Cutter, Ph.D.

Designed by Richard Stalzer Associates, Ltd.

Published by Behrman House, Inc.
235 Watchung Avenue
West Orange, New Jersey 07052

Library of Congress Cataloging-in-Publication Data:

Pasachoff, Naomi E.
      Great Jewish Thinkers: Their Lives and Work / by Naomi Pasachoff
          p.   cm.
      ISBN 0-87441-529-2
      1. Rabbis—Biography. 2. Philosophers, Jewish—Biography.
      3. Jewish scholars—Biography. 4. Philosophy, Jewish—History.
      5. Jews—Intellectual life. 6. Civilization—Jewish influences.
      I. Title
      BM750.P27 1992
      296.3'092'2—dc20
      [B]

                                                                    92-30148
                                                                          CIP

Manufactured in the United States of America

1 2 3 4 5 6
92 93 94 95 96

DEDICATION

To my father, Isaac Schwartz,
on the occasion of his eightieth birthday.
His lifelong dedication to Jewish learning
for its own sake
has been an inspiration.

CONTENTS

The author makes grateful acknowledgment to the following:

B'nai B'rith, for permission to quote from *Great Jewish Personalities in Ancient and Medieval Times*, ed. Simon Noveck, Copyright 1960 by the B'nai B'rith Department of Adult Jewish Education; from *Great Jewish Personalities in Ancient and Medieval Times*, ed. Simon Noveck, Copyright 1960 by the B'nai B'rith Department of Adult Jewish Education; from *Contemporary Jewish Thought: A Reader*, ed. Simon Noveck, Copyright 1963 by the B'nai B'rith Department of Adult Jewish Education; from *Great Jewish Thinkers of the Twentieth Century*, ed. Simon Noveck, Copyright 1963 by the B'nai B'rith Department of Adult Jewish Education; from *Reason and Hope: Selections from the Jewish Writings of Hermann Cohen*, trans. Eva Jospe, Schocken 1971, Copyright 1971 by the B'nai B'rith Department of Adult Jewish Education.

Columbia University Press, for permission to quote from *Studies in Medieval Jewish Philosophy*, Israel Efros, Copyright 1974, Columbia University Press, New York.

Farrar, Straus & Giroux, Inc., for permission to quote from *The Labyrinth of Exile: A Life of Theodor Herzl* by Ernest Pawel. Copyright © 1989 by Ernst Pawel. Reprinted by permission of Farrar, Straus & Giroux, Inc.

Georges Borchardt, Inc., for permission to quote from *Martin Buber's Life and Work: The Middle Years* (vol. 2) and *The Later Years* (vol. 3) by Maurice Friedman. Reprinted by permission of Georges Borchardt, Inc. on behalf of the author. Copyright © 1983 by Maurice Friedman.

Arthur Hertzberg, for permission to quote from *The Zionist Idea: A Historical Analysis and Reader*, A Temple Book, Atheneum. Copyright 1959 by Arthur Hertzberg.

Humanities Press International, Inc., Atlantic Highlands, N.J., for permission to quote from *Eclipse of God: Studies in the Relations Between Religion and Philosophy* by Martin Buber.

Louis Jacobs, for permission to quote from *Jewish Ethics, Philosophy and Mysticism*, Behrman House, Copyright 1969 by Louis Jacobs, and from *A Jewish Theology*, Behrman House, Copyright 1973 by Louis Jacobs.

James Clarke & Co., Ltd—Lutterworth Press, for permission to quote from *Martin Buber* by Ronald Gregor Smith, Copyright © 1975 by Ronald Gregor Smith.

Jewish Publication Society, for permission to quote from *Selected Poems of Jehudah Halevi*, trans. Nina Salaman, ed. Heinrich Brody, 1974; from *Three Jewish Philosophers*, eds. Hans Lewy, Alexander Altmann, Isaak Heinemann, 1960, with Meridian Books, Inc.; from *Selected Essays of Ahad HaAm*, trans. and ed. Leon Simon, 1970; and from Leon Simon, *Ahad HaAm—Asher Ginzberg: A Biography*, 1960.

Macmillan Publishing Company, for permission to quote from *I and Thou* by Martin Buber, translated by Walter Kaufmann. Reprinted with permission of Charles Scribner's Sons, an imprint of Macmillan Publishing Company. Translation Copyright © 1970 Charles Scribner's Sons.

New Directions Publishing Corporation, for permission to quote from Alan Unterman, *The Wisdom of the Jewish Mystics*. Copyright © 1976 by Alan Unterman. Reprinted by permission of New Directions Publishing Corporation.

Paulist Press, for permission to quote from *Zohar: The Book of Enlightenment*, Daniel Chanan Matt, trans. Copyright © 1983 by Daniel Chanan Matt. Used by permission of Paulist Press.

Random House, Inc. Alfred A. Knopf, Inc. for permission to quote from *Zohar, The Book of Splendor* by Gershom Scholem. Copyright 1949 and renewed 1977 by Schocken Books Inc. Reprinted by permission of Schocken Books, published by Pantheon Books, a division of Random House, Inc.; from *Franz Rosenzweig: His Life and Thought* by Nahum Glatzer, Copyright 1961 by Schocken Books Inc.; from *The Essence of Judaism* by Leo Baeck, Copyright 1948 by Schocken Books Inc.; and from *Israel and the World* by Martin Buber, Copyright 1948 by Schocken Books Inc.

Union of American Hebrew Congregations, for permission to quote from Leo Baeck, *This People Israel: The Meaning of Jewish Existence*, trans. Albert H. Friedlander. Copyright © 1964 by the Union of American Hebrew Congregations.

The author and publisher gratefully acknowledge the following sources of photographs for this book:

American Museum of Natural History, 55; Bill Aron, 25, 128; Beth Hatefutsoth, 21, 39, 131; Bibliotechque Nationale de Paris, 94; Bodleian Library, Oxford, 14; The British Library, 35, 181; German Information Center, 75; State of Israel Government News Office, 50, 59; Israel Board of Tourism, 103; Israel Office of Information, 171; Jewish National and University Library, 44; The Jewish Museum, London, 41; The Jewish Theological Seminary of America, 62, 174; The Library of Congress, 42, 52; Linda Mittel, 112; Tom McHugh/Photo Researchers, Inc.,120; New York Public Library, 76; Philadelphia Museum of Art/George W. Elkins Collection, 17; Eric Politzer, 148; Reconstructionist Rabbinical College, 190; Alan Reininger, 139; Superstock, 47; Jim Strong, 126; Jim Strong/Courtesy of the Leo Baeck Institute, 151, 155, 156; Suzanne Kaufman/JTS, 22; University of Judaism, 147; YIVO Institute for Jewish Research, 60, 160; Alan Zale/New York Times Pictures,197; Zalman Kleinman, 115; Zentralbibliotech Zurich, 81; Zionist Archives, 100, 105, 167.

FOREWORD

Change creates philosophy. Changes—in society, in technology, in ethics—all challenge old ideas and old ways of thinking. These challenges force religious and secular communities alike to understand and explain their beliefs to themselves and to the outside world. There will always be change, there will always be challenge, and there will always be philosophy.

Although we often forget, every age is a modern one when viewed through the eyes of those who live it. Even "ancient" worlds were modern in their own time. Each of these "modern times" introduces new technology, new social practices, and new ways of thinking. These, in turn, challenge traditional beliefs and practices. This was just as true in the ninth century as it is today, and it will be just as true in the centuries to come.

Two thousand years ago rural life was changing to city life, and Jews were meeting people from other cultures and societies who challenged their ideas of how to live and what to believe. Jews in turn challenged these cultures, in an endless cycle of influencing and being influenced. The earliest Jewish thinker mentioned in this book, Saadia Gaon, was the leader of an important community in Babylonia that had begun to settle there after the destruction of the Temple. He had to take ancient Jewish ideas, and find a way to fit them into his "modern" world. This process has never stopped, and never will.

Consider the changes that Jews have experienced throughout history: the encounter with the Arab culture and the Moslem religion during the early middle ages; the meeting with Catholic philosophers during the twelfth and thirteenth centuries; exposure to the fabulous commercial progress and cultural achievements of the Renaissance; and the more modern encounter with the diverse and free culture of Western Europe at the beginning of the twentieth century. All of these exchanges transformed society, forcing the leaders and scholars of the day to reexamine their beliefs. In many ways, the challenges faced by Judaism were no different from those faced by other cultures that interacted with the rest of the world.

But there was at least one unique aspect to the challenge facing the Jews: Judaism based its culture on a reverence for its history and its traditions and a belief that God's teachings were given at Mount Sinai. So Judaism had a special kind of problem: how to turn toward the future—adapt to it—while still facing the past with respect and with awe.

The development of Jewish thought is in many ways similar to the evolution we see in the world of music. Music is always presenting us with new rhythms and harmonies. But it is also deeply rooted in the achievements of past musicians. When I was growing up, jazz was revolutionary music, and my teachers had to point out to us that some of it had existed, in somewhat different form, in earlier classical music. Today various forms of rock music seem entirely new, but in fact grew out of some of the jazz sounds and rhythms that my parents considered revolutionary. In every aspect of life new ideas struggle against older ones. Jewish thought is no exception; it simply provides some of the more interesting examples.

This book, *Great Jewish Thinkers,* celebrates Judaism's ability to adapt and grow in response to new surroundings without giving up its precious history and legacy. The book honors the Jewish belief that the past is a model for the present. Dr. Naomi Pasachoff writes about sixteen individuals who struggled with changing times and who—because they were successful in their struggle—earned the label "great."

Some of the more modern people mentioned in the book are still writing and speaking publicly today. Because we continue to live through changes in our society, and because these modern thinkers are still wrestling with the problems of that change, we do not yet know who will earn the label "great." But we will all have the opportunity in the months and years ahead to learn about them and, perhaps, learn with them, as they continue to struggle with the challenge. And perhaps some of the readers of this book will be among the people who—tomorrow—help us think about Judaism and its future.

RABBI WILLIAM CUTTER
Professor of Education and Hebrew Literature
Hebrew Union College-Jewish Institute of Religion

Los Angeles, California
1 Elul 5752

ACKNOWLEDGMENTS

Many different people, playing a variety of roles, have had a hand in helping this book see the light of day. Particular thanks are due James A. Quitslund, who as Associate Director of the Institute for Advanced Study, enabled me to use the libraries not only of the Institute but also of Princeton University and the Princeton Theological Seminary. Professor Jacob Neusner, whom I met when he and my husband were members at the Institute, has been a source of professional and personal support ever since.

At Williams College, Professor Jacob Meskin's reading list for his course on modern Jewish philosophy helped shape my thoughts for the epilogue. Also for their contribution to the epilogue, I would like to thank the Jewish community in Honolulu, Hawaii, for their reactions to my 1990 Havdallah talk on post-Holocaust theology.

At Behrman House, Jacob Behrman agreed that the book was worthy of being written and helped me shape the initial chapters. Under David Behrman's expert guidance, the book assumed its present shape.

I owe a special debt of thanks to Rabbi William Cutter. While every chapter is better for his intellectual insights, I particularly appreciate his contribution to the shape and content of the epilogue. His friendship and support have helped sustain me throughout the writing of the book.

The members of my family also contributed to the development of the book in different ways. I would like to thank my daughter Eloise for class-testing the material on Leo Baeck in her tenth-grade English class at Princeton High School. I thank her, too, for inviting me some years later to hear her Harvard professor, Jay Harris, lecture on the Baal Shem Tov and on Ahad HaAm. My daughter Deborah's own research in preparing for the D'var Torah on the occasion of her Bat Mitzvah in 1990 shed light on my understanding of Maimonides' interpretation of the role of sacrifice. Her research also helped me understand the contribution to Jewish thought of the Buber-Rosenzweig translation of the Bible. My husband, Jay, patiently read all of the chapters in various stages, and made many useful comments.

Finally, I thank my parents, Anna Jacobson Schwartz and Isaac Schwartz. They not only provided me with an education at Ramaz School and at Camp Massad, but their devotion to scholarship in their own endeavors also made an indelible mark on me from an early age.

—N.P.

INTRODUCTION

Being Jewish means different things to different people. Some Jews insist that every religious law they observe must have a reasonable explanation. Some look to Judaism to help them in their personal search for God. Others think Judaism is less an individual matter than it is a community concern. For many, Judaism is not only a religion but also a civilization. National and political issues are as important to this view of Judaism as are purely religious ones.

Great Jewish Thinkers is an introduction to sixteen thinkers who, over a period of more than a thousand years, developed different approaches to what it means to be Jewish. In an epilogue, it presents three issues of concern to today's Jewish thinkers.

In trying to make sense of what it means to be Jewish and to live a Jewish life, the thinkers introduced here asked questions about God, about the Torah, and about the Jewish people. In one way or another, all of them address questions such as these: What is God like, and what role does God play in a Jew's life? What does it mean to say that God revealed the Torah to the Jews? Is the Torah fixed for all time? What do the Torah's *mitzvot* really signify? What exactly makes the Jews into a people—is it their religion alone, or do Jewish culture and Jewish nationhood in some larger sense also enter the picture?

Three strands of thought dominate the work of the thinkers presented here. Some thinkers stress the importance of reason in Judaism. They seek to identify the logic underlying each of the teachings of Judaism. Others find reason beside the point. Their concern is to find in Judaism a means for the individual Jew to make personal contact with God. For a third group of thinkers, it is the Jewish nation that is the basic ingredient in Judaism. They are all presented here in the order in which they lived—and made their contributions to Jewish thought and Jewish life. Each chapter discusses not only key aspects of a thinker's system of thought but also how the thinker's environment helped form that system, as well as the effect of that system on the Jewish community and the world at large.

A majority of the thinkers in this book formed their ideas in reaction to what was going on in the non-Jewish world. The word *philosophy* comes from the Greek for "love of wisdom." Most Jewish thinkers have combined traditional Jewish sources with ideas from other cultures. They have then shaped those ideas to make them uniquely applicable to the needs and concerns of the Jewish community. Some of them reacted to challenges from the Muslim or the Christian majority around them. Some responded to anti-Semitism and oppression of the Jews. Still others, seeing a decline in Jewish life, tried to shape Judaism in terms more meaningful for their times.

Obviously, not every thinker who is Jewish has been included in the scope of this book. Many wise and educated people who are born Jewish dedicate themselves to the life of the mind, but not all choose to deal with issues that are specifically Jewish. This book focuses on some of the best-known and most influential Jewish thinkers who developed systems of thought on Jewish themes. All those included helped shape the ways Jews have thought of themselves and continue to think of themselves. Many who lived at more or less the same time in the same country asked different questions about Judaism and reached very different conclusions. To many people, one of the most appealing aspects of Judaism is that it encourages people to ask questions, to continue to look at traditional texts in new ways. In fact, knowledgeable arguments are the foundation of Jewish learning. The Talmud, for example, records the opinions even of rabbis who deviate from the accepted conclusion. According to the rabbis of twenty centuries ago, "An argument for the sake of heaven must survive." Readers, then, should not necessarily be searching for the "right" approach to Judaism in this book. Indeed, not every reader will agree with all the methods or conclusions of every thinker. But readers may find help in defining their own Jewishness simply by paying attention to the questions asked. Perhaps readers will also find that both the lives and the thoughts of these thinkers can guide them in their search for a meaningful Jewish existence.

We are approaching the twenty-first century, a time when life will be different from today in ways we cannot imagine. How will the Jewish tradition, which was developed in an ancient time, adapt to the speed of our lives, the complicated relations among people, and the changing role of women and children? Is there still a place in a world of superhighways and rocket ships for the *mitzvot* that began in a world of camels and caravans? It is certain that *mitzvot* will have a place in tomorrow's world; the struggle to demonstrate that fact is what makes philosophy so interesting.

CHAPTER

1 SAADIA GAON

882 – 942

Born in Egypt, Saadia is often considered the father of Jewish philosophy. In fact, his many scholarly works explore a wide range of subjects: he produced the first Hebrew dictionary, and even today Arabic-speaking Jews use his translation of the Bible into Arabic. The only foreigner to be chosen head of one of the two great Babylonian academies of Jewish learning, he was the first important thinker to maintain that Judaism is a religion based on reason.

A Glimpse into Saadia's Times

Dangers Facing Judaism in a Changing World

Saadia was born about 250 years after the death of Muhammad, the founder of the Muslim (Islamic) religion. During those years, Muhammad's followers had undertaken a "holy war" to spread Islam, building a vast empire that extended from northern Spain to India.

Millions of Muslims, living in Iraq, Persia, Palestine, North Africa, Syria, and Spain, had established a strong civilization, translating and studying the works of ancient Greek philosophers and scientists, such as Aristotle. Building on the basis of these great forerunners, Muslim scholars were continuing to develop mathematics, astronomy, philosophy, and literature.

Increasingly, Arabic-speaking Jews began to feel that to be modern and well educated meant to be Muslim, and they saw the Jewish religion as lagging behind the times. Some of these Jews left Judaism altogether; others felt their faith was being undermined but were at a loss how to respond.

A large number of sects—small break away groups—sprang up among the Jews in the Islamic world. The most successful of these sects called itself the Karaites (from the Hebrew *Mikra,* or "Scriptures"). The Karaites felt that Jews should base their religion strictly on the Torah, that the Bible was the only text to live by, and that additional interpretations of the Bible were inauthentic. They rejected the authority of the Talmud, claiming it was the invention of the rabbis and did not reflect God's intent.

The challenge to Judaism thus came from two directions. Some Jews were attracted to Islam because it seemed more sophisticated than Judaism. Others were attracted to the Karaites' beliefs, since they seemed more central and fundamental than the Jewish heritage. Saadia rose to the challenge by weaving together a response that satisfied both sides.

Saadia Confronts the Muslim and Karaite Challenges

Saadia took several steps to show his Arabic-speaking fellow Jews that their religion and way of life were sophisticated, were not outmoded, and had not been supplanted by Islam. He not only translated the Bible into Arabic, but he also wrote a biblical commentary that helped answer some of the religious and philosophical questions

> " *Whatever is in the Scriptures must be taken literally except where it contradicts sensation, reason, other passages of the Bible, or tradition; in such cases, there is reward for a harmonizing interpretation.* "
>
> *Book of Beliefs and Opinions,* trans. Israel Efros

> **"** *I implore the scholar who may read this book to correct any mistake he will find and amend any obscurity of expression. He should not feel restrained because this is not his book, or because I anticipated him in shedding light on subjects which were not clear to him. For the wise care tenderly for wisdom and feel for it as members of the same family are attached to one another.* **"**
>
> Book of Beliefs and Opinions, trans. Trude Weiss-Rosmarin

of troubled readers. He also translated the Jewish prayers and organized them into an Arabic prayer book, adding explanations about their history and importance.

Taking note of the Muslim interest in language and grammar, and suspecting that Jews might feel Islamic scholarship outshone Jewish work in these areas, Saadia also compiled the first Hebrew dictionary and wrote a book setting up the basic rules of Hebrew grammar. He hoped that these works would help revive an interest in Hebrew studies. In general, Saadia did whatever he could to show that Judaism was a living faith and culture, capable of responding to the demands of the times.

Islam challenged Judaism to move forward, and Saadia was ready to meet that challenge. But the Karaite sect challenged Judaism by insisting that all but its most distant roots were inauthentic, by rejecting the Talmud and rabbinic interpretations in favor of total reliance on the Bible itself. In doing so, the Karaites threatened to make Judaism a religion of the past. For Saadia, to the contrary, Judaism needed to be reinterpreted in every age in order to keep up with new demands. The Talmud and later Talmudic commentaries were a way of keeping Judaism in step with the outside world. Saadia wrote several direct refutations of the Karaite position, and many arguments throughout his works were also aimed at Karaite beliefs.

In sum, Saadia's large body of writing had one general purpose: to make it possible for thoughtful Jews to feel that Judaism was a living culture, capable of continuous development in response to a changing world.

SAADIA'S PHILOSOPHY: REASON, FREE WILL, AND TORAH

Are the Torah and Human Reason Compatible?

Written in Arabic, the greatest of Saadia's works is his *Book of Beliefs and Opinions.* It was the first major effort to show that, far from conflicting with one another, reason and Judaism are both ways of reaching the truth. In fact, Saadia felt it was every Jew's duty to put even basic religious beliefs to the test of reason.

Saadia asks many of the questions that Jews today still ponder. Why, for example, did God bother giving the Jews the Torah? Couldn't they have achieved happy and fulfilling lives without it? Saadia observed that people take greater pleasure in their achievements, both simple and profound, when they feel they have earned them. For this reason, without the Torah's commandments to follow, Jews could not

Life Line by Winslow Homer

experience the joys and achievements that are the rewards of following those commandments.

Daily experience confirms Saadia's argument. Adults feel more secure with a job promotion if it really reflects their worth and is not merely the whim of an employer; similarly, students are more pleased with good grades that they feel they have earned than with those they did not deserve. Just as hard physical labor enhances the enjoyment people take in simple rewards like a cold drink, reasoned Saadia, people enjoy the pleasures of the world more after having observed the Torah's laws.

Still, however important the Torah may be as a basis for happiness, according to Saadia, human reason—the use of logic and common-sense judgment—is just as valuable a source of truth. This belief leads to another question: Why did God bother to give the Torah's laws if human minds alone are able to outline a similar code of life? The answer, says Saadia, is twofold. First, not everyone has fully developed powers of rational judgment. To follow the proper path, some require a Torah. Second, even good thinkers think slowly and sometimes make mistakes: it would have taken human beings a very long time to develop on their own a code as effective as the Torah's.

Saadia was a firm believer in free will. But free will implies choice, and Saadia wrote that "I saw men who were submerged in seas of doubt and covered by the waters of confusion, and there was no diver to raise them up from the depths and no swimmer to take hold of their hands and bring them ashore." Saadia said it was his "duty and obligation to help them and guide them toward the truth."

Saadia divides the Torah's laws into two groups. One group regulates behavior that human reason recognizes as good or bad, regardless of whether it is permitted or forbidden by the Torah. For example, common sense suggests that if murder were permissible, humanity's very existence would be threatened. As a result, the Torah forbids murder. But it also goes beyond basic common-sense principles—as do the Talmud and the teachings of later rabbis—furnishing details that help us incorporate the principles into our daily lives.

A second group of laws, such as observing the Sabbath and other holidays, controls behavior that human reason alone would consider neither right nor wrong: God's commandment is what makes such behavior one or the other. Saadia insists that careful examination would prove that each of these laws yields extremely beneficial effects. For example, setting aside certain days as nonworking creates the leisure time necessary for learning, and for developing friendships and family relationships.

Thus Saadia argues that even when people cannot figure out the purpose of such laws, they should gladly obey them. After all, reasonable people should be grateful for all that God has done for them. How better to show thankfulness than by obeying divine commands?

Committed Jews are sometimes upset to discover some Torah passages that seem not to make sense or seem to contradict other passages. Saadia, too, had such concerns, which led him to maintain firmly that wherever the Torah seems to conflict with reason, a Jew's duty is to *interpret* the text, to figure out what the real meaning is. He assumes that careful study will always reveal a sensible explanation.

For example, Saadia was troubled by the harshness of a passage from the Book of Proverbs (23:9), "Speak not in the ears of a fool, for a fool will despise the wisdom of your words." Saadia did not feel that intellectually gifted people should disdain those less gifted, and he could not believe that the Torah would recommend such disdain. So he interpreted the passage as follows: one must use an easier vocabulary and simpler explanations when talking to a less educated person.

Free Will and Responsibility

A key aspect of Saadia's thought is his strong belief in free will— that the choice between right and wrong is ultimately ours. In this respect, his thought contrasts starkly with the belief of many medieval Muslims that everything people do is the result of Allah's will. This belief was not reasonable to Saadia, and he offered three arguments to prove that even if God knows in advance how people will act, people themselves are still responsible for their own behavior:

■ If God determined the choices people make from the start, what purpose would the commandments serve?

■ If God were responsible for good deeds and for evil, shouldn't the sinner be as worthy of reward as someone who is pure and virtuous? After all, each person would simply be carrying out God's decrees.

■ If God were responsible for a person's sins, any type of criminal could avoid guilt simply by claiming inability to overpower the divine influence.

Saadia was well aware of several passages in the Bible suggesting that people do *not* have free will and that God causes us to act the way we do. In line with his general approach, Saadia argued that what is called for in such cases is proper interpretation. For example, Saadia turned his attention to the famous verse in Exodus (7:3) where it is said that God will "harden Pharaoh's heart." According to Saadia, the verse does not mean that God forced Pharaoh to prevent the Israelites from leaving Egypt but, rather, that God kept Pharaoh physically strong so that the plagues would not kill him as they did many other Egyptians.

Similarly, in the book of Isaiah (63:17) God is asked, "Why do You make us stray from Your ways?" Saadia explains that the question really means "Do not judge us as those who stray."

In fact, Saadia believed so strongly in underlying freedom of choice that he saw the authority of the Torah as stemming less from its origin with God than from the covenant by which the Jews freely agreed to accept it. From the people's declaration at Mount Sinai, "All that the Lord has spoken we shall do" (Exodus 19:8), Saadia concludes that they could have decided to reject the Torah. Likewise, each day every Jew decides whether or not to live by the Torah's laws.

A Man of Principle and Compassion

Man of Principle

Very few legends have come down to us about Saadia. Instead, we have a true and rather dramatic story. Partly transmitted from Saadia's own telling, partly from that of his contemporaries, and partly from later trustworthy accounts, this story offers us a glimpse of the complex and very human qualities that made Saadia the man he was.

In present-day Israel the citizens have both civil leaders, such as the prime minister, and religious leaders, such as the chief rabbis; and Babylonian Jews had a similar arrangement. The highest civil authority of the Babylonian Jewish community was the exilarch ("leader of the exiled"). One of the exilarch's responsibilities was to appoint the community's two official spiritual leaders, the heads of the two famous Talmudic academies of Babylonia, one at Sura and the other at Pumbedita. Each leader had the title *gaon* ("excellency"—in modern Hebrew, the word means "genius").

In 928 the Exilarch David ben Zakkai appointed Saadia *gaon* of the academy at Sura. Saadia was not ben Zakkai's first choice; the scholar to whom he first extended the honor turned it down because he was very old and also blind. When ben Zakkai asked the scholar whom he should appoint, the old man gave mixed advice, indicating that while Saadia was by far the best scholar, he was not easy to get along with. Nevertheless, after first having Saadia solemnly promise never to oppose him, ben Zakkai offered Saadia the position.

For a few years the Exilarch ben Zakkai and Saadia worked side by side in perfect harmony. But then a rupture occurred. The exilarch made a ruling about how a large inheritance was to be distributed, and as payment he was to receive 10 percent of the money involved. Saadia thought the arrangement was distasteful and unethical, and he refused as *gaon* of Sura to sign a document endorsing it. The *gaon* of Pumbedita had signed it without hesitation, and Exilarch ben Zakkai was putting increasing pressure on Saadia to follow suit. He sent his son several times to try to win Saadia's approval, to no avail. Finally, ben Zakkai's son lost patience and threatened Saadia with force, and he was thrown out of Saadia's house.

Naturally, ben Zakkai was furious, and after announcing that Saadia was no longer *gaon*, he appointed a replacement. In turn, Saadia named a different exilarch to replace ben Zakkai. For two years, the Babylonian Jewish community was in upheaval, with two men claiming to be exilarch and two others claiming to be *gaon* of Sura. Each side was supported by different influential Jews. Finally, ben Zakkai managed to have the Muslim ruler remove Saadia from office.

Saadia's *Book of Beliefs and Opinions* —a masterful reflection on the interactions between Torah and reason that influenced thinkers for the next several centuries—was the result of the ensuing period of forced retirement. If not for this apparent misfortune in his life, Saadia might never have had the time to lay the foundation for the work of future philosophers.

Man of Compassion

Somewhat later, Saadia showed the capacity to put bitterness behind him. In 937 an outside party was able to make peace between him and ben Zakkai, and Saadia once again became the unquestioned *gaon* of Sura. Then in 940 ben Zakkai died; his death was followed within the year by that of his son. Realizing that ben Zakkai's son—the man who had once violently threatened him— had left behind a young child, Saadia took the boy into his home and raised him as his own child. Saadia put the bitterness of the past behind him, behaving with charity and compassion.

While Saadia is not as well-known today as the great Jewish thinker Maimonides (born nearly 200 years after Saadia's death), Maimonides was fully aware of his predecessor's stature. Summing up Saadia's achievements, Maimonides wrote, "If not for our master, Saadia Gaon, Torah would have been forgotten in Israel." Saadia's kindness to the grandson of his former enemy is surely an example of the spirit of Torah applied in daily life.

Saadia was able to develop peaceful relationships with former antagonists. Here Saadia and the exilarch David ben Zakkai reconcile in the palace of the caliph in Baghdad. Ben Zakkai had removed Saadia from his position as *gaon* of Sura, but later Saadia raised ben Zakkai's orphaned grandson as his own.

The Kuzari by Yehudah HaLevi

המאמר השלישי

CHAPTER 2

YEHUDAH HALEVI

1085 – 1141

Yehudah HaLevi was born in Toledo, Spain, and lived most of his life in Cordova, where a street is named Calle Juda Levi in his honor. He died in Egypt. Although we know that he practiced medicine for a living, the details of his life are not too clear. What we do have are many magnificent Hebrew poems and a unique book of philosophy constituting a lasting record of his ideas and feelings. Whereas Saadia introduced the view that Judaism is a religion of reason, Yehudah HaLevi was the first thinker to base his arguments on Jewish history.

FROM LOVE POET TO PATRIOT AND PHILOSOPHER

A Poet Transformed by Politics

Yehudah HaLevi was an unusual thinker: he expressed his ideas about the Jews, their land, and their God through works of literature, not philosophy. In fact, he is thought of mainly as a poet. His early poems are about friendship, love, and wine, revealing a young man uninvolved in politics or the problems of his people. In several, he answers his older critics, who complain that he is wasting his talent on worthless topics; he responds that they are appropriate for someone his age:

> Shall one whose years scarce number twenty-four
> Turn foe to pleasure and drink wine no more?

Occasionally, however, even his early poems reveal a concern with Jewish problems. For example, in one wedding song he compares the young couple's hopes of being united to the Jewish hope for an end to exile from *Eretz Yisrael*.

The young Yehudah HaLevi enjoyed poetry as a game, entering poetry contests like other poets of his time. His later poetry became an outlet for deep religious and political beliefs. What happened to cause the change?

" *Whoever accepts the Torah without scrutiny and argument is better off than whoever investigates and analyzes.* **"**

A Poet Marked by History

The Jewish community in Spain had flourished for many years under tolerant Muslim rule. But now the Jews were caught between the rise of Christianity and the invasion of a new, militant Muslim sect. To most Jews, the new Muslims seemed the worse of the two evils, and some joined Christian armies fighting their advance. But this enlistment had an unforeseen, bitterly ironic effect. Whenever the Christians lost a battle, they would blame the Jews, and Christian mobs would then attack the so-called traitors. One such attack resulted in the murder of Solomon ibn Farissol, an important Jewish scholar, who was the leader of the Jews of Castile, in the central part of Spain.

These events transformed the central theme of Yehudah HaLevi's poetry from love and friendship to Jewish honor. He considered this transformation the end of his innocence.

HaLevi's Poetry of Longing

Yehudah HaLevi was a Zionist before there was such a word. The political events of his day convinced him that the Jews of Spain were doomed and that only by a return to the Land of Israel could they lead meaningful lives. To express his sense of urgency, he created a new type of Hebrew poetry, claiming in one famous poem that he could not be a whole person in Spain: "My heart is in the East, and I am in the uttermost West." East, of course, is the direction toward which Jews in much of the world face when they pray because it is the direction of *Eretz Yisrael.*

Despite his conviction that he had to "ascend" eastward, HaLevi knew he would be giving up much by leaving Spain. He would be leaving his only child, a daughter, and her only son, named Yehudah after him, in the tradition of Spanish Jews. *Eretz Yisrael* at this time was a hard, inhospitable land, in ruins.

But he was convinced that God would restore Zion to its former glory:

> Happy is he that waiteth, that cometh nigh and seeth the rising
> Of thy light, when on him thy dawn shall break—
> That he may see the welfare of thy chosen, and rejoice
> In thy rejoicing, when thou turnest back unto thy olden youth.

The greatest of Yehudah HaLevi's poems focusing on Zion is still chanted in Jewish congregations around the world. It is part of the service for Tisha B'Av, the fast day recalling the destruction in Jerusalem of both the First and Second Temple, and it poignantly contrasts different aspects of his poems about Zion—his sorrow over Jerusalem's destruction along with his hope for its future:

> To wail for thine affliction I am like the jackals;
> But when I dream
> Of the return of thy captivity,
> I am a harp for thy songs.

Yehudah HaLevi's words continue to be meaningful to Jews today. When Jerusalem was reunified after the 1967 Six Day War, a popular song—"Jerusalem of Gold"—was written. Part of its refrain—"I am a harp for thy songs"—refers back to the words Yehudah HaLevi wrote more than 800 years before. Jews have never forgotten his message of hope for his people and their land.

HaLevi's Jewish Faith

Yehudah HaLevi's poems also express his feelings about what it means to worship God. While we might at first easily mistake many of his religious poems for love poems, the loving couple turns out to be God and Israel.

Several poems also deal with the mystery of looking for God. One poem opens with an apparent contradiction:

> O Lord, where shall I find Thee?
> All hidden and exalted is Thy place;
> And where shall I not find Thee?
> Full of Thy glory is the infinite space.

Yehudah HaLevi's God is not a distant figure, to be thought about at a scholar's desk, but rather an object of yearning:

> Longing, I sought Thy presence,
> Lord, with my whole heart did I call and pray,
> And going out toward Thee,
> I found Thee coming to me on the way. . . .

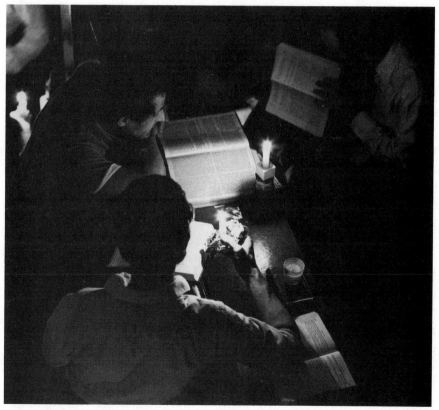

Tisha B'Av, Venice, California

HaLevi's poem ''Zionade'' is chanted throughout the world as part of the Tisha B'Av service commemorating the destruction of the First and Second Temples.

But while human beings can feel pangs of longing for the divine, they can never really comprehend its essence. The poet insists that since human understanding and reason are limited, people can never truly grasp the meaning of God's ways, which remain incomprehensible.

Another aspect of the religious theme in HaLevi's poetry is crucial to an understanding of his philosophy. In one poem he claims that his intimate relationship with God has deep roots in history—roots that extend back to the time when God gave the Torah at Sinai. According to the poet, his faith in God is so deep that it is as if he himself had been present at Sinai at the time of the giving of the Torah.

REASON IS NOT ENOUGH

Fiction Becomes Philosophy

Unlike the majority of Jewish thinkers, Yehudah HaLevi did not write books directly expressing his philosophy. Instead, he expressed his philosophy indirectly, through his poems and through a historical drama, *The Kuzari* ("The Khazar"). Like a play, *The Kuzari* consists of a series of conversations between Bulan, king of the Khazars, and a succession of scholars: a worldly philosopher, a Christian scholar, a Muslim scholar, and finally a Jewish scholar or rabbi.

King Bulan has twice had a disturbing dream—a voice from heaven has told him that although his intentions are good, his behavior is not. Seeking advice on how he should change his way of worship, he calls upon the worldly philosopher to advise him. When the philosopher tells him that the form of worship is unimportant, Bulan dismisses him. He invites the Christian and then the Muslim to argue the advantages of their religions, but each concedes that many of their beliefs are based on the Torah. Although the king has at first not intended to invite a Jew, knowing the Jews to be a despised people, he now changes his mind, and the arguments of the Jewish scholar convince him to accept Judaism, both for himself and for his people.

The Khazars were not a figment of Yehudah HaLevi's imagination. They were an actual Tartar tribe on the Volga River (in present-day Ukraine) who converted to Judaism in about the year 740. Yehudah HaLevi may have known about the tribe from two sources: a number of Jewish families in Cordova, where Yehudah HaLevi lived, claimed to be Khazarian descendants, and there were stories of a letter written about a hundred years before his birth by the great Spanish-Jewish statesman Hasdai ibn Shaprut to the last king of the Khazars. (The tribe was defeated by the duke of Kiev in 965.)

Although the existence of the Khazars and their conversion to Judaism are historical facts, the story as told in *The Kuzari* is a fictional version that reveals Yehudah HaLevi's philosophy. On the surface, the narrator of *The Kuzari* claims to be presenting historical research. He states, "As I found among the arguments of the Rabbi many which appealed to me and were in harmony with my opinions, I resolved to write them down as they had been spoken." In fact, there is no record of any discussion between a Jewish scholar and King Bulan. The arguments the scholar presents are HaLevi's own. He hints as much by having the narrator say, "The intelligent will understand me."

Why did HaLevi choose to present his philosophical views in this way? Was it simply a case of a poet's feeling more comfortable with storytelling? Was it a matter of caution in a time of growing religious warfare? We will never know for sure.

Certainly one possibility is that the story of the Khazars gave HaLevi the opportunity to imagine a contest between Judaism and the two world religions that had developed from it, Christianity and Islam. And he was sure that Judaism would prevail.

Revelation: Beyond Mere Reason

By profession, Yehudah HaLevi was a physician, and by virtue of his profession he believed that reason had a place in the world. For example, in mathematics and the sciences reason and experimentation are the proper tools for uncovering mysteries. But unlike Saadia, HaLevi also believed that God and Judaism require more than reason—more than the scientific or mathematical facts that reason can uncover—to be truly understood.

While reason can help people achieve faith in a single God, a God derived solely in this manner cannot care about human beings. In *The Kuzari,* HaLevi's views of the limitations of reason are shown in a scene in which King Bulan dismisses the worldly philosopher because of his "reasonable" arguments about God. The philosopher has told King Bulan that God cannot like or dislike human actions, cannot care about how people live their lives, and to make such a claim would indicate that the Holy One were less than perfect. The king knows better, however. After all, a heavenly voice has told him not once but twice that God is not pleased by his deeds even though his thoughts are good. Bulan tells the philosopher there must be a proper way of worshiping God.

The rabbi who convinces King Bulan to convert to Judaism does not argue against reason. To the contrary, he tells the king, "Heaven forbid that there should be anything in the Torah to contradict that which is manifest or proved!" On another occasion the rabbi says,

"Heaven forbid that we should assume what is impossible or that which reason rejects as being impossible." But the scholar refuses to use reason to prove the existence of God, since God will remain forever beyond reason's reach.

For Yehudah HaLevi, there is only one such proof: the revelation at Mount Sinai, when 600,000 Israelites heard God's voice. Prophets continued to experience God's presence during the biblical period, offering the Jewish people firsthand knowledge of God. Even after that historical period ended, the transmission of tradition continued, and continues to this day. For example, at the Passover seder every participant is instructed to imagine being one of those personally delivered

For HaLevi, the revelation at Mt. Sinai gave the Jewish people firsthand knowledge of the existence of God. HaLevi believed that this was the only possible proof of God's existence.

from slavery by God. Jewish tradition stresses that divine revelation was not a solitary event but something each generation is called upon to witness, and thus it provides each Jew with a direct link to God.

In other words, Judaism is based not on reason but on historical experience. The Israelites did not come to believe in God because they followed a logical argument. Rather, they experienced personal contact with God. And, unlike the God of the philosophers, who does not care about individual people and their deeds, the God that was revealed to the Israelites has a close relationship with humanity and desires an even closer relationship.

For Saadia Gaon, all Judaism's laws, even those laws not appearing so, can be defended on the basis of how rational they are upon deep reflection. But Yehudah HaLevi was not interested in proving that the commandments had such a basis; he believed profoundly that apparently unfathomable commandments are, in fact, *above* reason, which can never grasp the real purpose behind them. Jews should perform those commandments because doing so has spiritual consequences that reason also cannot grasp. For HaLevi, Judaism could never be explained by human reason alone—God and the Torah stand far above.

God of Reason and God of Revelation

The Torah refers to God in some places as *Elohim* and in others as *Adonai*, and Yehudah HaLevi believed that these two names reflected the limits of reason and the importance of revelation in understanding God. According to HaLevi, *Elohim* is the God of the philosophers, the God people find when they use their reasoning powers to analyze nature. This God is a distant one, not interested in human beings, and cannot be worshiped.

Adonai, on the other hand, is the personal name of the God of revelation. Those who know *Adonai* have experienced God in their own lives.

King Bulan claimed that only after listening to the Jewish scholar did he understand the difference between *Elohim* and *Adonai*: *Elohim* is the God of the philosophers, while *Adonai* is the God of Abraham. People can feel attached to *Elohim* on the basis of reason, since reason suggests that a divine intelligence rules the world. They may even feel awe for *Elohim* as ruler of the world. But *Elohim* demands nothing of them, and they will not suffer on behalf of this God. People who have experienced divine revelation long for *Adonai*. For this God, who demands much of them, they will even gladly give their lives.

> " *Man yearns for* Adonai *as a matter of love, taste, and conviction; while attachment to* Elohim *is the result of speculation. A feeling of the former kind invites its adherents to give their life for His sake and to prefer death to His absence. Speculation, however, makes veneration only a necessity as long as it entails no harm, but bears no pain for its sake.* "
>
> The Kuzari, trans. Louis Jacobs

LEGEND ROUNDS OUT HISTORY

To Egypt but Not Beyond

The Kuzari ends with the Jewish scholar telling King Bulan of his intention to leave for Jerusalem. *Eretz Yisrael*, he explains, is the most appropriate place for a Jew to be at one with God. Like the Jewish scholar, Yehudah HaLevi was drawn toward *Eretz Yisrael*.

A wealthy Egyptian Jew with worldwide trading connections helped HaLevi arrange an itinerary from Spain to *Eretz Yisrael*. The plan called for him to travel to Egypt by ship and to complete his journey by the land route to *Eretz Yisrael*. His poetry leaves behind a record both of the difficulties of the trip's first stage and of his faith in God. According to the poet, no sea voyager with a belief in God, the creator of the oceans, had any reason to fear.

After weathering stormy seas, the ship landed in Alexandria in early May 1140. The Alexandrian Jews received HaLevi with great honor and tried to convince him to stay. He spent several months in the house of a prosperous, well-known Jewish physician and judge. Then he moved on to Cairo, where the head of all the Egyptian Jews was his host.

Yehudah HaLevi's poems attest to the powerful effect Egypt had on him. After all, this was the land where many biblical miracles had taken place. Still, his verses make clear that not Egypt but only *Eretz Yisrael* is his ultimate goal and destination.

It seems, however, that Yehudah HaLevi never did get farther than Egypt. He died there, in July 1141, and was mourned by the local Jewish community.

Legend Achieves What History Did Not

Although Yehudah HaLevi died without fulfilling his dream, it was fulfilled in a popular legend that remains powerful today. In the late 1800s, more than 700 years after HaLevi's death, the German poet Heinrich Heine and the Hebrew poet Micah-Joseph Lebensohn each published a detailed version of the legend: When HaLevi first touched the soil of *Eretz Yisrael*, he removed his shoes so that his feet could make direct contact with the stones and dust. As he began to recite his poem to Zion, the one found in the Tisha B'Av service, an Arab horseman slew him.

Despite historical evidence to the contrary, this legend clings to the figure of Yehudah HaLevi. It seems to provide a suitable, if not a historically accurate, end to his life. His writings seem to foreshadow such a death. For example, the Khazar king's warning that the Jewish scholar's life will be at risk if he travels to the Land of Israel does not frighten the scholar. Death there, he claims, is more meaningful than so-called life elsewhere. Similarly, the scholar tells King Bulan that Jerusalem can be rebuilt only when Jews long so much for the city that they embrace her stones and dust. In the legend, Yehudah HaLevi does just that, thus suggesting that his death helped prepare for the re-building of Jerusalem.

It is not necessary to believe the legend, however, to see how Yehudah HaLevi helped bring about that goal. For more than 850 years his poems and philosophical work have helped instill a love of *Eretz Yisrael* in many Jews throughout the world.

CHAPTER

3 MAIMONIDES

1135 – 1204

Moses Maimonides was born in Cordova, Spain, moved to Morocco, and eventually settled in Egypt. He is generally considered the greatest Jewish philosopher; his masterpiece, *The Guide for the Perplexed,* was the first Jewish book since the Bible to become part of world literature. Written in Arabic and translated into Latin and Hebrew, it influenced Muslims and Christians as well as Jews. Maimonides is often called the Rambam, from the initial Hebrew letters of the words Rabbi Moses ben ("son of") Maimon; his father was an important Spanish rabbi and community leader.

REACHING UNDERSTANDING THROUGH REASON

Reason Should Guide the Perplexed

Maimonides knew that he was writing in the tradition of Saadia Gaon. In one of his shorter works, he praised the earlier philosopher for helping to save Judaism by using reason to solve questions troubling the "perplexed and misguided" Jews of that time. In *The Guide*, Maimonides seeks to help Jews of his own time who find themselves "perplexed and bewildered" by contradictions between what they find in the Bible and what they discover in their general reading.

Maimonides believed that as long as reason proves knowledge to be true and accurate, its source, the identity of the person teaching it—be he biblical prophet or non-Jewish scholar—is unimportant. Like Saadia, Maimonides felt that Jews have a religious obligation to use their intelligence to try to understand God. To make this point, he referred to the familiar section of the *Shema* commanding Jews to love God with their heart, soul, and very being. According to Maimonides, we cannot really love someone or something without first knowing that person or thing. The better we know God, the deeper our love of God can be.

> " *. . . on account of the Divine intellect with which man has been endowed, he is said to have been made in the form and likeness of the Almighty, but far from it be the notion that the Supreme Being is corporeal, having a material form.* "
>
> *The Guide for the Perplexed*, trans. M. Friedlander

Understanding the Bible's Anthropomorphisms

Maimonides believed that many Jews are frustrated in their desire to know God by the Bible's very language. People trying to understand abstract, complex things, often describe them in simpler, more familiar, and more concrete terms. For example, while electrons and planets are not really alike, students of physics can learn to think about invisible atoms by studying a model that compares electrons traveling around the nucleus to planets traveling about the sun.

When poets try to describe objects to their readers or listeners, they also use comparisons, often ascribing human qualities or features to nonhuman things. For example, in the *Iliad* the ancient Greek poet Homer says, "Rosy-fingered dawn appeared." Readers know that dawn does not have fingers, but the expression helps make the colors of sunrise vivid in the reader's mind. Such nonhuman objects described in human terms are anthropomorphisms, and Homer is talking anthropomorphically when he describes dawn as having rosy fingers.

In the same way, Maimonides said that the Bible uses many anthropomorphisms to help explain the abstract idea of God. The prophets, for example, use striking human comparisons, speaking in terms of God's jealousy or anger and describing God as seeing or walking.

Maimonides was concerned that many pious Jews corrupted their faith by taking anthropomorphisms literally. For Maimonides, God was purely spiritual. One of his goals in *The Guide for the Perplexed* was to offer a rational explanation for such language.

Maimonides begins by calling attention to the passage in the first chapter of Genesis (26), where God says, " 'Let us make man in our image.' " The Hebrew word used for image is *tzelem*. But if God is purely spiritual and invisible, how can there be a divine image?

Maimonides searches the text of the Torah itself for a solution to this problem. He discovers one in a second Hebrew word, *toar*. When the Torah is referring to an object's actual shape, image, or form, it uses the word *toar*. For example, when Joseph's good looks are being described (Genesis 39:6), we find the word *toar*.

Maimonides concludes that *toar* cannot be used for God, because God has no shape. Instead, the Bible uses *tzelem*, because that word points to an object's *essence*. When God made human beings in his *tzelem*, they were made to reflect the essence of godliness—namely, perception and intellect.

Maimonides also offers a unique approach to the idea of *homonyms* to explain much of the Torah's language about God. In daily use, a homonym is a single word that has two completely different meanings. For example, "mail" can mean either the correspondence the letter-carrier brings or the suit of armor a knight wears. Maimonides uses the idea of a homonym to underscore that words have one meaning when referring to human behavior and a totally different meaning when referring to God. Because of the distinction between human and divine, words like "life," "mercy," "knowledge," "speaking," "hearing," "standing," and the like can be used to speak about God. Each of those words, however, has a totally different meaning when used for human beings.

For instance, the idea of God having a voice is unacceptable to Maimonides; thus he reflects on what the Bible means when it says that God spoke to the prophets. His conclusion: God is the source of the words of the prophets, and therefore they did not make up their messages. Similarly, when the Bible says, "God stands," it means that God does not change, not that God has legs. And with "God descends," the Bible is not claiming that God literally comes down to earth, but rather tht God has an *effect* on the world.

Maimonides knew he was not the first to object to a literal understanding of the Bible's language. In *The Guide* he refers to the Talmudic saying "The Torah speaks according to the language of man"—that is, it uses examples from human experience to describe God because what we know of God is limited by our being human. But no one before Maimonides had analyzed the subject so thoroughly. He devoted forty-seven chapters of the first part of *The Guide* to this issue, considering every term the Bible applies to God and offering his opinion of the real intent of each.

Today most people accept the principle that God has no body and that truth is truth, whether spoken by a Jew or a Buddhist. Maimonides' thoughtful and systematic analysis went a long way toward convincing the world that this principle makes sense.

Understanding the Torah's Rationality

Maimonides believed there was a purpose for every commandment in the Torah. He claimed to have uncovered each and every purpose, knowing that his claim would be very controversial, and in fact it angered many of his readers.

Book Five, page 1, *The Mishneh Torah*

Maimonides believed that there is a purpose for every commandment in the Torah, and that each purpose can be identified through human reason and thought. Book Five of *The Mishneh Torah* explains the reasoning behind each of the laws of *kashrut*.

He made his argument by first taking his opponents' position. He asked what the implication would be if observant Jews demanded reasons for laws when the Torah itself had failed to provide them. Shouldn't the plain fact of the commandment be enough? Wouldn't having a rational purpose make the commandment seem less divine and more like a society's ordinary laws?

Having thus presented his opponents' case, Maimonides then revealed its shortcoming: the argument implies that God is inferior to human beings. After all, lawmakers try to make all of society's laws reasonable. The assumption that God's commandments do not have to be reasonable suggests that they are inferior to human laws. This, said Maimonides, cannot be true. Since it was written by God, every commandment in the Torah must be reasonable and must be for human benefit.

We can understand Maimonides' method of analyzing the Torah by reviewing his treatment of several parts of the Torah:

■ *Kingship.* According to Maimonides, it is not only the Torah's laws that are for human benefit. Even lists of the succession of kings are included to teach a lesson! When the Torah names the kings of Edom and the places of their origin, for example (Genesis 36:31–39), it is teaching us something. The kings listed were all non-Edomites who oppressed their subjects, and the Torah is thus teaching the Israelites not to appoint a non-Israelite as king. The point is later made explicit: "You must not appoint a foreigner" (Deuteronomy 17:15).

■ *Kashrut.* Today some of the reasons Maimonides proposed for various commandments are quite well-known, even if not all Jews accept them. He was the first, for example, to claim that the laws of *kashrut* have both physical and spiritual purposes. He said that the foods forbidden by the Torah are all in some way unhealthy and that the need to observe the laws of *kashrut* constitutes good training in self-discipline. In turn, such discipline promotes good citizenship, since getting along in groups demands the capacity to suppress individual whims. Furthermore, by prohibiting eating for mere physical enjoyment, the laws of *kashrut* also help focus on spiritual and intellectual matters, which give life its real meaning.

■ *Sacrifices.* Maimonides was the first philosopher to practice what we now call "comparative religion," looking outside the Israelite community to find clues to the underlying purposes of some of the Bible's laws. For example, if God is purely spiritual, why does the Torah call for sacrifices? A spiritual God would have no need for such material things. Maimonides found an answer in the rites of the pagan communities among whom the Israelites lived.

Many of the Torah's negative commandments, according to Maimonides, outlaw specific pagan practices, such as tattooing, that were common at the time the Torah was given. Although God could have forbidden sacrifices, the practice was so common at the time that the Israelites would probably have been tempted to follow the old customs. So instead, God made the pagan ritual more holy. Only priests would be allowed to sacrifice, and only in certain places. Furthermore, the people would be able to learn important values from the ritual. Just as only unblemished animals could be offered to God, so everything the people did in God's name would have to represent their best effort.

Maimonides compares God's leading the people out of slavery through forty years in the desert to the Torah's laws of sacrifice: the forty-year route gave the Israelites time to shed their past as slaves and grow into a people capable of ruling their own land. The road from paganism to worship of the one true God was equally indirect. While taking pity on human weakness and allowing the Israelites to cling to old habits, God changed the rules of sacrifice in ways that led the people toward God, the true object of worship.

Strikingly, in a passage on superstition Maimonides makes the same kind of concession to human weakness that he attributes to God in the arena of sacrifice. As we might expect, this champion of reason waged a constant battle with superstitious beliefs. Yet, like the rabbis of the Talmud before him, in his great code of Jewish law, he allows someone bitten by a snake to chant magical words over the wound. He affirms the rabbis' decision as their way of taking pity on a victim who, in dire danger from the bite, needs to do something to help stay sane.

> **"** *Whoever finds occasion to criticize me, or knows of a better interpretation of any of the laws, should call my attention to it and gracefully forgive me.* **"**
>
> Epilogue, *Commentary on the Mishnah*, trans. Isadore Twersky

MAIMONIDES' CHARACTER AND SPIRIT

Man of Community

Being deeply involved with the Jewish community in many ways, Maimonides showed himself to be more than just a great thinker. He was also a modest man who was kind and generous, devoted to charity and to helping others in many ways. In addition, his code of law helped Jewish communities in Europe, Africa, and the Near East live meaningful Jewish lives. Jews today honor Maimonides as much for his generosity of spirit and for his systematic summary of Jewish law as for his philosophy of reason.

The Philosopher and His Critics. Unlike many less important thinkers, Maimonides was known for his extraordinary modesty. At the end of his commentary on the Mishnah, he requests that critics call his attention to any problems they might find in his work. He justified their discoveries in advance by mentioning the conditions under which he did his research: during the ten years it took him to write the commentary, he and his family were constantly threatened by Muslim persecution. Being a refugee, Maimonides had no libraries to consult, and many of his explanations were written while he was on the road or on board ship. God would reward these critics, he said, because by pointing out his error, they would be doing godly work. On another occasion he claimed that not making mistakes was not something in which he took pride. He added that when others convinced him he had made one, or if he discovered one himself, he was prepared to amend his writings, his habits, and even his nature.

Consoling Victims of Religious Persecution.

Maimonides turned bar mitzvah just after a militant Muslim tribe raided his hometown of Cordova and demanded that all in their realm accept Islam or die. Like most Jews, the Maimon family tried to avoid both fates; most scholars believe they saved their lives simply by passing for Muslims. Both Maimonides and his father, however, felt great compassion for fellow Jews forced to pay lip service to Islam, feigning conversion in order to stay alive.

As a respected community leader, Maimonides' father wrote a letter comforting such Jews, offering assurance that as long as they continued to say their prayers (even in a short form) and do good deeds, they were still Jews. But an anonymous writer disagreed, insisting that even a pretense of accepting Islam was just as bad as actually converting. Perhaps he had in mind all the Jews who had in fact preferred death rather than speak, even falsely, words that betrayed their Jewish faith. In turn, both to defend his father and to calm the many Jews distressed by the anonymous dissent, Maimonides wrote his own public letter, dismissing the criticism and claiming that the writer had clearly never experienced persecution himself. He also encouraged Jews to flee lands where they were being persecuted. Ironically and sadly, after his remarks became public, Maimonides and his family themselves had to flee again. The fact that they themselves were Jews was all too clear now. It was impossible for them to pass as Muslims any longer.

Some time later, when Maimonides was living safely in Egypt, where he spent the last forty years of his life, the troubled Jewish community of Yemen wrote him for advice. His letter of response was so heartening that long after, the Yemenite Jews still included Maimonides' name in their daily prayers. Whatever concerns he had about his own safety, which might have kept him from writing, seemed insignificant when compared with the potential benefit to his fellow Jews.

Maimonides was famous in his time, and was welcomed by royalty. Here he treats a member of the family of the Sultan of Egypt. It was in Egypt that Maimonides helped heal the split between Karaite Jews, who accepted only the Torah as divine, and more traditional Jews, who also accepted Talmudic law and later commentaries.

Uniting the Community. Just as Saadia had faced a problem with the Babylonian Karaites, when Maimonides moved to Cairo, he found the Jewish community split: The traditional Jews had begun to fear that the Karaite sect's refusal to recognize Talmudic authority would destroy Judaism.

Having himself written one of the great codes of Jewish law, the *Mishneh Torah,* Maimonides, of course, was a firm adherent of Talmudic law and the later commentaries and codes. However, instead of fighting with the Karaites, he tried to bring the sect back into the Jewish fold—and to a remarkable extent his policy succeeded. Wisely arguing that the Karaites, like the Jews, are descendants of Abraham, obey the Torah, and worship only one God, Maimonides ruled, as community leader, that members of the sect might be visited except when they were celebrating holidays traditional Jews did not observe. Furthermore, their children were to be circumcised and their dead buried like other Jews. His gentle rulings succeeded in bringing many Karaites back into the Jewish community.

Maimonides' wish to unite the Jewish community is also apparent in his attitude toward converts to Judaism. Obadiah, a man who had converted from Islam, wrote Maimonides to ask if it was proper for him to say prayers referring to a Jewish past in which he did not share. For example, in the *Amidah,* can a convert say, "Our God and God of our fathers"? In his formal letter of reply (called a *responsum*), Maimonides assured Obadiah that by adopting Judaism, a convert becomes one of the household of Abraham and acquires all the rights and responsibilities of one who is born Jewish. He compared the convert to

Abraham himself, who also left his family behind in order to embrace his new belief in God. Maimonides reassured Obadiah by saying that his lineage was in no way inferior to that of those born into Jewish families.

Interpreter of Jewish Law.

Maimonides developed a complete code of Jewish law in his *Mishneh Torah*. This work helped Jewish communities in Europe, Africa, and the Near East maintain cohesion and a sense of purpose. For many Jews today, Maimonides is important primarily for his interpretation of the laws of Jewish practice. The *Mishneh Torah*, along with later codes such as the *Shulhan Arukh*, remains an important guide for traditional Jews. Above all other aspects of Maimonides' life, his legal code is probably viewed as his major contribution to Jewish communities everywhere.

Maimonides is also famous for his teachings on *tzedakah*, the Hebrew word meaning "justice" that is usually translated as "charity." He said that while helping the poor is important, so is the manner in which aid is given. Accordingly, the philosopher listed eight degrees of *tzedakah*:

1. *Reluctant.* The least worthy method of supporting the poor is to give grudgingly.
2. *Meager.* Somewhat better is to give graciously but less than one should.
3. *Hesitant.* A slightly higher form of *tzedakah* is to give an appropriate amount but only after being asked.
4. *Forthcoming.* It is better to give an appropriate amount even before being asked.
5. *Anonymous recipient.* A higher degree of *tzedakah* occurs when the receiver knows who the giver is while the donor remains ignorant of who receives. In Talmudic times, explains Maimonides, the rabbis would toss sacks of money over their shoulders without looking. The poor could take what they needed without being embarrassed.
6. *Anonymous donor.* Even higher is a donor who knows who will receive the aid while the receiver remains unaware of who the donor is. Maimonides says that the rabbis of the Talmud would often leave money in secret at the doors of the poor.
7. *Anonymity on both ends.* Still higher is when neither the giver nor the receiver knows the other's identity. Maimonides compares this arrangement to one functioning at the time of the Jerusalem Temple. In a special room there, charitable people could leave their *tzedakah* in secret, and the poor could secretly go there to take what they needed.
8. *Self-help.* The highest form of *tzedakah* is the least conventional: putting someone back on the road to self-reliance by coming up with a job or even by going into partnership with the person.

Maimonides also taught that no one should give so much as to risk becoming poor oneself. We need to balance our duty to ourselves with our duty to society.

The Community Mourns Maimonides' Death

Maimonides worked without stop, in spite of years of wandering as a refugee and his busy schedule as court physician in Egypt. How fitting, then, that he died while working, dictating the final chapter of the revised edition of his most popular medical writings.

In Egypt, Jews and Muslims joined in three days of public mourning for Maimonides. In Jerusalem, mourning spread throughout the entire Jewish community, the mourners fasting and meeting in their synagogues.

Before dying, Maimonides had let it be known that he wished to be buried in Tiberias, considered one of the four holy cities in *Eretz Yisrael*. According to legend, while his body was being transported, a large group of bandits stopped the procession, but try as they might to hurl the coffin into the sea, it would not budge—a sign that it contained a holy man. Upon learning that the body was Maimonides', instead of harming the Jews in the procession, the bandits asked to join them in carrying the coffin to Tiberias. His tomb still rests there, visited from year to year by those wishing to honor the greatest of Jewish leaders and thinkers.

Maimonides taught that the highest form of *tzedakah* is putting the recipient back on the road to self-reliance. When this is not possible, he said, the next highest form is when neither the giver nor the receiver knows who the other is. The inscription on the painting reads ''and the holy God is sanctified by charity.''

The Zohar

4 MOSES DE LEON

1250 - 1305

Moses de Leon wrote his most important book,
The Zohar, in Guadalajara, a town northeast of Madrid.
The Zohar, which means "The Splendor," is considered
the most sacred mystic text by the Kabbalists, or Jewish
mystics, who rank it with the Bible and the Talmud.
Jewish mystics believe their approach to the mysteries
of God and the universe is based on an accumulated
tradition, handed down over the generations. The
Hebrew word for mysticism, *Kabbalah*, actually means
"Tradition."

WHO WROTE THE ZOHAR?

The Zohar's Mysterious Appearance

Unlike the other figures in this book, Moses de Leon did not wish to be remembered as a thinker. In fact, he did not even publish his most important book in his own name. He claimed, instead, that it was written by a rabbi who had lived eleven centuries earlier in *Eretz Yisrael*.

Starting in about 1280, Moses de Leon began to circulate and sell passages of mystical commentary on the Bible. Written in Aramaic, the language of the Talmudic rabbis, these passages had never been seen before. De Leon insisted that his role was only that of a scribe, that he had found an old manuscript of Rabbi Shimon ben Yohai, a famous teacher living in *Eretz Yisrael* over 1,000 years earlier.

According to legend, Rabbi Shimon ben Yohai and his son lived in a cave for thirteen years to escape the Romans (who controlled *Eretz Yisrael*), and the prophet Elijah visited them twice daily to instruct them in the Torah's mysteries. De Leon claimed that *The Zohar* contained those mysteries and that after Rabbi Shimon died, the book was secretly handed down from teacher to student, over the generations. The work had only recently arrived in Spain from its land of origin, and de Leon was making it his task to copy out parts and sell them, in order to spread its mystic understanding of the Torah.

First Suspicions

Shortly after the "ancient" Aramaic commentary emerged on the scene, a refugee named Isaac ben Samuel arrived in Spain from *Eretz Yisrael*. Parts of ben Samuel's diary have survived, and we can read of his growing interest in the commentary and of his efforts to contact its distributor, Moses de Leon. De Leon was traveling, but he assured ben Samuel that in fact he owned the original manuscript. Wanting to see it for himself, ben Samuel arranged to meet de Leon at the latter's home.

As fate would have it, de Leon died before he could return. Ben Samuel, however, proceeded to de Leon's hometown, where he heard an amazing story that was being told by the dead man's widow. She was claiming that her husband had confessed to her that *The Zohar* was his own invention. When asked why he would pretend to be copying ancient secrets from a manuscript, she said he did it to earn more money: people would naturally pay more for the words of the

> *Rabbi Simeon said: If a man looks upon the Torah as merely a book presenting narratives and everyday matters, alas for him! Such a torah, one treating with everyday concerns, and indeed a more excellent one, we too, even we, could compile. . . . But the Torah, in all of its words, holds supernal truths and sublime secrets.*
>
> The Zohar, trans. Gershom Scholem

This sixteenth-century drawing shows a man holding a tree with the *sefirot,* the ten different divine characteristics through which the nature of God can be understood. *The Zohar* describes the *sefirot* without actually using the term.

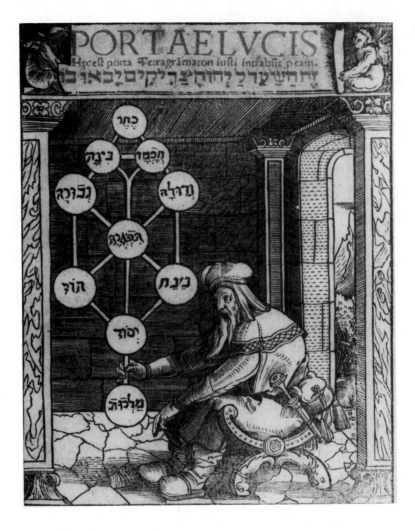

revered sage Rabbi Shimon ben Yohai than for those of the unknown Moses de Leon.

Too upset by this news to accept it easily, Isaac ben Samuel continued his travels, and he came across many Jews who were willing to support de Leon's claim that the commentary originated in ancient times.

Ben Samuel also noted that Moses de Leon never distributed the entire *Zohar*, only selections. In fact, to date no entire manuscript has ever been found. When the book was first printed in the sixteenth century, it consisted of several incomplete manuscripts that had been put together. A legend arose that the 2,000-page printed book was only a small portion of the original work, which was said to weigh the equivalent of 40 camel loads.

As time passed, Moses de Leon's name began to fade, more and more people maintaining that *The Zohar* was an authentic work from the second century. They recognized that the book mentioned rabbis living hundreds of years after Shimon ben Yohai and contained other evidence that it was written later, but these anachronisms—or errors in chronology—did not alter their conviction that the book was an ancient one. To the contrary, they argued that the anachronisms merely proved how holy a man ben Yohai was. As one rabbi from the early nineteenth century said, "Through his torah, Rabbi Shimon ben Yohai attained the hidden light, in regard to which there is no distinction between the present and the future."

De Leon's Authorship Emerges

By the mid-1600s *The Zohar* was widely accepted as a holy and ancient book. But Leone Modena, an Italian rabbi and scholar, had concluded it could not have been written before the beginning of the fourteenth century. Modena had written a book carefully presenting his case, but he was afraid to publish it, and only a few people read his ideas in private manuscripts. The book appeared for the first time two centuries after Modena's death.

During the nineteenth century Moses de Leon's name was again connected to *The Zohar*. First, one scholar pointed to its containing an Aramaic version of a Hebrew text by Moses de Leon—surely this suggested that he was the author of at least part of *The Zohar*. Later, the famous Jewish historian Heinrich Graetz claimed that the work was written entirely by Moses de Leon. Graetz had nothing good to say about *The Zohar*, dismissing de Leon as a forger who kept generations of Jews from seeing that Judaism was a religion of reason.

By the late 1930s the distinguished German-Jewish scholar Gershom Scholem had also concluded that Moses de Leon was in fact the sole author of *The Zohar*. Unlike Graetz, however, Scholem did not consider de Leon a forger, emphasizing the Spanish Jew's great creative achievement. *The Zohar*, Scholem noted, was neither the first nor the last book that was claimed to be written by someone other than the true author. English has even borrowed the Greek word for literary or religious works falsely attributed to another author: *pseudepigrapha*.

Scholem's research is not the last word on *The Zohar* for everyone; some scholars still think it possible that earlier mystic literature found its way into *The Zohar* as we know it. And many Hasidic Jews, as well as those of Yemenite descent, continue to read it as part of the holy Kabbalah they believe has been transmitted from ancient times.

The Zohar arouses strong passions. By thinking about the work's content and its purpose, we can start to understand the fascination and power it has held for so long.

A RESPONSE TO HUMAN NEED

The Zohar Filled a Gap

Philosophers develop systematic explanations for the physical and intellectual world: they describe why things appear the way they do. Mystics take a different approach: they attempt to describe God's behavior more directly. While the two approaches are quite different, they can enrich each other a great deal.

The ancient philosophers were well acquainted with mystical literature, as mystics were with philosophy: Saadia wrote a commentary on an earlier mystical work, and Yehudah HaLevi referred to the same work in *The Kuzari.* The first piece of solid evidence we have of Moses de Leon's life comes from a Hebrew translation made for him in 1264 of Maimonides' *Guide for the Perplexed.* The translator or scribe dedicated the manuscript to "the learned Rabbi Moses de Leon."

The mystics found that philosophers had not satisfied some basic human needs. As one author noted, Maimonides' *Guide* "did not save all from perplexity"—many found that the emphasis on reason in that book sapped the life out of Judaism. They longed for myths, like those of the ancient Greeks, that would make God seem more available to human beings. Myths often use stories about deities to explain customs, rituals, or facts of nature and allow people to feel closer to those deities.

Others saw an unexpected problem with Maimonides' works: instead of furnishing inspiration to observe the commandments, works of philosophy often seemed to provide excuses for failure to observe them. In one of his Hebrew works, Moses de Leon attacks those Jews who hide behind Maimonides and other thinkers to excuse their lack of religious observance: "They claim: 'Do you think we have to bless God? Does He need this? Foolishness!' "

The Zohar thus wooed some Jews back to the observance of Judaism. It did so in at least two ways: by giving a very different explanation for the commandments, and by describing a very different sort of God from that found in the works of systematic philosophers.

Intimacy with God Through the Commandments

Saadia and Maimonides looked for the rationale behind each commandment to prove that God would not expect people to perform empty acts of ritual. They also claimed that performing many of the

mitzvot would encourage us to live moral lives. In *The Zohar*, however, the commandments have an additional role: they bring the Jew into a close relationship with God.

For Maimonides, God commanded the Jews to make sacrifices as a way of weaning them from pagan customs. Compare this approach with the mystical view of *The Zohar*: Rabbi Shimon ben Yohai meets the prophet Elijah while on the way to Tiberias. According to the prophet, God has sent him to ben Yohai to learn the answer to a troublesome question: Why, since there is no eating or drinking in heaven, do people offer sacrifices and expect that God will find them acceptable? Ben Yohai offers the following explanation: "When a man's newly wedded bride wants a bite to eat, isn't it appropriate for the groom to join her at the table? In the same way, God, out of love for the chosen people, accepts the sacrifice of food and drink."

For *The Zohar*, then, commandments create as intimate a personal relationship with God as the relationship between a bride and groom.

But the commandments play another role in *The Zohar*. By observing them, Jews on earth have the opportunity to influence the universe directly; every *mitzvah* acts like a rope anchored at one end

In *The Zohar*, de Leon argued that fulfilling the commandments brings people into a closer relationship with God. Performing *mitzvot* is like pulling on a rope that connects earth and heaven; the action on earth is noticed above.

on earth and at the other in God's heavenly sphere. When Jews perform a *mitzvah*, it is akin to wiggling the rope, sending a wave of energy along it toward the heavens.

In the language of *The Zohar*, "Through an action below, an action above is aroused. The lower world depends upon the upper world, and the upper world functions in accordance with the behavior prevailing in the lower world." By observing *mitzvot*, Jews help to bring about "unifications" in heaven. These "unifications" make it possible for God's mercy to flow down upon the entire people. Similarly, failure to observe the commandments causes heavenly "blemishes" that prevent "unifications." As for the individual Jew performing a *mitzvah*, according to *The Zohar* "the Divine Presence walks with him constantly and never departs from him."

God: Light Without End

The concept of God in *The Zohar* manages to combine Maimonides' idea that human beings can never understand God with the sort of anthropomorphic divine picture that Maimonides worked so hard to destroy. How does *The Zohar* manage to do both?

According to the Kabbalah, human thought can never grasp God's ultimate reality, which it calls *Ayn Sof*, or "the Infinite." Only God can understand the world of *Ayn Sof*. *The Zohar* rarely mentions *Ayn Sof*.

The world of *Ayn Sof*, however, is connected to a second world, through which human beings can get to know God. This is the world of God's *sefirot*, or "emanations"—the light that *Ayn Sof* gives off. According to *The Zohar*, the different *sefirot* represent different characteristics of God.

The world of *Ayn Sof* and that of the *sefirot* are actually a single world. As *The Zohar* says, the relationship between *Ayn Sof* and the *sefirot* is like that between a lump of coal and its flame. A piece of coal can exist without giving off a flame. We become aware of the energy it contains, however, only when we see it burn. *Ayn Sof* is like the coal. The *sefirot* are the light given off as the hidden nature and energy of *Ayn Sof* make themselves apparent to humans.

The Zohar's description of the *sefirot* is full of anthropomorphisms. Maimonides understood expressions like "the arm of God" as comparisons with human arms, the only ones that really exist. But in the world of the *sefirot*, God really has a body, which is the model for the human body. *The Zohar* claims that God can actually be understood in terms of the human image, because that image is a reflection of God's. "None can see the real and authentic image. The reproduction nearest to it is that of man. But all the upper and the lower worlds are comprised in the image of God."

A Different Idea of the Torah's Meaning

"The True Torah"

Like Saadia and Maimonides, *The Zohar* interprets the Torah by examining each word very closely. *The Zohar* sometimes also uses comparisons recalling those used by Saadia and Maimonides to stress the need for deep study of the Torah. The kind of interpretation the two philosophers had in mind, however, is often very different from what is at work in *The Zohar*.

Both Maimonides and *The Zohar* talk of the net or veil that obscures Torah's meaning. Maimonides compares the Torah to a golden apple enclosed in a silver net. The apple has an outer face, which shines like silver, and an inner face, which shines like gold. A person who examines the apple superficially or from a distance sees only its silver face. Only the person who studies Torah deeply and seriously sees its golden inner face.

A famous passage in *The Zohar* makes a similar comparison. It compares the Torah to a beautiful woman who covers her face with a veil. She hides her beauty from the eyes of strangers and allows only those who love her to see her face. This passage tells us that only truly devoted students of Torah can see beyond the veil of symbols covering the words.

In another famous passage, Rabbi Shimon ben Yohai expresses his dismay that so many Jews mistake the Torah for nothing more than a collection of stories and ordinary words. In a daring statement he says, "If that were so, we could compose a better Torah right now." Rabbi Shimon goes on to say that the stories told in the Torah are only the Torah's clothing. Just as a liquid must be enclosed in a container, the Torah must be enclosed in its garment of words and stories, and people who mistake the garment for the true Torah are just as foolish as those who judge others by their clothes.

But while Maimonides and *The Zohar* agree that the Torah needs to be interpreted, they differ when it comes to what form the interpretation should take. Like Saadia before him, Maimonides looked for the philosophical ideas behind the Torah's words. Their work resulted in sophisticated concepts and abstractions. *The Zohar*, to the contrary, describes the inner life of God and the true inner meaning of the Torah, which reveals that life.

> " *[The Torah] may be compared to a beautiful and stately damsel, who is secluded in an isolated chamber of a palace, and has a lover of whose existence she alone knows. . . . She thrusts open a small door in her secret chamber, for a moment reveals her face to her lover, then quickly withdraws it. . . . So it is with the Torah, which discloses her innermost secrets only to them who love her.* "
>
> *The Zohar*, trans. Gershom Scholem

Moses De Leon claimed that *The Zohar* had been written by Rabbi Shimon ben Yohai a thousand years earlier. Visitors crowd the rabbi's tomb in Meron on *Lag B'Omer*, the anniversary of his death.

Hidden Meaning: The Inner Life of God

A brief glance at how *The Zohar* treats the opening of Genesis shows its use of the Torah to understand God's inner life.

Everyone is familiar with the Torah's first words, *Braysheet bara Elohim*, usually translated, "In the beginning God created." *The Zohar*'s interpretation is different. It describes the beginning of creation as a process in which a flame sprang forth from *Ayn Sof*, the unknowable aspect of God. A single point of light shone out, beyond which nothing could be known or understood. *The Zohar* calls this point of light *Raysheet*, or "Beginning." From this beginning point, God began to unfold into the various *sefirot*, or emanations of divine light.

What the words *Braysheet bara Elohim* mean in *The Zohar*, then, is that at the moment when the point of light, *Raysheet*, broke through, the *Ayn Sof* unfolded. In doing so, it created Elohim. In terms of grammar, Elohim is not the subject of the verb *bara*, as it is in the usual translation. Instead, Elohim becomes the object of the verb.

The Zohar explains the meaning of Elohim by dividing the word and scrambling its letters a bit. The result is two other Hebrew words: *eleh*, which can be translated as "these," and *mi*, or "who." For *The Zohar*, Elohim is the name of God representing the connection between *eleh*—what can be known in the world—and *mi*—the great Who, God Who knows everything.

A second example of how *The Zohar* finds hints about God's life in the Torah involves another passage from Genesis, examined in the previous chapter. Recall Maimonides' suggestion that the Torah listed the names of the kings of Edom as a way to warn the Israelites not to have foreign kings. For *The Zohar*, each name on this list hints at a previous world of stern judgment: God destroyed these worlds because each contained too much of this divine quality of judgment.

For Saadia and Maimonides, the idea that God had a past or an inner life would have been scandalous. For mystics, *The Zohar*'s most important insights are found in passages offering evidence for such an idea.

5 ISAAC LURIA

1534 - 1572

Isaac Luria was born in Jerusalem and educated in Egypt. Although he died at the age of 38, his work created a new way for Jews to look at the world. Luria's version of the Kabbalah had at least as much influence on Jewish thought and history as Maimonides' *Guide*, and modern Hasidism bases much of its thinking on the system he developed. In fact, in the whole history of Jewish mystical thought, only *The Zohar* itself had as much of an impact. His tomb in the Galilee town of Safed is still a place of pilgrimage for many Jews.

THE HISTORICAL SETTING

Expulsion from Spain

Although Jews had lived on Spanish soil for centuries, as the lives of Yehudah HaLevi and Maimonides indicate, they began to suffer in religious wars during the 1100s. As a result of these wars, the Christians drove the Muslims out of Spain.

For over a century Jews prospered in Christian Spain. They engaged in commerce and became scholars, politicians, professionals, and even army generals. Some official Spanish documents have come down signed with a Hebrew name or even in Hebrew script. But in 1391, major anti-Jewish riots spread through the country; many Jews were killed or forced to convert.

In the 1400s the situation gradually deteriorated. The Marranos—a Spanish word for "swine," as the Christians labeled the Jewish converts to Christianity—found no security in their new religion. Often the Christians around them resented the fact that these former Jews now had the same rights as Christians. In the early part of the century the government attempted to force all Jews to live in a single area, and Jews began to leave the country. Many fled to nearby Portugal, which had a similar language and culture. Finally, in 1492 a decree expelled the Jews from Spain. It was issued by the same rulers who sent Columbus on his voyage to America.

In 1497, only five years after the Spanish expulsion, a similar decree in Portugal demanded that Jews convert to Christianity or leave. Jews and Marranos streamed out of Portugal during the next two centuries. In fact, the first Jews to come to what is now the United States arrived in 1654 as refugees from Brazil, which was under Portuguese control.

The two expulsions made Jews living everywhere feel threatened and insecure and filled them with longing for the arrival of the Messiah—the figure who, the biblical prophets taught, would come at the end of time to usher in a new era of peace. The prophet Isaiah had described this era so: "No sound of weeping, no voice of crying, shall ever be heard in it; no child shall die there anymore in infancy, nor any old man who has not lived out his years of life" (65:19–20). In addition, the Messiah would finally end the exile of the Jewish people and return them to *Eretz Yisrael*.

> " *Once the Master, the holy Ari, passed a large synagogue in Tiberias. He showed the disciples a stone built into the wall and said: 'In this stone is incarnated a soul which asks me to pray for it.'* "
>
> From *The Wisdom of the Jewish Mystics*, trans. Alan Unterman

A Community of Exiles in Safed

Many Spanish Jews, including many Marranos, went to *Eretz Yisrael*, where they were welcomed by the Muslim ruler. The Marranos thought the biblical homeland would be an appropriate place to repent their conversion and return to Judaism. Caught up at first in the problems of resettlement, such as finding new homes and new ways of making a living, the Jewish settlers did not have much time to contemplate the meaning of the expulsion and of Jewish existence in the world.

Eventually, however, the refugees and their offspring became well enough established to take time to wonder, Why, if God loved the Jewish people, were they forced to suffer so? In another form, this question had troubled the biblical figure Job; now it became a question of Jewish national destiny. The group of Jewish mystics that settled in the 1500s in the small hillside town of Safed, in the Upper Galilee region of *Eretz Yisrael*, offered answers to this question that appealed to many Jews around the world.

There were several reasons why the Spanish-Jewish refugees chose Safed as a place to settle. Neither Islam nor Christianity considered the town a holy place. At the same time, it was close to Meron, where the tomb of Shimon ben Yohai, the supposed author of *The Zohar*, was located. It was also a good location for business, near the commercial centers of Syria to the north. Soon Safed became a center of trade in grain, textiles, and clothing.

By 1522 there were as many Jews in Safed as in Jerusalem. As the community grew economically secure, learning began to flourish. There were schools for the study of Talmud, and many small groups met regularly to study Kabbalah. The worlds of learning and of business overlapped: Isaac Luria himself dealt in pepper and other goods.

Forty years after the expulsion from Spain, Safed had become the center of a thriving movement of Jewish mysticism. Isaac Luria lived among the town's Spanish refugees for only two years, from 1570 to 1572, but his version of the Kabbalah would spread out from there to Jewish communities throughout the world, giving them a new sense of hope and purpose.

Luria addressed basic questions troubling the Jews of his day: Why is there evil? Is the exile of the Jewish people from their homeland only a punishment for their sins? Do Jews as a group have a meaningful role to play in this world? Can the individual Jew affect the forces that change history? He answered these questions by connecting the Jews' condition with the history of the universe.

The Retelling of Cosmic History

Contraction and Creation

Luria began by developing an older idea about creation that few had taken seriously until then. Recall that *The Zohar* had called God *Ayn Sof*, or "the Infinite"; at the moment of creation the *Ayn Sof* sent forth a ray of light that became the *sefirot*, or emanations of divine light. But for Luria, there was a problem with this picture: if the *Ayn Sof* were infinite, then God filled everything; there was no place that was not God. How, then, could there be room for the universe as we know it?

According to Luria, in order to create the universe, God first had to withdraw from it. Luria called this first action of creation *tzimtzum*, which is Hebrew for "drawing back."

Most people have experienced a type of *tzimtzum* in their personal lives. *Tzimtzum* can be an act of love on the part of a parent or teacher. For example, when a child learns to ride a bicycle, at some point the teacher must draw back, refrain from holding on to the bike to steady it, while the novice learns to balance alone. A modern scholar has pointed out that for Luria, the universe really began when God withdrew from it: There could have been nothing but God if God had not contracted to create space for the world.

Luria believed that God is infinite, and that in the first step of creation God had to withdraw from the world to make room for the *sefirot* and all of creation. Luria called the withdrawal *tzimtzum*.

The Source of Evil

Only after *tzimtzum* could the *Ayn Sof* radiate the divine light to form the *sefirot*. For Luria, each one of the *sefirot* is really a vessel for light. The vessels were intended to contain the light beamed forth from the *Ayn Sof.*

The first three *sefirot* were able to contain the light as it radiated from the *Ayn Sof.* However, the light struck the remaining *sefirot* all at once. In Luria's view, too much divine light poured out into the vessels all at once, and the vessels broke. The Hebrew term for this occurrence is *Shevirat HaKelim*, "the breaking of the vessels."

Shevirat HaKelim explains why there is evil in the world. When the vessels broke, sparks of divine light became mixed up with pieces of the shattered vessels. The broken pieces became husks or shells, forces of evil that trapped some of the sparks. As a result of *Shevirat HaKelim*, since the moment of creation, nothing in the universe—divine or human—has been what it was meant to be nor is where it belongs. Everything is in exile. Since sparks of God's light are not where they belong, even part of God is in exile. Before the world can be as God initially intended it to be, everything needs to be restored to its proper place. Everything must be repaired.

The Jew's Role in Repairing the World

Luria argued that the purpose of human existence is to make these repairs. The Hebrew word for this process is *tikkun*. Although part of the divine light that spilled out of the dishes made its way back to *Ayn Sof,* God has reserved the rest of the task of *tikkun* for human beings. By performing these tasks, people will eliminate evil from the world and, by liberating the divine sparks that remain trapped, will also put God back together properly.

Luria suggests that Jews have a very special role to play in the process of *tikkun*: every *mitzvah* is part of this process. Literally, the word *mitzvah* means a commandment given by God. More generally, it has come to mean a good deed. For Luria, both senses of the word are at work in *tikkun*. The crucial point is that Jews themselves are responsible for redeeming the world.

In addition, each Jew has a specific job to perform in the process, and no one can assign the job to someone else. If any refuse to perform it, or perform it badly, that marks a setback to the process. By carrying out their individual, personal assignments properly, the Jewish people contribute to the world's perfection.

In Luria's version of the Kabbalah, the idea of exile has become more hopeful than it was previously. First, Jews share the experience of exile with the universe and even with God. Second, there is a purpose to Jewish exile: by performing *mitzvot,* and thereby finding and gathering all the divine sparks scattered throughout the world's remotest corners, every Jew becomes a significant participant in the world's development.

For Luria, it is not the Messiah's job to redeem the Jews and the world. Instead, the Messiah will come only when Jews have completed the job of *tikkun* and will merely confirm that the world finally matches God's original intention.

LURIA IN HISTORY AND LEGEND

A Brief Life with Enduring Influence

Like Maimonides and many other important figures in Jewish history, Luria is often referred to by a name that comes from putting together initials. His nickname, HaAri, stands for HaElohi Rabbi Yitzhak, or "the godly Rabbi Isaac," a reflection of his force of personality and way of life. At the same time, the name means "The Lion." Luria died before he turned 40 and left behind no important writings. Nonetheless, his system of mystical thought affected Jewish life for centuries, as powerfully as a lion's roar affects the stillness of a jungle.

He was born more than forty years after the expulsion from Spain. His father, whose family came from Germany or Poland, moved to Jerusalem, where he met and married a woman of Spanish-Jewish origin. His father died while he was still a boy, and he moved on with his mother to Egypt. There he was raised in the home of a wealthy uncle, who was so fond of him that he later gave Luria his daughter's hand in marriage.

Young Luria excelled in nonmystical studies but was drawn to the Kabbalah. He developed the habit of spending the week alone in a house owned by his father-in-law on the banks of the Nile. He claimed to be visited there by the prophet Elijah, who taught him previously unheard of secrets of the Torah. Each Shabbat, however, he would return to civilization so that he could fulfill the Talmudic responsibility to spend the holy day with his wife.

On one of his Shabbat visits in the year 1570, Luria informed his wife that Elijah had told him to move to Safed right away: The prophet wished him to use Safed as a base for spreading the Lurianic Kabbalah. The move was urgent, Elijah explained, since Luria had only two more years to live. Luria and his wife made the move, and before two years were out, he died during an epidemic.

> *Once when the Master, the holy Ari, was sitting in the House of study with his disciples, he looked at one of them and said to him, 'Go out from here, for today you are excommunicated from heaven. . . . It is because of the chickens you have at home. You have not fed them for two days. . . . God will forgive you on condition you see to it that before you leave for prayers in the morning you give food to your chickens.'*

From *The Wisdom of the Jewish Mystics,* trans. Alan Unterman

In Luria's brief sojourn in Safed, he made a tremendous impression on the community of mystics. He taught his system of Kabbalah orally, believing his thoughts overflowed in a way that prevented their being organized in books. After his death, however, one of his followers, Hayim Vital, wrote *Tree of Life*, not only explaining Luria's system of Kabbalah but also combining legend and fact in an imaginative account of the great mystic's life.

Hesitation Delays the World's Redemption

A legend told about Luria underscores his idea that each Jew has the power to advance or delay the processes of *tikkun* and redemption.

One Friday afternoon, Luria and his followers went to welcome the Sabbath in the fields outside Safed. The master suddenly turned to his companions and said, "I see that the time has come to usher in the era of the Messiah. Come right now with me to Jerusalem. We shall begin by rebuilding the Temple."

But his companions did not respond with the enthusiasm Luria had hoped for. A good number of them simply rejected his suggestion. "Jerusalem is too far off," they said. "We're comfortable in our homes here, and we can't know what dangers await us there."

Others seemed prepared to act on Luria's advice, saying, "We are ready to join you." But even they begged off for the immediate moment. "Just give us a while to go home," they said, "to put our affairs in order."

Luria turned to his followers with tears in his eyes and spoke: "Heaven and earth will bear witness that from the time of Rabbi Shimon ben Yohai to the present, no moment has been more fitting for redemption than now. If you had agreed to join me, the Temple would have been rebuilt. The period of exile would have ended with all the world's Jews coming together in Jerusalem. While you hesitated, however, the moment for redemption passed. The period of exile has begun again."

For Luria, of course, the idea is that God works in wondrous ways, and no one should ever miss the opportunity to assist in the world's redemption. There might be a less theological and more practical way to look at the story, however. If the opportunity to do something important arises, perhaps we should act more swiftly than we usually do. It is always easy to find excuses for not taking a Sunday afternoon to visit an elderly relative, for example. Nor is it hard to come up with reasons for not helping the homeless or contributing to the relief of earthquake victims. But "reasonable excuses" may be the ones that tip the balance away from redemption.

The ark of the Sefardic synagogue of HaAri in Safed. During
Luria's lifetime Safed was the
center of the Jewish mysticism
with which he was associated.
Luria is buried in Safed, and to
this day his tomb attracts many
visitors.

6 BAAL SHEM TOV

1700 – 1760

Israel Ben Eliezer, the founder of modern Hasidism, is more commonly referred to as the Baal Shem Tov— often translated as "the Master of the Good Name," and often shortened to the Besht. He left behind even fewer written works than Isaac Luria, but, as with Luria, after his death the Besht's followers wrote down many of his statements, as well as stories and legends about him. The Besht's ideas, transforming Judaism into a joyous religion in which people could delight, won over not only common people but also many Jewish intellectuals.

A Spiritual Healer

Eastern European Jewry on Its Sickbed

Just as a crisis in Spanish Jewry prepared the way for Isaac Luria and his system of thought, several crises in Eastern European Jewry prepared the way for Israel ben Eliezer. The fifty years before the Baal Shem Tov's birth were tragic ones for the Jews of Poland.

From the eleventh century on, Poland had become a haven for Jews fleeing oppression elsewhere in Europe, including England, Germany, and France. The kings of Poland welcomed the Jewish immigrants, who took an increasingly important role in the Polish economy. In the century from 1500 to 1600, the Jewish population increased tenfold, from 50,000 to 500,000.

In 1648 the situation changed. Groups of peasants, called Cossacks, rose up against their Polish landlords. The Cossacks hated the Poles for charging high rents, and they blamed the Jews for being the agents of these hated landlords.

During a two-year period the Cossacks committed the types of atrocities against the Jews now associated with the Nazis. They seized Torah scrolls from synagogues and defaced them. Then, forcing Jews to lie on the shreds of the scrolls, they tortured and butchered their victims. They also seized thousands of Jewish infants, whom they threw into wells or buried alive. In this way, the Cossacks wiped out over 700 Jewish communities, killing at least 100,000 Jews.

This physical calamity for the Jewish people paved the way, in turn, for a crisis in religious belief. According to tradition, the Messiah's arrival will be preceded by a period of suffering. So when a Turkish Jew named Shabbetai Zvi announced he was the Messiah, many Jews were prepared to believe him. By 1665 the news of this self-proclaimed redeemer had reached Jews all over the world. Many were so ready to believe the Messiah was at hand that they sold all their worldly goods in preparation for returning to the Land of Israel under his leadership.

Realizing that Shabbetai Zvi's claims threatened his throne, the Turkish sultan offered him a choice: immediate death or conversion to Islam. In the fall of 1666, Shabbetai Zvi converted to Islam. The effect on his Jewish followers was devastating. Some went so far as to continue to believe in him. Basing their faith on Lurianic Kabbalah, they claimed that Shabbetai Zvi had to become a Muslim in order to free the holy sparks scattered among the Muslims. Some of them also converted to Islam, but for most Jews, disappointed in their deepest hopes, there no longer seemed to be anything definite in which to believe.

> " *Rabbi Israel Baal Shem Tov said that when a man reads the Torah and sees the light in the letters of the Torah, even though he does not know how to pronounce the words accurately, then God does not mind even if he does not read correctly since his reading is with great love and with a heart on fire.* "
>
> From *Sefer Baal Shem Tov,* Satmar, 1943, trans. Louis Jacobs

Gloom and depression settled over the Jews of Eastern Europe. They would gather in their synagogues and weep over the deaths and disappointments they had witnessed, denying themselves normal comforts and pleasures in the name of religion. Against basic Jewish ideals, some began to whip themselves until they bled, while others starved themselves to death. Feeling sinful, many Jews began to fear evil spirits and demons.

Shabbetai Zvi, a Turkish Jew who claimed he was the Messiah in the 1660s and attracted a large following of Jews around the world. Shabbetai Zvi converted to Islam after the Turkish sultan threatened to kill him, and thereby provoked a crisis of confidence and belief for his followers. The Baal Shem Tov helped revive Judaism following this crisis.

Crisis in Jewish Leadership

The Jews of Poland were desperate for leaders who would make some sense of what they had lived through, who would make it possible for them to get on with their lives and with their belief in God. But the heads of the Jewish community, perhaps overcome themselves by despair and disappointment, failed to provide the necessary leadership. Many retreated into their books instead of facing the issues troubling the Jews of their time; some even busied themselves with research on sacrifices for the long-destroyed Temple.

There was a huge gap between the rabbis and scholars on the one hand and the common people on the other. Although they lived in the same communities, the people did not feel they could turn to the rabbis except for advice on how to carry out rituals. Many rabbis criticized ordinary Jews for not taking more time to study Torah, ignoring the fact that they needed to work to earn a living. Such criticism made working-class people feel they were inadequate Jews because they were not scholars.

Rabbis rarely even addressed the people in sermons. When they did, they were more likely to deal with a dry topic of interest only to other scholars. Who else could be interested in an elegant proof that two seemingly contradictory statements of Maimonides were not really in opposition? Such sermons lacked all emotion and did not touch the troubled Jews at the source of their pain. A dynasty had developed that overlooked the people and their needs.

Master of the Good Name

So it was to a Jewish world crying out for a new type of leadership that the Baal Shem Tov appeared. Individuals using the title *Baal Shem*, or "Master of the Name," had been circulating in Jewish communities from as far back as the 1100s, when Yehudah HaLevi criticized them in *The Kuzari.* They claimed to have special knowledge of God's names, which enabled them to work magic.

From the 1500s on, there were many people called Baal Shem at work in Germany and Poland. Some were rabbis and Talmudic scholars. Others were disciples of the Kabbalah. Still others were not educated at all but attracted followers because of their supposed ability to heal the sick. They would often write God's names on a slip of paper for ill and frail people to wear on their bodies as a charm.

There are different opinions as to just how the term *Baal Shem Tov* should be translated. For some, the Besht was the "Good, or Kind, Master of the Name." Unlike the many charlatans claiming healing powers just to make money, this Baal Shem proved he was *tov* (or

According to one tradition, at the age of thirteen the Baal Shem Tov became an assistant to a schoolmaster. In this painting he leads his young students to school in an Eastern European village.

"good") by trying to cure people because he truly loved them. For others, *Baal Shem Tov* means "Master of the Good Name" or "Possessor of a Good Reputation." According to a famous Hebrew proverb, *Tov shem tov mi shemen tov*—"a good name, or reputation, is better than good oil," a symbol of wealth.

Today, nearly three centuries after the Baal Shem's birth, it matters little if he was indeed a wonder-working medicine man. The main point is that his personality and way of life managed to revive a dying people.

"There Is No Place Where God Is Not"

God's Presence and God's Absence

Underlying the Besht's interpretation of Judaism is the belief that God is in everything. "Let people realize," he taught, "that when they look at the things around them, they are in reality seeing God's Countenance, which is present everywhere. Keeping this in mind, people will find it possible to serve the Lord in all things, even in trifles."

Although God is everywhere, when a person sins, God is blocked. The Besht saw a hint of this situation in the spelling and pronunciation of the Hebrew word for "sin," *het*. In English, some words have silent letters. For example, the letter *a* in the English word "dead" is silent; we pronounce the word as if it had no *a* at all. In the same way, the letter *alef* in the Hebrew word *het* is silent. According to the Baal Shem Tov, the *alef* stands for God. Just as *alef* is the first letter of the alphabet, God is the first aspect of the universe. So God is present, but silent, in the word "sin." By sinning, a person suppresses God.

Since God is in everything, there is good in all things. The Besht taught his followers to remember that God is present even in suffering, which serves as a kind of garment, covering God. By becoming aware of God's presence everywhere, we can remove the garment and make the suffering disappear.

This idea is related to the concept of sparks of holiness that we find in the Lurianic Kabbalah. Indeed, many of the Besht's teachings are later developments of ideas that Isaac Luria taught 200 years earlier. For example, the Besht taught that the things we consider our possessions are really given to us so that we may liberate the sparks of holiness in them; for that reason, we must treat our possessions with respect.

Just as there are sparks of holiness in all things, there are such sparks in all people, even the wicked. The Baal Shem himself was often criticized for keeping company with people others disdained as wicked. When a father once asked him how he should treat a son who had given up on God, the Baal Shem answered, "Love him more."

Approaching God with Joy

The Baal Shem Tov was able to rouse the Jews of Eastern Europe from their deathbed by stressing joy as the heart and soul of Judaism, rather than self-denial. To all those who fasted and whipped themselves in the name of holiness, the Baal Shem spoke sternly. Such behavior, he said, only caused God to judge the rest of the world more harshly, since most people were not capable of performing such acts. In addition, he said, fasting weakens the body so much that it cannot serve God properly. Instead of fasting, a person should study Torah and pray with full strength.

Eating and drinking should, in fact, be considered holy activities. Whenever we taste something, we should be aware that what we are enjoying is "nothing other than God Himself, from whom all pleasures derive." In other words, people serve God through all their activities, not only through those usually considered religious.

Sadness in general, said the Besht, puts up a barrier between human beings and God, who is the creator not merely of heaven and earth but also of delight and joy. Jews who do not rejoice in their

Jewishness are being ungrateful to God and have not properly under-stood what it means to be a Jew.

The Besht believed that a person who worships God in joy is also likely to be full of love for other people. A story from the Talmud he particularly liked tells of a rabbi who met the prophet Elijah in the marketplace one day. The rabbi asked Elijah if any of the people around them would merit a place in the world to come. Elijah surveyed the crowd and answered, "No." Just then two men walked by them. Elijah said to the rabbi, "These two men will merit a place in the world to come." Curious as to what accounted for their future reward, the rabbi asked the men what they did for a living. "We are jesters," they answered. "Whenever we come across depressed people, we do our best to cheer them up."

Like a superb jester, the Baal Shem Tov raised the spirits of many Jews of his time by turning Judaism into a religion of joy. He showed Jews of his time a way to rise above both ordinary sadness and the dreadful experiences of the recent past, to achieve that joy.

THE VALUE OF PRAYER

The Importance of Concentration

The Besht taught that the best way to gain true closeness to God is to pray. But there is a difference between praying mechanically and praying with *kavannah*, or real concentration. Praying with *kavannah* means being so intensely caught up in prayer that everything else is forgotten. Every athlete, artist, or writer knows what it is like to do something with *kavannah*, to be completely absorbed in a single activity.

By the time the Besht came on the scene, for many Jews praying was simply a matter of routine. The Baal Shem Tov reminded them of the importance of being spontaneous, of really feeling the meaning of prayer. One day he refused to enter a synagogue. When his followers asked him why, he answered: "I cannot go in there. The place is full of prayers." When asked to explain, he said: "All those who prayed here went through the motions in a lifeless manner. As a result, the prayers had no wings; they couldn't go up to God. With all those prayers stuck down here, there is no room in the synagogue for me."

Achieving Closeness with God

When prayers are spoken with *kavannah*, worshipers may close the gap they otherwise feel between themselves and God. They may achieve *devekut*, a feeling of intense oneness with God.

Many people wonder why some Jews sway back and forth while praying. The answer lies in the Besht's teaching about the road to *devekut*: in order to achieve this feeling, worshipers must pray whole-heartedly, involving their whole bodies, not simply their lips.

Some modern Jews are amused or embarrassed by this style of prayer. The Besht was aware of such reactions in his own day, explaining that the swaying was perfectly appropriate in times of both despair and joy. In times of despair the worshiper is like a drowning swimmer who tries to attract attention in every possible way. And to explain a worshiper's swaying in times of joy, the Besht offered a story:

A wedding feast was taking place inside a house. In a corner sat musicians playing their instruments. The guests danced to the music, joyfully swaying back and forth. A deaf man passing by peered in the window. Unable to see the musicians in their corner or to hear the music, all he observed were people wildly leaping about the room. He naturally concluded that the house was filled with madmen.

Two Paths of Judaism: Praying and Studying

For generations, the Polish Jewish community had revered its scholars and dismissed the uneducated as insignificant. In emphasizing the value of prayer as a way of achieving *devekut*, the Baal Shem Tov gave ordinary Jews the sense that they, not only great sages, could have a meaningful relationship with God. The Besht did not mean to suggest that intense study of Torah and Talmud was unimportant, but simply that many scholars were so caught up in the pride of their own achievements that they belittled less educated Jews. And what was the use of all such intellectual labor, if it came at the cost of forgetting that physical laborers, as well, are creatures of God, deserving respect?

The Besht refused to accept this elitist point of view. Two legends about the Besht illustrate his belief that the prayers of simple Jews can sometimes be more effective than those of great scholars.

The first describes how once, on Yom Kippur, during the concluding service, the Baal Shem Tov went up to the gates of heaven. There he found a pile of prayers uttered by scholars and rabbis during the previous fifty years. These prayers had not made it through the gates of heaven. The Besht then asked the Messiah for help, and together the two of them succeeded in bringing the prayers to God's attention.

> " *The Baal Shem Tov commented on the saying of* The Zohar *that a man is judged in each heavenly palace and that he is driven out of the palace. He explained it to mean that the words of the prayers are the heavenly palaces, for in them thought dwells. When a man prays, he proceeds from letter to letter and word to word and if he is unworthy he is driven away.* "
>
> From *Sefer Baal Shem Tov*, Satmar, 1943, trans. Louis Jacobs

The second tells of the Yom Kippur prayer of a disabled boy. Although his father regularly worshiped at the Besht's synagogue on the High Holy Days, he never bothered to take his son with him, since the boy had never been able to learn the *alef-bet*, much less the meaning of the prayers. Still, this year the boy had become bar mitzvah and was now responsible for carrying out the *mitzvot*. Worried that he might break the holy fast out of ignorance, his father decided it would be better to bring his son with him to services, so that he could keep an eye on him.

What the father did not know, however, was that the boy had brought a whistle with him in his pocket. Several times during the service he asked his father if he could contact God by blowing the whistle; horrified at the thought, the man firmly placed his hand over both pocket and whistle. But during the concluding service the boy was so overcome by the wish to pray that he managed to push away his father's hand, grab the whistle, put it to his lips, and blow loudly.

The sound startled all the worshippers. Suddenly, having grasped what happened, the Baal Shem Tov called out, "The sound of this child's whistle has convinced God to judge us with mercy."

By raising the importance of prayer, and by insisting that abstract study that does not lead to consideration for other people is worthless, the Baal Shem Tov made it possible for all Jews to feel worthy of God's love.

THE PROPER ROLE OF JEWISH LEADERS

Leaders and Followers Need Each Other

While the Baal Shem Tov was well aware that only some people are meant to lead and that not all people are similarly gifted, the kind of leadership he provided was unique, based as it was on a recognition that the leader and his flock needed one another. The leader became known as the *Tzaddik*, or "righteous one," while the followers were called *Hasidim*, or "pious ones." The relationship between the Hasidim and *Tzaddik* was very much like that between pupils and a good teacher. Good teachers help bring out the best in their pupils by guiding them along an unfamiliar path until they can find their way alone. Once this point is reached, the teacher stands back to let the pupils work out problems for themselves.

The teacher–student relationship is not one-sided, however: teachers also need the help of students to achieve their own goals and potential. When students ask questions, for example, they often help the teacher answer in a way that sheds new light on old problems—an illuminating process for everyone. Teachers often insist that they learn at least as much from students as from books or other adults.

An Illustrative Story

The Baal Shem told a story to explain the role of the community in helping the *Tzaddik* develop himself. A group of men stood under a high tree, but only one of them could see that resting at its top was a magnificent bird. He very much wanted to reach the bird but realized he could not do so alone. Since there was no ladder nearby, he asked the group to form a human ladder, with each person standing on the shoulders of the one beneath him. In this manner, he reached the bird. While the others remained unaware of its existence, if any had left their place in the human ladder, he never would have succeeded.

According to the Baal Shem Tov, the *Tzaddik* should be a model for the Hasid but should not stand in the way of the Hasid's own development. Likewise, the *Tzaddik* can fulfill his potential only by working with the community, not by keeping aloof. The kind of leadership the Baal Shem Tov offered his followers was a healthy change from the distant, unemotional leadership that was common in the Polish-Jewish community before his day.

Hasidism Then and Now

Perhaps no form of Judaism has been as intriguing to modern Jews as the Hasidism that began with the Baal Shem Tov. The beautiful ideas of Hasidic leaders strike many Jews and non-Jews alike as remarkably modern and universal. Strikingly, these ideas are wedded to a very traditional way of life, shared with other extremely observant Jews in Hasidic communities in Israel and the United States. To some, however, the universal themes sounded in the thought of the Baal Shem Tov and his followers seem undercut by the Hasidic way of life, which keeps its adherents bonded together in closely knit, exclusive communities.

These seeming contradictions only add to the intrigue of the legacy of the Baal Shem Tov. While most modern Jews do not choose to live in the extremely traditional manner of today's Hasidim, they recognize that some of the most authentic values were sown and harvested by the Baal Shem Tov's movement more than 200 years ago. These values continue to enrich Judaism and to remind us of the varied possibilities within the Jewish tradition.

7 · MOSES MENDELSSOHN

1729 – 1786

Moses Mendelssohn was born in the Jewish ghetto of Dessau, Germany, and died in cosmopolitan Berlin. Despite a humpback and a stammer, this son of a poor scribe became famous throughout Europe. His goal was to bring the worldly culture he had acquired to his fellow Jews. His reputation grew from works for a general, not specifically Jewish audience. In fact, he might never have published his philosophy of Judaism had he not been challenged to do so by Christians, and he was deeply admired by Jews and Gentiles alike.

A Bridge Between Cultures

Life in Two Worlds

While throughout his life Moses Mendelssohn signed his Hebrew name as *Moshe mi-Dessau*—"Moses of Dessau"—he was generally known as Mendelssohn, or son of Mendel. His father earned a meager living in Dessau as a *sofer*, a copier of Torah scrolls and other religious documents. Dessau is only thirty miles from Berlin, where Mendelssohn spent most of his life, but vast distances separated the world into which he was born from the world he was part of at the time of his death some 56 years later.

Overcoming Cultural Isolation.   For many centuries, Jews in parts of Europe had been forbidden to live outside of ghettos. Jews throughout Europe were also forbidden to hold many types of jobs and were forced to pay special taxes by their non-Jewish "protectors." In addition, Jews were isolated culturally. Hardly any Jews even spoke the language of those around them; rather they spoke Yiddish or other similar mixtures of Hebrew and the local language. Unable to read the works that European culture was producing, Jews were in many ways out of touch with the changes that were moving Europe from the Middle Ages into modern times.

As someone actively participating in European culture while remaining a loyal Jew, Moses Mendelssohn was the single most important force in helping the Jews of Europe overcome cultural isolation. In this way, he was a bridge between two worlds.

Mendelssohn left the Dessau ghetto and his parents' home when he was only fourteen. Education was the magnet. He followed his hometown rabbi and teacher, David Frankel, to Berlin, where the situation of the Jews was different from that in Dessau, though not necessarily better. Berlin's wealthier Jews had rights that the poorer Jews lacked, and many of them spoke German. But even wealthy, German-speaking Jews had to endure taunts and prejudice.

Six categories of Jews, determined by wealth and occupation, had official permission to live in Berlin:

1. A tiny group of Jews with "general privileges" were permitted to live wherever they chose, to own property, to pursue business on an equal footing with Gentiles, and to bequeath these privileges to all their offspring.

> **"** *I believe that Judaism knows nothing of a revealed religion in the sense in which Christians define this term. The Israelites possess a divine legislation— laws, commandments, statutes, rules of conduct, instruction in God's will and in what they are to do to attain temporal and eternal salvation. . . .* **"**
>
> *Jerusalem*, trans. Alfred Jospe

2. "Protected Jews" were allowed to own property and engage in business but could not move from place to place. In addition, only one child from each family could inherit the status of "protected Jew," although other children could buy entry into it.

3. A lesser class of "protected Jews," including professionals such as physicians, had the same status, but only for themselves; none of their children could inherit it.

4. A still lesser class of "protected Jews," including rabbis, cantors, and other community officials, were permitted to perform their religious roles but forbidden to participate in business.

5. "Tolerated Jews" included the children of Jews of the four higher classes. They were excluded not only from business but also from the professions, and they maintained their status only if they married into one of the two highest classes.

6. The lowest class of Jew included employees who were permitted to remain in Berlin only while they were employed.

When the teenaged Mendelssohn arrived in Berlin, he fit none of those official categories. For seven years he lived a hand-to-mouth existence. His rabbi found him an attic room in the home of a wealthy Jew and gave him an occasional manuscript to copy. During these years, he educated himself.

The standard education of a Jewish boy consisted almost exclusively of training in Talmud. Nonreligious subjects, and even the non-Talmudic Hebrew heritage, were ignored. Students were not taught biblical Hebrew or the poems of such important poets as Yehudah HaLevi, and they were rarely encouraged to study works of Jewish philosophy. Mendelssohn rebelled against this system as a young boy, learning biblical Hebrew and reading the Bible on his own, even memorizing large sections. He also managed to lay his hands on some of Maimonides' works. Maimonides' emphasis on reason appealed to him.

In Berlin he met young Jewish professionals who took him under their wing and introduced him to modern and ancient languages as well as mathematics. Books were expensive, so Mendelssohn was limited to what he could borrow or barely afford. He learned both Latin and philosophy, for example, when he came upon a Latin version of a work by the English philosopher John Locke. He also improved his German and got his first introduction to Christian thought when he came upon a book by the German Christian thinker Gustav Reinbeck.

After spending seven lean years in Berlin, Mendelssohn had a stroke of luck: a wealthy Jewish silk manufacturer hired him to tutor his children. Now his life became more comfortable; he had more time to pursue his studies and more money to buy books. He impressed his employer so much that in less than twelve years he rose from tutor to clerk to manager of the silk-manufacturing business. After his employer's death, Mendelssohn, along with the widow, took charge of the business.

Mendelssohn's employer had a hand in shaping not only his professional and financial future but also his personal life. About the time that he became manager of the firm, his employer's daughter introduced him to Fromet Gugenheim, whom he would marry. Professionally, he gradually became respected even outside his firm, and finally, toward the end of his life, was commissioned to write a report on the silk-manufacturing business for the state. But Mendelssohn's is a much more complex tale than how a ghetto boy rose from rags to riches.

A New World: Berlin's Writers and Intellectuals.   When Mendelssohn was 24, a friend introduced him to the young German playwright and critic Gotthold Ephraim Lessing. The ensuing friendship between the two—ending only with Lessing's death—helped launch Mendelssohn on a literary career that would spread his fame throughout Europe.

In mid-century Germany, friendships between Jews and Gentiles were extremely rare; transactions between the two groups usually involved only business. Lessing might have been predicted to have an unusually open mind, since he had already revealed his religious tolerance when he was twelve years old, in an unusual place: a Latin exam. He had been asked to translate a piece about how the Christians in ancient Rome dealt with foreigners. After completing his task, he added his own thoughts about how all people can help each other, stating that it is wrong to condemn Jews or Muslims for their religion. Likewise, before meeting Mendelssohn, Lessing had written a play called *The Jews*, whose central characters were favorably drawn.

With Lessing's encouragement, Mendelssohn began to share his remarkable talents for expressing himself in German. Shortly after they met, he published his first German essay, a defense of Lessing's *The Jews*, in response to a nasty review that questioned whether the decent Jews portrayed in the play could exist in real life. Lessing also quietly undertook to publish Mendelssohn's first book, on the English philosopher Shaftesbury. Together with other friends, Mendelssohn and Lessing became partners in a literary magazine that was published regularly over a six-year period.

In 1763, twenty years after he left the Dessau ghetto, Mendelssohn won first prize for a philosophical essay in a contest sponsored by the Berlin Royal Academy. Second prize went to Immanuel Kant, who would eventually become one of Germany's greatest philosophers. It is generally agreed that Mendelssohn's superior German style

> **"** *Adopt the mores and constitution of the country in which you find yourself, but be steadfast in upholding the religion of your fathers, too. Bear both burdens as well as you can.* **"**
>
> *Jerusalem*, trans. Alfred Jospe

led to the selection of his essay over Kant's. Four years later he published a book on the immortality of the soul, which established his reputation in Europe as a first-rate thinker. He was compared to the Greek philosophers Plato and Socrates, and the book was translated into several languages.

Remaining an Involved Jew.

Mendelssohn's growing fame as a German thinker and writer never led him to turn his back on his Jewish roots. He made an effort both to educate non-Jews about the glories of the Jewish heritage and to involve the Jewish community in the latest political and social developments. For instance, he translated into German several Hebrew poems celebrating the military victories of Prussia's Frederick the Great, and when the wars ended, he wrote a German sermon celebrating peace, based on a saying from the Talmud. Like the poems, the sermon was read as part of the synagogue service in Berlin, Prussia's capital. German poems by Mendelssohn celebrating other joyful occasions in the life of the royal family were also read in synagogue.

In dealing with Gentiles, Mendelssohn made no attempt to hide or ignore his Jewishness; he even ended some letters abruptly with the explanation that Sabbath was about to begin and Jewish law permitted no writing on the Sabbath. On at least one occasion, when he and his wife were entertaining a group of philosophers and poets, the Mendelssohns left the living room to light Sabbath candles. When writing for non-Jewish audiences, Mendelssohn often included Hebrew sayings in translation, hoping both to show the wisdom and poetic value of Jewish literature and to chip away at anti-Jewish prejudice.

One episode in Mendelssohn's extraordinary life underscores the way in which he bridged two worlds. In the autumn of 1771 he was summoned to the royal palace in Potsdam, just outside of Berlin. Frederick the Great had no love for Mendelssohn: some years before, the philosopher had criticized the king's poems in the literary magazine he and Lessing published. The king had already displayed his dislike by vetoing Mendelssohn's appointment to the Royal Academy. One of the king's visitors, however, expressed a wish to meet Mendelssohn, and so an invitation—an order, really—was issued to the Jew.

Mendelssohn had a problem, however. He was observing the holiday of Shemini Atzeret, at the end of Sukkot, when observant Jews are not permitted to ride. Yet the distance to the royal palace was much too great for him to walk. He consulted the rabbis of Berlin, who came up with the following compromise: On this occasion, in response to a specific order of the king, Mendelssohn was to be permitted to ride to the palace. Some Jews of Berlin or Potsdam might be unaware of the special circumstances, however, and might think Mendelssohn was

openly violating Jewish law by riding on the holiday. For that reason, the rabbis asked him to go through the Berlin gate on foot and to leave the carriage before it entered Potsdam.

Mendelssohn Brings Modern Culture to the Ghetto

Mendelssohn was convinced that German Jews could benefit from participation in the world around them. His attempts to open up the ghetto to modern culture fell into three categories: improving the Jews' skills in German, renewing their interest in Hebrew, and reforming the type of education offered to Jewish children.

Offering Jews the German Language. Mendelssohn was convinced that Germans would not take Jews seriously until they could speak, read, and write German. The mixed German-Jewish ghetto dialect, he felt, simply would not gain them access to the cultured world beyond.

Mendelssohn felt that the best way to encourage German Jews to learn German was with a first-rate translation of the Torah. He knew that some translations existed, but none seemed satisfactory. In translations done by Jews, the German was crude; neither the original beauty of the Bible's Hebrew nor the poetry of which German was capable came across. And in the standard Gentile translations, the translator often interpreted the Torah along Christian lines.

Frederick the Great invited Mendelssohn to the Royal Palace at Potsdam on *Shemini Atzeret* in 1771. Mendelssohn received special rabbinical dispensation to be driven from Berlin to the palace on this holiday.

Die

fünf Bücher Mose

חמשה חומשי תורה

übersetzt

von   A. M. Bank.

Moses Mendelssohn.

Für Bibelfreunde

aller Konfessionen, und zunächst für Israeliten
bestimmt.

Herausgegeben

von

D. Fränkel,

Herzogl. Anhalt-Dessauischem Direktor der Israelitischen Schulen

und von

M. H. Bock,

Doktor der Philosophie und Vorsteher einer Lehr-Erziehungs-
und Pensions-Anstalt in Berlin.

Dessau,
zu haben bei dem Direktor Fränkel.
Berlin,
in Kommission bei Fr. Nicolai.
1815.

Mendelssohn's translation of the
Torah into German introduced
many Jews to the German
language, allowing them to
participate in the world of
German culture.

What began as Mendelssohn's effort to tutor his German-speaking children led to a landmark in modern Jewish history: his own German version of the Five Books of Moses transliterated into Hebrew, published between 1780 and 1783. For many young Jews, this German Torah, written in the Hebrew alphabet, opened the door to German culture. After working their way through it, they found themselves able to read the German masterpieces, along with other great works of world literature in German translation.

Germany's rabbis did not all celebrate the publication of Mendelssohn's translation. Although many, including the chief rabbi of Berlin, hoped that it would help end Jewish ignorance, others objected, fearing that time spent on German literature would be at the expense of religious study. In some communities, rabbis used their religious authority to ban the work.

Making Hebrew into a Modern Language.

Today Hebrew is the language of the state of Israel and of its poets, novelists, and thinkers. In Mendelssohn's time, however, most Jews considered the language part of the past. Although many could read the Bible in Hebrew and knew the Hebrew prayers, few had the fluency to use it as a living language.

Mendelssohn felt that Hebrew had as much expressive potential and flexibility as German or any other modern language. It, too, could be a tool for entering the modern world. After all, biblical Hebrew had produced one of the masterpieces of world literature. He wanted Jews to learn German, but not to feel that Hebrew was less rich.

To promote this goal, Mendelssohn included a Hebrew commentary, written by either himself or one of his colleagues, in his translation of the Torah. In addition, throughout his career he sponsored Hebrew journals that introduced Hebrew readers to both religious subjects and secular culture.

Changing the Educational System.

Today Jewish day schools proliferate in the United States. There, Hebrew language and religious subjects are taught, along with English, math, computers, and sports. Before Mendelssohn's time, such schools did not exist anywhere.

In 1781 one of Mendelssohn's younger colleagues opened a new type of Jewish school in Berlin with Mendelssohn's encouragement. Yiddish was no longer the classroom language, and the Jewish students were offered a free, well-rounded education with courses in Hebrew, German, and other languages, in addition to subjects ranging from bookkeeping to geography. Starting with this experiment, under

Mendelssohn's influence the nature of Jewish education would slowly change. Young Jews were learning how to live in the world beyond the ghetto, breaking down the barriers between themselves and non-Jews.

MENDELSSOHN AS A JEWISH ADVOCATE

Defending the Mishnah

Mendelssohn was never afraid to use his position on behalf of his fellow Jews. More than once the literary journal he directed with Lessing served as a platform for the support of Judaism. Although the journal's writers did not sign their names, regular readers knew who they were and could identify them by style. In one instance, Mendelssohn pretended to be a Gentile recalling an encounter with a scholarly Jew at a spa: the Jew had carefully explained to him what the Talmud was really like, suggesting that what non-Jews think they know of it is often totally inaccurate.

In 1759 the German literary community learned that a German chaplain was preparing a translation of the Mishnah, a basic part of the Talmud. In the journal, Mendelssohn put on a mask of anonymity to defend the Mishnah. He wrote that, like his readers, he was looking forward to the translation, but probably for different reasons. He said that many of them probably relished the idea of making fun of the work's odd qualities, which they expected the new German translation to make apparent. In his Gentile disguise, Mendelssohn begged to differ. "On no account can I persuade myself that the best minds of a nation (and, surely, the Jewish nation is not short of very good minds) should have occupied themselves throughout so many centuries exclusively with a work consisting of insipid rubbish. The immense diligence with which they study it and the . . . ardor that I have so often seen displayed when they argue some of its subjects would seem proof to me that a person of genius can find all that is necessary for nourishment in this kind of study."

To Mendelssohn's relief, the first volume of the translation deserved much praise; the criticism he offered was received gracefully; the translator even included Mendelssohn's review in the preface to the second volume. It was this Christian who was first to say of Mendelssohn that "from Maimonides until this Moses, there has been no Jew like him."

Defending Judaism with Self-Restraint

A distinguished Swiss preacher named Johann Kaspar Lavater was an admirer of Mendelssohn and had visited him more than once in Berlin. During one encounter Mendelssohn, when pressed, had made some polite remarks about Jesus.

Lavater was among those Christians who believed that when the Jewish people converted to Christianity, the so-called second coming of Christ would occur and eternal peace would then reign on earth. He also believed that if Mendelssohn converted, other Jews might follow his example. Lavater could thus hasten the second coming by encouraging Mendelssohn to convert.

Lavater set about his task by translating a French book into German, then published under the title *An Examination of the Proofs for Christianity.* Imagine Mendelssohn's surprise to find that the translation was dedicated to him and that in the preface Lavater challenged him either to explain why the book's arguments were not convincing or to convert to Christianity.

At the end of 1769 Mendelssohn sent Lavater a printed letter in which he stated, "If I ever became convinced that my religion was not the true one, I would feel compelled to leave it." But for three reasons, he said he would not enter a debate with Lavater. First of all, arguments Jews might offer on behalf of their religion were less likely to change non-Jewish attitudes than was dignified Jewish behavior; Mendelssohn considered it beneath his dignity to argue with Christians whose "expert" knowledge of Judaism came from anti-Semitic books. Second, Judaism has never sought to encourage non-Jews to convert. On the contrary, it taught that God rewards even those lacking all belief, as long as their actions are good. If Mendelssohn stated his objections to Lavater's arguments, he might be seen as trying to convert Christians. Finally, Jews everywhere were dependent on the kindness of their rulers. If Mendelssohn found fault with Christian arguments, Christian rulers might see his criticism as a sign that Jews lacked gratitude toward their protectors.

The following spring Lavater sent a letter of apology to Mendelssohn. But the entire episode convinced Mendelssohn that more needed to be done on behalf of the Jewish people.

Jewish Communities Turn to Mendelssohn

Mendelssohn had become the most influential Jew of his time. As a result, Jews everywhere turned to him for help in time of distress, sometimes forcing Mendelssohn to put aside his own needs. A case in point is an appeal on the part of the Jews from two Swiss villages, about five years after the Lavater incident. In an attempt to eliminate the Jewish population, the village governments had forbidden Jews from marrying. Mendelssohn realized that his most influential Christian-Swiss connection was none other than Lavater, whom he persuaded to intervene. With Lavater's help, the Swiss Jews' right to marry was restored.

In 1780 an anti-Semitic judge wrote a pamphlet viciously attacking the Jews of Alsace, France. The leading Jew from that region contacted Mendelssohn, requesting that he write a letter to the French authorities. But Mendelssohn felt such a petition would be more effective if it came from a Christian. In Berlin he had met a young man—Christian Wilhelm von Dohm, a preacher's son—whose tolerance had impressed him, and he asked Dohm to work with him to improve the situation of the Jews of Alsace. Inspired by Mendelssohn, Dohm would end up writing the first significant work by a non-Jew arguing that Jews be given full rights of citizenship.

MENDELSSOHN'S PHILOSOPHY OF JUDAISM

The Cornerstone: Argument Against Excommunication

The joint effort by Mendelssohn and Dohm on behalf of the Alsatian Jews also led to a major work by Dohm, one having an important effect on Mendelssohn's own writing over the next several years. Although Mendelssohn agreed with most of what Dohm said, he could not accept one line of thinking: that Jewish religious leaders, like church leaders, should have the right to excommunicate—that is, banish from the community—those who violate Jewish beliefs, and a similar argument that Jewish leaders, like other religious leaders, should be permitted to ban books they found inappropriate.

He wondered how he could best express his differences with Dohm regarding excommunication. The solution occurred to him when he reread a work written over a century before called "The Vindication of the Jews"—a letter from Rabbi Manasseh ben Israel of Amsterdam to the leaders of England. Ben Israel had argued that the Jews were worthy of being readmitted to England, from where they had been banished in 1290. Since Mendelssohn found these views still important, he asked a German friend to translate them into German. Mendelssohn himself wrote a preface to the translation. The title of the work, when it was published in 1782, indicated that his preface was "a supplement" to Dohm's earlier work.

After he gained prominence, Mendelssohn was challenged by the Swiss theologian Johann Lavater to prove the merits of Judaism. Mendelssohn declined to debate the merits of Judaism and Christianity, and Lavater later apologized to him. Here Mendelssohn, on the left, plays chess with Lavater, while Gotthold Lessing looks on. Lessing is often considered the father of modern German literature, and was an important force in launching Mendelssohn's philosophical and literary career.

Before dealing with the excommunication issue, Mendelssohn used the preface to charge the Christian world with extreme unfairness in its dealing with Jews: "People continue to keep us away from all contact with the arts and sciences or with trades and occupations which are useful and have dignity. They bar all roads leading to increased usefulness and then use our lack of culture to justify our continued oppression. They tie our hands and then reproach us that we do not use them."

Mendelssohn ended the preface by appealing to Jewish religious leaders directly. Using a psychological approach, he asked them to give up the right of excommunication, the only type of power their oppressors had left them. Perhaps, he said, Jewish leaders get some satisfaction out of treating their own people with as little tolerance as all of them have been treated as a group. Mendelssohn seemed to be expanding on the advice the ancient sage Hillel had offered nearly 1,800 years earlier. Said Hillel, "What is hateful to you, do not do to others." Mendelssohn, in turn, advised Jewish religious leaders, "If you wish to be sheltered, tolerated, and spared by others, you ought to shelter, tolerate, and spare each other."

Jerusalem: A Controversial Philosophy of Judaism

Mendelssohn had written the preface to Manasseh ben Israel's work as a way of partially rebutting Dohm. He did not anticipate that it would lead to further challenges, similar to the one Lavater had issued earlier. These led Mendelssohn, in turn, to write *Jerusalem, or Religious Power and Judaism*, in which he outlined his full, and controversial, philosophy of Judaism.

In 1782 an anonymous pamphlet appeared called "The Search for Light and Right: An Epistle to Moses Mendelssohn Occasioned by His Remarkable Preface to Rabbi Manasseh ben Israel's 'Vindication of the Jews.'" The pamphlet did not disagree with Mendelssohn's position that no religion should have the power of excommunication. But, it said, if Mendelssohn truly believed that all people should be free to practice religion according to their own consciences, what was Mendelssohn's attitude toward all the laws of the Torah and Talmud, which a Jew is supposed to observe? In the pamphleteer's words, "Clearly, ecclesiastical law armed with coercive power has always been one of the cornerstones of the Jewish religion."

The author of the pamphlet then issued a challenge: Mendelssohn must explain how the position in his preface conformed to Jewish beliefs or else explain why he refused to convert to Christianity. The book *Jerusalem* is Mendelssohn's response.

In the first section of the work, Mendelssohn argued that no religious institution has the right to use force. While governments can compel people to obey laws even if they disagree with them, neither religious institutions nor governments are justified in controlling people's thoughts or beliefs. Religious institutions may try to persuade, and they have the right to instruct. But they may neither use force to make people accept those beliefs nor punish them for failing to accept them. What makes a person good or bad is behavior, not belief.

In *Jerusalem*'s second section, Mendelssohn took up the question of whether Judaism does permit religious leaders to use force. He began with his famous explanation of what Judaism and the Torah are. Mendelssohn believed that God gave all people, not just Jews, the ability to use their powers of reasoning to figure out how to behave toward one another. What is special about Judaism is the specific set of laws listed in the Torah, which only Jews are required to observe. According to Mendelssohn, what God revealed to the Israelites through Moses "were rules and precepts" instructing them in how to behave, rather than "doctrines" or "saving truths." He pointed out that none of the commandments or laws begins "Thou shalt believe" or "Thou shalt not believe." Instead, they all say "Thou shalt do" or "Thou shalt not do." In other words, Judaism from the outset was interested in guiding people's behavior, not their thought.

Mendelssohn then completed his answer about the use of force in Judaism. When the ancient Israelites had a nation, God was its monarch. Every offense against one of the Torah's laws was also an offense against the nation's laws. Violating the Sabbath, for example, weakened the authority of God, the nation's monarch, and thus weakened the state itself. Therefore, the state could punish such violations.

Once the Temple was destroyed, the Jewish state came to an end. At that time and forever after, Judaism lost its power of force; religious violations no longer constituted crimes against the state. The Talmud specifically indicates that after the Sanhedrin—the ancient Jewish court—ceased to function on the Temple grounds, Jewish courts could no longer put people to death or use bodily punishments. From then on, "Our religion … knows no punishment, no penalty save the one that the repentant sinner voluntarily imposes upon himself."

Mendelssohn argued that, with the end of the Jewish state, some of the Torah's laws lost their binding effect. For example, the laws of the Temple and the priesthood have no meaning. But Jews must continue to observe all the other laws. He offered three reasons for the continuing need to observe the Torah: (1) The Torah was given by God, and it would be arrogance to say that its laws are no longer needed. If that time ever comes, God will make it clear in some obvious way. (2) Observance of the Torah's laws keeps the Jewish people united.

(3) Even though all people are capable of using reason to arrive at religious truths, the human spirit tends to lead people toward errors, such as idol worship. Judaism's laws preserve the pure belief in God.

Mendelssohn ended *Jerusalem* with an argument against blending all the world's religions into one. Such a step would destroy freedom of thought. It would also go against God's intention to have a varied world. Just as God gave people different faces, so different religions are part of God's plan.

Flaws in Mendelssohn's Arguments

Kant, the most important philosopher of the German Enlightenment, was only one of a number of non-Jews who were impressed by *Jerusalem*. He wrote to Mendelssohn, "I hold the book to be the announcement of a great, if a slowly advancing reform, which affects not only your own nation but all others." Still, the Jewish community had trouble with Mendelssohn's philosophy of Judaism. The idea that Judaism was only a body of laws, given by God in a supernatural act, did not sit well. Mendelssohn in effect argued that everything that was reasonable about Judaism was not specifically Jewish, while everything that was specifically Jewish was supernatural.

There were other problems as well. For example, if human reason is capable on its own of figuring out the proper way of living, why is reason not able on its own to come up with God's plan for the Jews? If all people can come to the same idea of religion as the Jewish idea, why did God give the Torah only to one people? And if all human beings have the gift of reason, why does error persist? Why is Jewish law needed to protect the "religion of reason" from perversion?

MENDELSSOHN'S PLACE IN JEWISH HISTORY

Evaluating the First Modern Jewish Thinker

Mendelssohn, who never tried to hide his Jewishness in order to succeed in German society, is important as a trailblazer for all thoughtful Jews wishing to live in the modern world without giving up their lives as Jews. At the same time, his colorful life and personality have led to more poetic assessments of his importance. In the nineteenth century more than one writer saw Mendelssohn as fulfilling part of God's design. In a Hebrew biography published within two years after his death, the author stated that God sent Mendelssohn to free the minds of the Jews from the slavery of the ghetto.

The German poet Heine, who died 70 years after Mendelssohn, failed to follow Mendelssohn's example in the most crucial way of all: in order to advance his career, he converted from Judaism to Christianity in his late twenties. Never ceasing to consider himself truly a Jew, he later bitterly regretted the decision and wrote many works with Jewish themes. He remarked that God had made Mendelssohn a hunchback in order to teach common people that everyone should be judged by inner worth, not by outward appearance.

The modern scholar Eva Jospe incorporates both of these reflections—that Mendelssohn liberated Jews from slavery and was a hunchback by divine intent—into a unified evaluation. How accurate is the claim on behalf of Mendelssohn that "from Maimonides until this Moses, there has been no Jew like him"? According to Jospe, Mendelssohn can be compared to the biblical Moses as liberator: his contributions to freeing European Jewry from the ghetto were many, and like the biblical Moses he overcame personal problems to fulfill his task. According to legend, the biblical Moses had a speech defect, and according to the Torah, he felt hesitant when God called upon him to be a leader. Moses Mendelssohn not only stammered and had a humpback, but he also hated controversy. But both the biblical Moses and Moses Mendelssohn put aside their personal concerns to help their people when need arose.

8 THEODOR HERZL

1860 – 1904

More than any other individual, Herzl changed the course of modern Jewish history. Neither an observant Jew nor rigorously trained in Jewish studies, he focused on the Jews as a people, not on Judaism as a religion. As the first Jewish statesman in nearly 2,000 years, he was an activist, transforming his ideas into reality. He thus created political Zionism and became the father of the modern Jewish state.

FROM MENDELSSOHN TO HERZL

Three Solutions That Caused New Problems

Herzl was born nearly 75 years after the death of Moses Mendelssohn. During this period, a great deal had happened to the Jews of Europe, much of it resulting from Mendelssohn's work, and much of it leading to Herzl's. Jews had moved toward citizenship, broadened their learning, and expanded their definition of religion. Each of these advances toward modernity created strains on Jewish life and did nothing to lessen the dangers of the modern world.

Emancipation.   In the years following Mendelssohn's death, many Western European governments began to abolish laws limiting the freedom of Jews. This process of "emancipation" began in France, as a result of the French Revolution of 1789 and Napoleon's subsequent rise to power.

In Austria-Hungary, where Herzl lived much of his life, Jewish emancipation began only a few years before his birth; completed when he was seven years old, it enabled Herzl's father to leave the ghetto and become a wealthy businessman in Budapest. During the 1850s and 1860s the last restrictions on the Jews of England, Germany, and Italy were lifted. The Jews of the Eastern European countries lived in hope that their government would become more liberal and emancipate them as well.

But there was a paradox at work. To merit emancipation, it seemed that the Jewish communities of Europe were expected to give up their claim to ties with worldwide Jewry—in other words, to deny that there was such a thing as a Jewish nation to which they belonged. They had to accept the principle that they were English, French, or German like any of their fellow citizens and that all that made them different was the religion they followed.

Haskalah: The Great Enlightenment.   Mendelssohn believed that education was the key to society's acceptance of the Jews: if they learned to speak like their neighbors and studied modern science, literature, and so on, they would eventually be accepted as equals. Out of this belief grew a movement called *Haskalah*, which is Hebrew for "Enlightenment." Its aim was to bring Jews and Judaism into the modern world. In addition to broadening Jewish education, the *Haskalah* movement led to the rebirth of the Hebrew language.

> *Now everyone knows how steam is generated by boiling water in a kettle, but such steam only rattles the lid. The current Zionist projects and other associations to check anti-Semitism are teakettle phenomena of this kind. But I say that this force, if properly harnessed, is powerful enough to propel a large engine and to move passengers and goods.*
>
> The Jewish State, trans. Arthur Hertzberg

Mendelssohn and those who followed in his footsteps hoped that emancipation and *Haskalah* would make it possible for Jews to blend—or assimilate—into European society. But all too often, assimilated Jews moved into European culture by converting or marrying non-Jews. Some members of Mendelssohn's own family followed that route after his death.

The Reform Movement.

Today we are familiar with the several branches of Judaism—Orthodox, Conservative, Reform, and Reconstructionist. But in Mendelssohn's time there was only one branch, which today we would call Orthodox. In the years following his death, and into the early 1800s, the Reform Movement was begun by a group of German Jews. Among their goals were to show that Judaism was just as modern and acceptable as the Christian faiths (primarily Lutheranism and Catholicism) adhered to by most German citizens, to make Jewish worship more compatible with that of these faiths, and to improve the image of Jews in the eyes of non-Jews.

The Reform Movement stressed the centrality of the ethical teachings of Judaism over the observance of specific rituals, which was not considered so important. It also put a more optimistic face on one crucial element in Jewish life. In traditional prayer books, Jews read that they had been exiled from the Land of Israel because of their sins. The Reform Movement interpreted the tradition to mean that Jews were not really in exile but instead were in the "Diaspora"—scattered across the face of the earth. Diaspora Jews had a role to play for the benefit of all humanity—namely, to spread the ethical teachings of the one God.

From Germany, the Reform Movement spread to other European countries and to the United States, where in 1885 it adopted the position that Jews were strictly a religious group and not a national community.

Anti-Semitism.

Unfortunately, Mendelssohn's hopes were not fully realized. Modern Jews might dress, speak, and worship in ways more familiar to Gentiles, but emancipation and enlightenment did not lead to their full acceptance in European society. Old hatreds did not disappear; they just changed. While emancipated Jews and the Reform Movement insisted that Judaism was only a religion, anti-Semites insisted otherwise—that Jews were a race whose attributes (which they believed were foreign and a menace) were fixed, passed on from generation to generation, any efforts to mask them through conversion notwithstanding. They consequently believed assimilated Jews to be the most dangerous, since they looked and behaved like other people and could not be readily recognized as Jewish.

A new word was coined to describe this "scientific" Jew-hatred. In 1879 a German journalist first used the term "anti-Semitism" in a pamphlet accusing the "Semitic race" of attempting to destroy "Germandom."

A great deal of study has been devoted to the causes of this new, virulent anti-Semitism and to its connections with the more traditional variety. In part, it was an unexpected result of the emancipation. As Jews poured into fields that had formerly been closed to them, their non-Jewish competitors felt threatened. In part, it was an offshoot of the rise of national movements in Europe at this time. The modern countries of Germany and Italy had just been formed out of collections of separate states. Poland was trying to free itself from the hold of the Russian czar, parts of the Turkish Ottoman Empire were seeking freedom, and Hungary was trying to break free of Austria. As these national movements developed and grew, they focused on the qualities that made groups of people different from one another, rather than on those that joined them. Also, the fact that Jews lived scattered around the globe led to suspicions that they had sinister plans to dominate the world.

Everywhere, even in educated circles, there was sudenly talk of a "Jewish problem." During the final decades of the nineteenth century this so-called problem was one of the most hotly debated topics. In 1880 a former professor at the University of Berlin published *The Jewish Question as a Question of Race, Morality, and Culture.* It became respectable to hate Jews even if they were like other people in every respect other than religion. Surrounded by such talk, many Jews began

When Israel's Declaration of Independence was read by its first prime minister, David Ben-Gurion, on May 14, 1948, a portrait of Theodor Herzl hung prominently in the center of the room.

to experience self-hatred, feeling that there must be something desperately wrong with themselves to warrant such general contempt. Rich Jews blamed poor Jews and poor Jews blamed rich Jews for the negative impression the non-Jewish world had of them as a whole.

The situation was bad enough in Western Europe, where anti-Semitism existed but was not encouraged by governments. But it was even worse in Eastern Europe, where governments began to stir up anti-Jewish uprisings. In this way, Jews became the scapegoats for whatever dissatisfactions people felt. When the czar of Russia was assassinated in 1881, a period of bloody, violent anti-Jewish pogroms spread across the country. Jews in more than 160 cities and villages were victims. Not only did the government support the pogroms, but few educated people objected, some even joining in. The hopes of Eastern European Jews for eventual emancipation were shattered.

The sympathy of assimilated Western European Jews was mixed with other emotions. They did not want to give up their belief in the goodwill of governments and of civilized human beings everywhere, but many Western Jews thought of their Eastern European counterparts as old-fashioned and foreign. To escape the violence, Russian Jews began to move in great numbers to other countries, and the Westerners worried that the arrival of these strange Eastern Jews would only worsen the "Jewish problem" in their own countries. Furthermore, the pogroms were leading many Russian Jews to become involved in the revolutionary, anti-czarist movement, and Western European Jews were afraid such behavior would justify one claim of the anti-Semites: that Jews everywhere were conspiring to topple rightful governments.

Early Zionist Stirrings

Another effect of the 1881 Russian pogroms was that they led many Russian Jews to Zionism. The word "Zionism" came into use toward the end of the nineteenth century. The Hibbat Zion, or "Love of Zion," movement was a reaction to the loss of faith in emancipation and enlightenment. The movement's members called themselves Hovevei Zion, or "Lovers of Zion," and they began to set up small colonies in *Eretz Yisrael*. Their efforts were financed by the wealthy Jewish philanthropist Baron Edmond de Rothschild.

Eretz Yisrael was not a universal choice for a homeland. Another Jewish philanthropist, Baron Maurice de Hirsch, decided it was too close to Russia for a huge colony of Jews, and the fact that it was part of the unstable Turkish Ottoman Empire also made him hesitant. In any event, the Turks had barred the entrance of Jewish settlers to *Eretz Yisrael*, so the Hovevei Zion had to sneak in illegally.

The group did not represent the first Jews to have plans for resettling *Eretz Yisrael*. Earlier in the century the national movements in Europe steered Jewish thinkers in a similar direction. Among these early Zionists were Rabbi Yehudah Alkalai (1798–1878), Moses Hess (1812–1875), and Leo Pinsker (1821–1891).

Yehudah Alkalai.   Alkalai was the rabbi of Serbia, which at the time was part of the Turkish Empire. The Serbs were beginning to demand independence from the Turks, and the nearby Greeks had already shaken off Turkish rule.

Beginning in 1834, Alkalai began to publish his thoughts on resettling the Land of Israel. Very strict rabbis then believed it an act of impiety to suggest that Jews should try ending the exile on their own by returning in large numbers to *Eretz Yisrael*. They felt that only the Messiah could bring about "the ingathering of the exiles." Alkalai, however, interpreted several biblical texts to justify "self-redemption," or going ahead without waiting for the Messiah.

In 1840 a "blood accusation" was raised against the Jews of Damascus. This scurrilous accusation—that Jews use Christian blood in the baking of Passover matzot—dates back to 1171. (Since then it has been raised in many countries, including the United States.) Now firmly convinced that Jews would find a secure life only in their own homeland, Alkalai wrote a series of books and pamphlets outlining his program.

Just as the biblical Abraham had been able to buy land from Ephron the Hittite (Genesis 23:10–20), Alkalai hoped to buy the Land of Israel from the Turks. He also spoke of calling together a "Great Assembly" of Jewish representatives from all over the world and setting up a national fund to purchase land.

Almost no one knew of Alakai's writings, and there was little reaction to them.

Moses Hess.   Hess, a German Jew, was from a much less traditional background than Alkalai. Although he was himself an assimilated Jew, once his wide reading introduced him to the new anti-Semitism, he began to feel that the tendency to view Jews as a race would prevent them from becoming part of the nations where they lived. Hess argued that the Jews are in fact a nation and that with the help of the liberal European nations they could establish their own country in *Eretz Yisrael*.

In 1862, impressed by the way the Italian states had banded together to form the nation of Italy, Hess wrote his Zionist book, *Rome and Jerusalem*. Modeling their dream on Virgil's epic poem the *Aeneid*, the Italians imagined that Rome would be the center of a new world of nations. In Hess's biblical vision, Jerusalem would become the center of the new world. The Jewish people would return to *Eretz Yisrael*, where they would establish a Jewish state based on social justice and other Jewish values.

As was the case with Alkalai, Hess's book had little immediate impact.

Leo Pinsker.   The most important Zionist work to follow fast on the pogroms of 1881 was published anonymously by the Polish-born physician Leo Pinsker. Before the pogroms, Pinsker, who had been honored by the czar for his service during the Crimean War, believed that the Jews could assimilate within Russia. But the involvement of both the government and educated classes in the slaughter changed his mind. Anti-Semitism was permanent, he felt, and the only solution for the Jews was to establish their own state, in *Eretz Yisrael* if possible but elsewhere if necessary.

In his pamphlet "Auto-Emancipation," Pinsker argued that emigration to other nations was not a solution because anti-Semitism would eventually arise there. Because the rest of the world rejected the Jews, they must renew their old national ties, directing their energies toward finding a country of their own.

Pinsker wrote "Auto-Emancipation" in German, hoping to spread his views among Western European Jews. But he found no support. The Orthodox community felt it was heresy to talk about auto-emancipation or self-redemption; they believed that instead Jews must patiently await the coming of the Messiah. The liberal community condemned him for losing faith in brotherhood's triumph over hatred, which they believed was surely coming. Only those who already shared his views welcomed his statement. In 1893 Pinsker joined the Hovevei Zion.

THE FATHER OF POLITICAL ZIONISM

The Making of a Zionist

If the blood accusation confirmed Alkalai's Zionist views, if new racist theories of anti-Semitism turned Hess into a Zionist, and if the pogroms of 1881 converted Pinsker into one, what made a Zionist out of Herzl?

He knew nothing of the Zionist activity preceding him. He also knew precious little about Judaism in general, and until he became a Zionist leader his views of Eastern European Jews were shaped by anti-Semitic stereotypes. He came from a well-to-do, assimilated home in which only a few traditions were observed. While growing up, he attended Reform services at a Budapest synagogue near his family's apartment. Rather than becoming bar mitzvah in the synagogue, it seems he was confirmed at home. In his diary, he records a negative impression of his early Jewish education.

It is thus not surprising that Herzl's early ideas on the future of the Jewish people were similar to those of other assimilated Jews. He felt that history meant progress, that eventually the process of assimilation would be completed, and that Jews would be fully accepted by non-Jewish society.

After Herzl decided on a career in journalism, he turned down an offer to write for a newspaper that would have forced him to use a less Jewish-sounding pen name. But this incident did not shake his faith in the power of assimilation to overcome anti-Semitism.

He soon moved to Paris as the local correspondent for an influential Viennese newspaper, and he began covering a series of anti-Semitic incidents in France, the very first country to emancipate its Jews. In late summer 1892 he wrote an article entitled "French Anti-Semites," noting that the author of a two-volume best-selling anti-Semitic book, published a few years earlier, had just founded a weekly dedicated "to the defense of Catholic France against atheists, republicans, Free Masons, and Jews." Herzl's conclusion was that anti-Semitism was being used everywhere to divert people's attention from the real problems of society.

The Dreyfus Affair.

What Herzl later called the event that made him into a Zionist began to unfold in the mid-1890s. In October 1894 Captain Alfred Dreyfus, a Jew in the French army, was arrested on charges of high treason. Eventually it became clear that he had been framed by anti-Semites, but for nearly a decade the "Dreyfus affair" tore French society apart. Although the trial itself was closed to both the public and journalists, Herzl was present at the ceremony, in January 1895, at which Dreyfus was stripped of all his military honors. Herzl wrote a vivid description of the scene for his newspaper.

In general, Herzl's biographers today consider it an exaggeration to say that the Dreyfus case turned him into a Zionist. Still, it is clear that over the next few months a fundamental change came over him. While he was in Vienna in 1895, an anti-Semitic party came extremely close to winning an election. Herzl returned to Paris in a confused state of mind. For the first time as an adult, he attended synagogue services, which he found "solemn and moving." He began to be obsessed with the thought that he had "to do something for the Jews."

In 1894 Captain Alfred Dreyfus of the French army, a Jew, was convicted of treason based on false evidence and perjured testimony. The explosion of anti-Semitism in France, a country that had been considered enlightened, convinced Herzl that Jews would be safe only when they had their own homeland. Herzl became a committed Zionist.

By spring, Herzl had come independently to the idea that the Jews needed a home of their own. In the two liberal Western European countries he had called home, Austria-Hungary and France, emancipation seemed to be failing. With great boldness verging on madness, he approached Baron Maurice de Hirsch, who was already supporting Jewish settlers in Argentina. As Herzl put it, quite rudely, he wanted to give the baron the chance to do something really important. The baron, not surprisingly, declined to become involved with Herzl.

Instead of giving up, Herzl retreated to his desk. Over a period of five days he made diary entries, which amounted to a rough draft of the book that was to change modern Jewish—and world—history.

The Degradation of Captain Dreyfus

A JEWISH STATE FOR THE JEWISH QUESTION

First Stirrings of a Jewish State

When Herzl wrote *The Jewish State* in June 1895, there had been no such state for over 1,800 years—only Jewish communities scattered across the globe. Wherever Jews lived, they were a minority. Although they prayed in Hebrew, they otherwise spoke different languages, and little seemed to unite them. Whereas only a few months earlier Herzl had seen this process as leading to complete assimilation, when writing *The Jewish State* he proclaimed that "we are a people: one people." He now saw proud Jews of Western Europe as facing the same dilemma as the more obviously oppressed Jews in the East. Everything else in Herzl's book stemmed from that central point.

Speaking from the perspective of an assimilated Western European Jew, Herzl thought the anti-Semites themselves had transformed the Jews into a single people: "Our enemies have made us one whether we will or not, as has repeatedly happened in history." Furthermore, anti-Semitism would provide the motive for founding a Jewish state; the misery and suffering at the hands of anti-Semites would encourage Jews to abandon the Diaspora and settle in a homeland of their own.

Herzl came up with his own explanation for modern anti-Semitism: Having been forced to live together in ghettos during the Middle Ages, Jews had to develop financial skills in order to eke out a living. Once allowed out of the ghetto, these skills enabled them to compete successfully with their non-Jewish neighbors, who came to resent and fear their financial power. Anti-Semitism was thus based on economic competition. This being so, thought Herzl, once the Jews had begun to leave for the new state, anti-Semitism would draw to an end. And since the Jewish exodus would take place slowly, there would be no economic upheavals in the countries they left.

The truly original aspect of Herzl's theory was his assertion that both the Jews and the anti-Semites would benefit from Zionism. As Herzl put it, "The world needs the Jewish state; therefore it will arise." In his opinion, since anti-Semitism not only caused Jewish suffering but also disturbed the peace of Gentile society, the governments of Europe would agree to establish a Jewish state.

Herzl honestly believed, as he would later say, that "Zionism is simply a peacemaker. And it suffers the usual fate of peacemakers, in being forced to fight more than anyone else." However questionable this definition, it is worthwhile to follow Herzl's reasoning. If governments tried to protect Jews from anti-Semites, they would arouse the anger of the masses; if they turned their backs on the Jews, however, there would be economic consequences. Only by helping the Jews set up their own nation could governments restore peace within their own borders.

Whether or not Herzl was accurate in the details of his analysis is beside the point. Its main historical value is that *The Jewish State* transformed people's understanding of anti-Semitism. It could no longer be considered purely a problem of Jewish suffering, but rather was an international issue worthy of the attention of heads of state. Herzl's Zionism is called "political Zionism," because from the outset he intended to secure a homeland through diplomatic contacts with government officials.

Herzl acknowledged that there were already other Zionist projects, as well as other attempts to deal with anti-Semitism, but he dismissed them as inadequate. He criticized the small-scale settlements of the Hovevei Zion in *Eretz Yisrael* and of Baron de Hirsch in Argentina. The failure of these settlements could only "inspire doubt among the Jews themselves as to the capacity of Jewish manpower." But, he claimed, his Zionist plan could succeed because it was on a larger scale.

What distinguished his plan from earlier ones was his confidence that the nations of the world would help the Jews set up their state, since Zionism was to their advantage. On their part, the Jews would no longer need to sneak into *Eretz Yisrael* to set up their colonies. What Herzl sought from the outset was a homeland set up with international approval, to which the Jews would have an acknowledged right and where they would be a majority.

What he did not insist on was that the homeland be in the Middle East. "Is [*Eretz Yisrael*] or Argentina preferable? . . . Argentina is one of the most fertile countries in this world, extends over a vast area, is sparsely populated and has a temperate climate. . . . [*Eretz Yisrael*] is our unforgettable historic homeland." It was only later, when the Hovevei Zion joined Herzl, that he became committed to this "homeland" as the site of the Jewish state.

The Jewish State also described two institutions that Herzl saw as necessary first steps toward a national homeland. The first, the "Society of the Jews" would be a form of government in exile, taking the place of the state until the state came into being. The second, the "Jewish Company," would deal with Jewish economic interests. It would help Jews close their businesses in countries they were leaving and would reimburse those countries for the loss of Jewish income and taxes. In addition, it would purchase land in the new country as well as provide financial help and equipment for settlers.

The Second Zionist Congress was held in 1898. A year earlier, Herzl had predicted that the Jewish state would be founded within 50 years. He was almost exactly right—Israel was founded 51 years later on May 14, 1948.

Gathering Support for a Jewish State

Reactions to *The Jewish State* were at first not very encouraging. Herzl had intended the book as a speech he would give to the Rothschild family of philanthropists. But Baron Edmond de Rothschild, supporter of Hovevei Zion settlements in *Eretz Yisrael*, rejected Herzl's plan, feeling that it threatened Jews in the Diaspora, whose patriotism would now be questioned. He also thought it put his own settlements at risk.

The publisher of Herzl's newspaper also felt that the book's arguments would support anti-Semitic claims that Jews could never be assimilated. The newspaper ignored the book and, in fact, never printed the word "Zionist" until it published Herzl's obituary in 1904. Other newspapers gave the book unfavorable reviews.

Orthodox rabbis opposed Herzl's plan because it seemed contrary to the tradition that only the Messiah would restore the exiles to *Eretz Yisrael*. Reform rabbis opposed it because it contradicted their belief that Jews had a mission to perform in the Diaspora—to teach Jewish ethics. Even some Hovevei Zion opposed the book, fearing it would lead Turkey to wipe out the Jewish settlements already existing in *Eretz Yisrael*.

But Herzl had a sense of his own mission. Having been rejected by the social elite, he turned to the Eastern European Jews, who welcomed him and his message. Because of czarist censorship, most of these Jews were unable to read *The Jewish State*, but the network of Eastern European students studying at universities in England and throughout Western Europe helped spread Herzl's message of pride. Herzl was rapidly transforming Zionism from an idea into a democratic mass movement.

Convoking a Jewish National Assembly.   In August 1897, a year and a half after *The Jewish State* was published, Herzl chaired the First Zionist Congress, the first Jewish parliament in modern history. About 200 Jews from twenty countries participated, among them businessmen, lawyers, physicians, writers, and students. The Congress issued a statement of the goal of political Zionism: to establish a publicly recognized, legally secured homeland for the Jewish people in *Eretz Yisrael*. The flag of the modern state of Israel made its debut at the Congress, held in the Municipal Casino of Basel, Switzerland, and the now familiar blue and white banner hung over the entrance to the building. The inspiration for the colors came from the *tallit*, the Jewish prayer shawl.

The Congress also set up the World Zionist Organization and the basic institutions that were to serve the Zionist movement for the next half-century. These institutions carried out functions similar to those Herzl assigned to the Society of the Jews and the Jewish Company in *The Jewish State.*

In a diary entry made after the Congress, Herzl summed up the significance of the three-day meeting: "At Basel I founded the Jewish state. If I said this out loud today I would be greeted by universal laughter. In five years perhaps, and certainly in fifty years, everyone will perceive it." In his second estimate, Herzl very nearly had the number of years right. On May 14, 1948, the state of Israel was established.

Putting Political Zionism into Effect.   Herzl not only transformed the Jewish people into a political unit, but he also made the world's nations acknowledge there was such a thing as a Jewish nation, to be dealt with on political terms. Each time Herzl met with a minister, a sultan, or a king, that person was in effect saying that there was a Jewish nation and that Herzl was its representative.

In the hopes that he could buy a Jewish state from the Turkish Empire, Herzl arranged meetings with the sultan. Hoping that Germany could help secure a homeland, he met with the German kaiser. After the czarist government encouraged a new wave of Russian pogroms in 1903, Herzl met with the Russian minister of the interior, one of those involved in starting the slaughter. He gave Herzl a written statement in which his government agreed to help the Zionist effort.

Herzl's greatest diplomatic triumphs were with Great Britain. Ironically, his dealings with the British also nearly destroyed the Zionist movement. After the pogroms of 1903 Herzl felt it necessary to help the suffering Russian Jews immediately. If *Eretz Yisrael* was not available right away, perhaps some other place could be found. The British offered the possibility of a homeland in East Africa. Although Herzl claimed that he did not support substituting this region for the historical Jewish homeland, the suggestion led to a walkout of many delegates from the Sixth Zionist Congress in 1903. Herzl managed to pull things back together, publicly quoting the words from Psalm 137: "If I forget thee, O Jerusalem, may my right hand wither." But the rift aggravated his poor health, and some months later he died.

Although Herzl's diplomatic ventures did not secure immediate results, the connections he established with the British helped bring about the Balfour Declaration in November 1917. Signed by the British foreign secretary, Lord Arthur James Balfour, this document stated that the British government viewed "with favour the establishment . . . of a national home for the Jewish people, and will use their best endeavors to facilitate the achievement of this object." Other countries, including the United States, approved the Declaration. In July 1922 the League of Nations reaffirmed it. Thus, twenty-five years after Herzl presided over the First Zionist Congress, the predecessor to the United Nations gave recognized legal status to Herzl's dream.

After Herzl's death, one of his supporters who had broken with him over the East Africa issue summed up his unique blend of thought and action: "Those who came before him carried the ideal in their hearts but only whispered about it in the synagogues. . . . Herzl brought us courage and taught us to place our demands before the whole non-Jewish world."

Other people, and two world wars, also played important roles in the development of the modern Jewish state. But Herzl's unique blend of thought and action cleared the path for one of the key events in modern history.

> " *To create a new State is neither ridiculous nor impossible. . . . The governments of all countries scourged by anti-Semitism will be keenly interested in obtaining sovereignty for us.* "
>
> *The Jewish State*, trans. Arthur Hertzberg

9 AHAD HAAM

1856 – 1927

Ahad HaAm, the pen name of Asher Ginzberg, means "One of the People." Just as most people are familiar with the author Samuel Clemens as Mark Twain, Asher Ginzberg's pen name has replaced the name he was given at birth. Many Jewish thinkers have tried to show that Judaism is a rational religion, but Ahad HaAm's goal was to prove it a national religion. Ahad HaAm is considered the father of *spiritual* Zionism; he believed that the return of the Jews to *Eretz Yisrael* was the best way of restoring spiritual dignity to the Jewish people.

THE EVOLVING JEWISH NATIONAL SPIRIT

The Need for a National Homeland

Ahad HaAm was born in a small Russian town in 1856 to a wealthy Hasidic family. His formal education was strictly traditional but, like Moses Mendelssohn, he managed to educate himself more broadly. In Ahad HaAm's case, however, his self-education led him away from a belief in God. Although he remained quite observant, believing that one had no right to tamper with the "holy things" of the nation, throughout his life his Jewish practice was based primarily on loyalty to both Jewish history and the Jewish people. He broke new ground by substituting a belief in what he called "the Jewish national spirit" for a belief in God.

Is One's Judaism a Matter of Choice? Ahad HaAm believed that Jewishness is neither voluntarily embraced nor surrendered. Rather, it is an intrinsic part of the very being of every Jew. His philosophy was thus different from that of Mendelssohn, who believed that remaining Jewish was a matter of choice. When a Christian suggested that Mendelssohn seemed to have given up his Jewishness without coming out and saying so, he politely retorted that if, after considering the arguments for Christianity, he were ever to conclude that he had to give up his Jewishness, intellectual honesty would compel him to do so. In other words, he suggested that he remained a Jew out of choice.

For Ahad HaAm, however, the question "Why do I remain Jewish?" was a meaningless one. "I know why I remain a Jew, or rather, I can find no meaning in such a question, any more than if I were asked why I remain my father's son." One might as well ask a tree why it is an oak rather than an elm. In all three cases, the identity is a fact, not a matter of choice: a Jew being a Jew, a child belonging to a particular family, and a tree being a certain type. "It is within us; it is one of our laws of nature."

The Jewish National Spirit. Ahad HaAm's philosophy of Judaism is based on a comparison between nations and individuals. Just as each individual has a particular personality, each nation has a "national spirit" that makes it unique. For Ahad HaAm, the essence of the Jewish national spirit was the idea of absolute righteousness—the idea that the biblical prophets had preached to the ancient world. Ahad HaAm, an agnostic, was not even sure whether or not a God existed. He thus considered it irrelevant whether or not the prophets actually

> " *The secret of our people's persistence is-... that at a very early period the Prophets taught it to respect only the power of the spirit and not to worship material power.... As long as we remain faithful to this principle, our existence has a secure basis, and we shall not lose our self-respect....* "

"The Jewish State and the Jewish Problem," trans. Arthur Hertzberg spoke with God. The important aspect of the prophets was that they expressed the highest ideals of the Jewish people by demanding the pursuit of justice.

The National Will to Live.

According to Ahad HaAm, a nation's spirit is formed from outside pressures that threaten the nation's survival. Just as each of us has certain instincts enabling us to survive, so does each nation. He called these instincts "the national will to live."

In ancient times, Israel responded to outside threats in such a way that the uniquely Jewish national spirit formed. The ancient Hebrews were a weak people surrounded by stronger neighbors. They were forced from their land and lost their political independence. Under similar circumstances, other conquered nations were swallowed up by their conquerors. What enabled the Jewish people to survive over the centuries was their belief in right rather than might—their clinging to the Book (the Torah) in the face of the sword.

The Need for a National Homeland.

Ahad HaAm was troubled because he felt that the national will to live had become so weakened by the lack of a homeland that Jewish survival itself was threatened. Just as a person's spirit develops in a physical organism— the body—so a nation's spirit should have a physical organism in which to develop—a land. But the Jews had lost their land 2,000 years earlier, and many elements of the national spirit that would have grown, changed, or developed naturally were simply frozen in a centuries-old condition. This was the case with old beliefs and practices, to which Jews continued to cling in order to protect themselves from extinction. The result was that many young Jews felt imprisoned by the rituals forced upon them in the ghetto, and they would abandon Judaism altogether when exposed to the culture of the outside world.

For Ahad HaAm, this new threat to Jewish survival could be overcome only if national life were reestablished in *Eretz Yisrael*. Only there would the Jewish national spirit once again be able to develop naturally.

Ahad HaAm was impatient with the claim that God had scattered the Jews among the nations so that people everywhere would learn about justice. To the contrary, he felt that Jews could reassume moral leadership only in their own land. Since Ahad HaAm was a businessman for most of his career, he summarized the difference between the two views with a business image. Jews scattered throughout the world trying to teach the importance of righteousness could command the respect only of a peddler carrying all his wares with him. Those based in their own land, however, would be respected like company representatives of an established firm displaying samples of their products.

Ahad HaAm was also impatient with those who saw hope for national renewal in the Land of Israel but rejected all the values of Jewish life developed during 2,000 years of exile. Jews with such a view looked down on everything connected with the exile, considering it a sign of weakness. Ahad HaAm worried that by trying to create a nation like all the others, they would strip away the moral basis that made the Jewish national spirit unique.

Two Ways to Face Tyranny

Wishing to show that Jewish spiritual growth can lead to national survival, Ahad HaAm turned to Jewish history. He compared two types of resistance to the Roman occupation of *Eretz Yisrael* in the first century C.E. On one hand he pointed to the Zealots, a party of Jewish patriots. Rather than yield to the Romans, the Zealots committed mass suicide at Masada, the famous fortress on the west shore of the Dead

Ahad HaAm believed that the Jewish national spirit could be preserved by removing Jewish life from the political realm. He cited the example of Yohanan ben Zakkai, who after the destruction of the Temple in the year 70 persuaded the Romans to allow him to establish a school, which eventually became the nation's spiritual center. Ahad HaAm contrasted this action with the approach of the Zealots, a group of Jewish patriots who committed mass suicide at Masada rather than surrender to the Romans.

The fortress at Masada

Sea. While their gesture seemed heroic to many, Ahad HaAm did not view them as role models. If all Jews were to react to outside pressures as they did, there could obviously be no chance of national survival.

On the other hand, Ahad HaAm noted the activities of the famous scholar Yohanan ben Zakkai, who foresaw the victory of the Romans over the Jews and understood that it would mean the destruction of the Temple. (This in fact occurred, in 70 c.e.) But in ben Zakkai's view, loss of the Temple and the way of life that had developed around it for 500 years did not have to signal the end of the Jewish people. Survival of the national spirit was the prime concern, and to achieve that goal, he was willing to submit to the Romans. Ben Zakkai managed to convince them to let him establish a school in the town of Yavneh, near Jaffa on the Mediterranean coast.

After Jerusalem fell, the school in Yavneh became the nation's spiritual center, and the scholars who taught there helped to define a new way of Jewish life. Yohanan ben Zakkai's emphasis on spirit thus enabled the people to adjust to life without the Temple.

Ahad HaAm's goal was to restore to *Eretz Yisrael* the role it had played in ben Zakkai's time, as the focus of Jewish spiritual life.

SPIRITUAL ZIONISM

A Critical Lover of Zion

Ahad HaAm was nearly thirty when he left his father's house and moved with his wife and family to Odessa, the second largest Ukrainian city after Kiev and an important center of Jewish rebirth. There, Ahad HaAm joined the Hibbat Zion movement and also became deeply involved in the movement to modernize the Hebrew language and literature.

From the outset, it was clear that Ahad HaAm was no mere romantic, dreamily enchanted with the idea of resettling an ancient land. If the idea was worth pursuing—and he had no doubt that it was—it was worth doing in the most effective way. From his earliest days in the movement, Ahad HaAm felt it his duty to point out flaws in resettlement policies and to suggest better ways of reaching Hibbat Zion's desired goal.

"The Wrong Way."   After the pogroms of 1881, Hibbat Zion began to encourage Eastern Europe's persecuted Jews to settle in *Eretz Yisrael*. Baron Edmond de Rothschild, the wealthy French-Jewish banker, agreed to finance several of the movement's early agricultural settlements. In 1889 Ahad HaAm published his first important article, "The Wrong Way," in which he criticized both Hibbat Zion and Rothschild for going about the resettlement improperly.

The main problem, Ahad HaAm explained, was that the Hovevei Zion had rushed into resettlement without the necessary advance preparation—it was obviously impossible to rebuild a nation without devoted, selfless workers. The Hovevei Zion thus needed to conduct an educational program to "prepare the hearts" of their fellow Jews for the task of rebuilding the nation.

Baron Edmond de Rothschild

Ahad HaAm's spiritual Zionism emphasized the importance of a Jewish state in preserving the Jewish culture and spirit, and creating a center where Jewish ideals of justice and righteousness would flourish. It was in contrast to Herzl's *political* Zionism, which emphasized the need to protect Jews from outside threats. When Baron Edmond de Rothschild, the wealthy French banker and philanthroplist, financed early agricultural settlements in Palestine, Ahad HaAm was critical—he believed that the hearts and spirits of the settlers should be prepared carefully before they moved to Eretz Yisrael.

But in their eagerness to get the resettlement process started, the Hovevei Zion had lured unprepared Jews into volunteering as settlers, offering incomplete and misleading information. It thus came as no surprise to Ahad HaAm that many settlers were disappointed after arriving in *Eretz Yisrael* and that many had left the country.

Ahad HaAm was also dissatisfied with the commitment of the Jews who stayed. He felt that by pouring money into the settlements,

Rothschild had taken away the settlers' initiative. Not forced to work their problems out for themselves, they hardly provided the nucleus of committed patriots needed to build a national spiritual center in the land.

While Ahad HaAm did not feel that the process of preparing the hearts of the people had to be complete before resettlement began, he urged that quality, not quantity, be the governing concept. It was the level of the settlers' commitment that was key, not their number. One model settlement was a worthier beginning than ten colonies simply propped up by the money of a well-meaning but distant benefactor.

"The Wrong Way" did not overcome the problems that Ahad HaAm outlined, but his insistence on facing facts provided an important challenge. If Zionist dreams were to become a reality, Zionist thinkers would have to educate the people and depict accurately the situation in *Eretz Yisrael.*

Collecting Data to Reveal the Truth.   Not wanting to be an armchair critic, Ahad HaAm made two early trips to *Eretz Yisrael*, in 1891 and 1893. Following those visits, he published two articles called "Truth from *Eretz Yisrael.*" He did not mince words: "One's first sight of Jews tilling the soil of our ancestral land gladdens the heart, but the numerous and fundamental shortcomings which an observant eye detects cannot but cause disappointment. . . ."

In the first of the articles, Ahad HaAm drew a distinction between the economic and spiritual problems facing the Eastern European Jews. Those individuals more interested in overcoming personal economic problems would do well, he said, to emigrate to America rather than to *Eretz Yisrael.* But "if there is any hope of a solution" for the spiritual problem, "it is to be found only in *Eretz Yisrael.*" Building a national center thus meant "that both Jews and their enemies may know that there is somewhere in the world a place where . . . a Jew can . . . create his own conditions of life in his own national spirit."

The data Ahad HaAm collected during his two visits confirmed his dissatisfaction with the Jewish settlers as a group. Not only did they rely too much on charity and too little on inner conviction, but they also often treated the Arab inhabitants of the land with disrespect and indulged in petty arguments among themselves.

Such shortcomings in the resettlement process were critical. Without basic changes, instead of solving "the problem of Judaism"—the need to revitalize the national spirit—the misguided settlers were bound to cause hatred of the Jews. In Ahad HaAm's words, "We shall simply create 'a problem of the Jews' in a country in which it has not hitherto existed—in our ancestral land."

Ahad HaAm Responds to Political Zionism

When Herzl arrived on the scene, the entire scope of the Zionist movement changed. Herzl's emphasis on diplomacy to achieve the Zionist dream was different from Hibbat Zion's emphasis on agricultural settlements. In a short time, what was a small-scale effort in Eastern Europe became a world Jewish organization dealing with heads of states. Ultimately, the Hibbat Zion movement dissolved by joining the World Zionist Organization.

Just as Ahad HaAm had identified flaws in Hibbat Zion policies and suggested more effective approaches, he also saw problems in the new movement. He criticized its understanding of Jewish nationalism, its vision of a rebuilt Zion, its goals for the Jewish national character, and its policy for achieving its aims. As a result, he never felt comfortable enough with political Zionism to join the movement.

What Is the Proper Goal of Jewish Nationalism?   For Herzl and the political Zionists, "the problem of the Jews"—what most threatened their survival as a nation—was anti-Semitism, a threat from the outside. Herzl thought that anti-Semitism could be overcome only by transferring the Jews from all the places of their exile to a Jewish homeland, and accomplishing this became the central goal of Jewish nationalism.

Ahad HaAm felt that nothing would overcome anti-Semitism, which would persist as long as the unique Jewish people did. For Ahad HaAm, what most threatened the Jews was not anti-Semitism but, rather, "the problem of Judaism"—a threat from within, characterized by a decline in the national spirit. The goal of Jewish nationalism should be to create a cultural and spiritual center in *Eretz Yisrael*, where a new type of Jew would develop—a Jew with deep attachment to Judaism, who took pride in being Jewish. A large Jewish community would continue outside of the national Jewish homeland, but Jews in the Diaspora would be strengthened in their spiritual identification by the model set for them in the national spiritual center. From there, the prophets' ideals of justice and righteousness would spread around the world.

How Jewish Was Herzl's View of Zion?   In the eyes of Ahad HaAm, and of many other Eastern European colleagues in Hibbat Zion, Herzl's view of Zion was simply not Jewish. Herzl did not have a traditional Jewish education and seemed out of touch with the very Jews whose salvation he sought. In Herzl's initial conception of a national Jewish homeland, the Jewish state did not even have to be located in *Eretz Yisrael*. Argentina would do. Nor was it important that

> " *The Jews as a people feel that they have the will and the strength to survive whatever may happen, without any "ifs" or "ands." They cannot accept a theory which makes their survival conditional on their ceasing to be dispersed, because that theory implies that failure to end the dispersion would mean extinction, and extinction is an alternative that cannot be contemplated in any circumstances whatever.* "

"The Negation of the Diaspora," trans. Arthur Hertzberg

the language of this state be Hebrew, or that its institutions be somehow linked to the Jewish past. Ahad HaAm believed that Herzl's movement, by ignoring basic Jewish values, undermined the national Jewish spirit that had enabled the Jews to survive for centuries.

When Herzl's novel *Altneuland* appeared in 1902, Ahad HaAm's worst fears were confirmed. Jewish readers everywhere were thrilled by this glowing vision of a modern Jewish state in *Eretz Yisrael*. But in his review of the book, Ahad HaAm dared to ask what made this state Jewish rather than just a modern technological wonder. After all, in the novel, Hebrew is used only in the synagogue and in a children's song, and nothing about the culture is distinctively Jewish at all.

Are Jews to Be Like All the Other Nations?   Ahad HaAm also worried that the aim of Herzl's Zionism was a Jewish state that would cease to respect "the power of the spirit" and would begin, like all other nations, "to worship material power." Such a shift in values would break "the thread that unites us with the past" and thus undermine "our historical foundation." Ahad HaAm feared that Herzl's followers would try to prove that they were no different from any other people.

As early as 1897 he saw evidence of this when a group of Zionist students used "fists and sticks" to publicize their cause, seemingly with the support of Herzl's weekly Zionist paper. After the First Zionist Congress of that year, Ahad HaAm worried that Herzl's policy would lead to a future "which would put the greatness of our past to shame."

But despite his emphasis on ethics and his avoidance of force, Ahad HaAm did not believe that Jews should submit to abuse. In 1903, after the severe pogroms in Russia, he became involved in efforts to help Jews defend themselves against such attacks.

But he did strongly object to the attitude of many Zionists toward the Arab inhabitants of *Eretz Yisrael*. From his first trip in 1891, he noted that these Zionists overlooked the fact that it was not an empty land. Ahad HaAm deplored the fact that many of the Jewish settlers "treat the Arabs with hostility and cruelty, deprive them of their rights, offend them without cause, and even boast of these deeds." He advocated dealing with the Arab inhabitants on terms of mutual respect.

Shortly after moving to *Eretz Yisrael* in 1922, Ahad HaAm wrote a famous letter to the daily Hebrew paper *HaAretz*. A group of young Jews had murdered an Arab boy to avenge several Arab attacks. Ahad HaAm wrote, more in sorrow than in anger: "Is this the dream of the return to Zion which our people dreamt for thousands of years: that we should come to Zion and pollute its soil with the spilling of innocent blood?" He expressed his pain at the willingness of Jews "to sacrifice, on the altar of the 'revival' . . . the great moral principles for which our people lived and suffered and for which alone it thought it worthwhile to labor to become a people again in the land of its fathers."

How Realistic Was Herzl's Policy? Ahad HaAm found Herzl's plan for achieving a Jewish state unrealistic. As was described in *Altneuland*, overnight millions of poor Jews would create a wealthy society on a barren land. How could this possibly happen, particularly since Herzl's movement had at first discouraged the development of small agricultural settlements? Herzl had advocated a different route, convincing the Turkish government to grant the Jews a charter to develop *Eretz Yisrael* into an independent Jewish state. Ahad HaAm felt there was no chance the Turkish government would agree, but even if it did yield to the Jewish request, he argued, how could all the Jews of Europe thrive in a completely undeveloped land?

EVALUATING SPIRITUAL ZIONISM

Did Ahad HaAm Want a Jewish State?

As a result of Ahad HaAm's arguments, many people concluded that he was opposed to a Jewish state. But in fact, Chaim Weizmann, who was to be Israel's first president, consulted Ahad HaAm behind the scenes regularly while negotiating with the British about the Balfour Declaration (see Chapter 8). He was thus involved in the first real political success of the Zionist movement.

Far from opposing a state, Ahad HaAm merely believed that it would be more difficult to found one than the political Zionists were claiming. Organizing such a state would be difficult, and only slowly would it overcome the economic and social problems of the Jewish people. Ahad HaAm also feared that such a state would not resist the temptation to become like other nations, thereby betraying the national spirit of the biblical prophets.

Was Jealousy a Factor?

Many people thought that Ahad HaAm was jealous of Herzl and that his attacks on Herzl's political Zionism were motivated by this less-than-noble quality. The evidence does not support such a conclusion, however. To many, Herzl became "the secular messiah," and Ahad HaAm was doubtless frightened of the messianic attraction of Herzl's personality. He did not want a failure of Herzl's movement to leave despair in its wake, just as the Shabbetai Zvi affair had ended in chaos (see Chapter 6).

A collection of Ahad HaAm's essays appeared shortly after Herzl's death in 1904. In the preface, Ahad HaAm showed no understanding of the lasting significance of Herzl's work, nor was he even sure that the World Zionist Organization would last without its founder. All the same, he wrote that in the course of time Herzl would become a national Jewish hero and a source of inspiration to the nation in its struggle to survive.

During Herzl's life, too, Ahad HaAm took pains not to attack him on personal grounds. Ahad HaAm was editor of an important Zionist journal during most of Herzl's brief Zionist career. He refused to publish letters dealing with shortcomings in Herzl's personality rather than with those of the movement, and he criticized another of Herzl's opponents for personal attacks against Herzl. For Ahad HaAm, it was enough to attack what he saw as the crucial weaknesses of political Zionism.

Has Israel Fulfilled Ahad HaAm's Vision?

How can we evaluate Ahad HaAm's spiritual Zionism in the light of today's world? And how would he regard today's Jewish state in the light of his ideals?

Ahad HaAm believed that the Jewish state must be prepared gradually, that before a state could emerge there must be a massive educational movement to "prepare the hearts" of the Jewish people for such a need. Clearly, he could not have foreseen the rise of Hitler. The Holocaust did away both with the need to prove that a state was necessary and with the possibility of a gradual approach. The Jewish state was forced to develop rapidly.

If events have proved him wrong in this respect, he has been proved right on other grounds: the emergence of the Jewish state did not spell the end of either the Diaspora or anti-Semitism, and the Arab inhabitants of the land had a claim to it as well.

Anti-Semitism continues in the old forms, with neo-Nazi movements active in the United States and elsewhere. Ironically, in addition to these traditional threats, the emergence of Israel has also led to new anti-Semitic claims, such as the equation of Zionism and racism. As for the relationship between Arabs and Jews, Ahad HaAm refused to ignore the serious potential problem. Other Zionist leaders claimed that *Eretz Yisrael* was "a land without a people" waiting "for a people without a land." But Ahad HaAm correctly understood that Jewish settlers in *Eretz Yisrael* could not simply ignore the Arabs who were there.

Ahad HaAm's practical explanation for why the Jews would continue to live in the Diaspora was not quite right, however. The Jewish state, he felt, would never be able to absorb all the world's Jews. As it turns out, many Jews in the Diaspora choose not to move to Israel even if they feel emotionally connected to it.

With regard to other aspects of Ahad HaAm's philosophy of spiritual Zionism, the final answers are not in. Was he right about who the ideal Jewish hero is? Some of his younger critics felt that if the nations of the world idealized brute force, the Jewish state should do so as well and should choose a military figure. Ahad HaAm, however, was reluctant to give up the heritage of the prophets of old, preferring the *Tzaddik*—the righteous man—as his Jewish ideal. Most Jews today take pride in stories of Israeli military successes, but some Jews question, as Ahad HaAm might have, whether military strength alone represents the Zionist ideal.

Ahad HaAm also asked whether Israel should be just a nation like all the others. Perhaps it should judge itself, and be judged by the world, according to higher moral standards. Jewish voices are heard on both sides of this question. There are many who insist that the world is hypocritical for criticizing the Israelis for acting the way other nations routinely act. Other Jews, however, argue that it is appropriate to demand higher moral behavior of Jews and inexcusable for Jews not to demand it of themselves.

Finally, we have to ask whether Israel has become a "national spiritual center" of the sort that Ahad HaAm envisioned. Do Diaspora Jews look to Israel as a source of pride, a symbol of Jewish strength and survival? Or do they pride themselves mainly on providing the money to support Jews in need there?

In the end, evaluation of Ahad HaAm's dream of a national spiritual center may depend on our understanding of his use of the word "spiritual." If he meant that Jews in the Diaspora would feel connected to the Jewish state and determined to work for its progress, his dream has certainly been realized. Ahad HaAm's belief in the importance of "preparing the hearts" of Diaspora Jews for a love of the Jewish nation has also taken root. In Jewish day schools and after-school religious schools throughout the United States, children and their parents become familiar with Hebrew language and literature, Jewish history, and Israeli culture.

If, however, the most important aspect of Ahad HaAm's philosophy of Judaism and of Zionism is his emphasis on the teaching of the prophets, it is not clear that his philosophy is a practical one. Will the Middle East ever be a place where absolute righteousness is more than a dream? Can Jews play a role in world history if the rules of the game are different for them than for the other players? What would Ahad HaAm tell us if he were alive today?

10 HERMANN COHEN

1842 – 1918

Like Mendelssohn, Hermann Cohen was born in a German town—in his case, the small town of Coswig—and died in Germany's intellectual and political center, Berlin. His work helped demonstrate that Judaism was a world religion with teachings of universal value, centered on a single God as the model for moral behavior and on the overriding importance of helping the unfortunate. Cohen's thought shaped the way Jews think about themselves and their culture.

A SOCIETAL GOD AND A PERSONAL GOD

The Heart of Judaism: Ethical Monotheism

While Cohen's religious ideas changed during the course of his life, he maintained a strong belief in the importance of ethics, or moral principles, identifying Judaism with ethical monotheism—a moral religion based on a belief in one God. Cohen based his philosophy of Judaism on three main ideas: monotheism itself, or how the belief in one God shaped Jewish moral behavior; prophetism, or how the teachings of the Jewish prophets helped focus Jewish moral awareness; and messianism, or how the belief in a better future for all humanity affected ethics.

Monotheism.   Whereas most people define monotheism simply as a belief in one God, for Cohen the importance of Jewish monotheism lies in its insistence on a unique God, a God bearing no similarity to anything else.

Such an insistence is at the heart of the Jewish prohibition against worshiping idols. Idol worship implies that God can be identified with certain familiar features or aspects of nature. But by identifying God with familiar objects, we might come to the conclusion that things in this world are satisfactory the way they are and do not need improvement. Only a unique God, said Cohen, one totally different from nature and unlike anything familiar, can demand that human beings refuse to be satisfied with things as they are. Only such a God can set high ethical standards—standards that encourage humanity to do better and better and to seek a more perfect world.

The unique God of monotheism cannot be described, said Cohen. Instead of describing God's essence, the Torah identifies God's actions. Anyone familiar with the song "Who Knows One?" from the Passover Haggadah has heard of God's so-called Thirteen Attributes. The answer to "Who knows thirteen?" is, "I know thirteen. There are thirteen attributes." The rabbis found thirteen distinct attributes of God listed in the Book of Exodus (34:6–7). For Cohen, these attributes provide an ethical ideal, Judaism teaching that each person's behavior should be modeled on God's mercy, righteousness, and love. In Cohen's words, "Not what God is has God to teach me, but what humankind is," or, more precisely perhaps, what each person can and should be.

Likewise, when the Torah instructs us, "Ye shall be holy for I the Lord your God am holy" (Leviticus 19:2), the intention is that people

> " *. . . Judaism . . . makes no distinction between religion and ethics. For the God of Judaism is the God of morality. That means that His significance lies wholly in His disclosure as well as His guarantee of ethics. He is the author and the guarantor of the moral universe. The significance of God as the ground of the moral universe is the meaning of the fundamental principle of God's unity.* "
>
> 1907 address, trans. Eva Jospe

should model their behavior on God's. Cohen calls attention to the two different grammatical tenses in the Torah's words: the present tense is used to describe God's holiness ("am holy"), while the future tense is used for people ("shall be holy"). The different tenses emphasize that God's holiness is an accomplished fact, while human holiness is a goal that is forever in the future. We can strive toward holiness only by behaving ethically.

According to Cohen, "Holiness in God would be pointless if it did not find its practical application in [people]." He interprets the words of the prophet Isaiah, "And God the Holy One is sanctified through righteousness" (5:16), to mean that only by our living moral lives does God's sanctity become meaningful.

In Cohen's interpretation of Jewish ethical monotheism, holiness is not equated with a mystical understanding of God but rather with a continuous effort to improve human life.

Prophetism. Cohen the philosopher had a deep knowledge of both Jewish sources and philosophy in general. He knew that the Greek philosopher Plato had laid down important ethical principles. But his knowledge of Plato's ethics led him to appreciate just how important the contributions of the Jewish prophets were to the field of moral philosophy. For example, Plato felt that a person who had lost physical strength and good looks forfeited all claim to being human, and he argued in *The Republic* that a government should drive out its poor "to purge the land of these animals," leaving behind the sick among the poor to die. Plato also argued that only upper-class Greeks were entitled to rights and that the ideal government owed nothing to foreigners or even to Greek workers.

Cohen pointed out that the Jewish prophets were the first thinkers to broaden the scope of ethics to include all of humanity. For example, they direct our attention to the rights of the underprivileged classes of society. Instead of focusing on God's might, they insist that God is the lover of the outcast and the stranger, that all human beings have rights, and that we should improve the lot of the downtrodden not because they deserve our mercy but because they have been denied justice.

In accord with his views on ethical monotheism, Cohen maintained that the prophets were not interested in analyzing God's nature. Instead, they focused on the crucial aspect of humanity's relationship to God. The prophet Micah, for example, summarizes all that human beings need to know of God: "What the Lord requires of you: only to do justice, and to love mercy, and to walk humbly with your God" (6:8). God's function, as the prophets interpret it, is to help us live ethical lives.

Messianism.   The prophets, Cohen explained, were not only the first to proclaim that all human beings should have the same rights; they were also the first to look forward to a better human future. Before the prophets, people tended to look back nostalgically to a golden age that could never be attained again. Through this momentous shift of focus, connecting the way people behave in the present with how things can and will be in days to come, the prophets foretold that today's behavior affects humanity's future. In short, they developed the messianic ideal, belief in the messianic age resting on confidence in human efforts to achieve a better world for all in the future.

Cohen describes the idea of messianism as passing through several stages of development. At first, achieving a better world depended on an individual who would restore Israel from defeat. Even at this early stage, however, the Messiah was associated with better times not for Israel alone but for all humanity. Eventually, as the idea of messianism matured, it lost its connection with a single human savior, broadening into what Cohen called "a calendar concept," or "the days of the Messiah," an era of history in which the condition of all human beings will be bettered.

Some individuals believed in the arrival of an individual Messiah. However, Cohen spoke of the arrival of the Messianic age, which will remove wordly obstacles to continued ethical development. He cautioned that it will not be a time of perfection; the work will never be completed, but rather ethical improvement will become a more central and meaningful part of all human life.

Significantly, the messianic era is not a time of perfection when ethical struggles are over. For Cohen, ethical perfection can never be attained; things can always be improved. But during the messianic era, ethics become a part of life in a new and more meaningful way, and the task of ethics is clearly advanced.

Cohen's idea of messianism was not just an abstraction. He believed that even in his own lifetime the messianic age could be brought about if Jews led the way in showing the world the ethical God of monotheism. His student Franz Rosenzweig (Chapter 11), who was to become a distinguished thinker himself, describes an incident underscoring how real this idea was. Already in his seventies, Cohen was walking with Rosenzweig one day. Fully serious, the older man turned to the younger and said, "I still hope to live to see the coming of the messianic age." Rosenzweig, taken aback, did not quite know what to say but mumbled something indicating doubt that even he, though much younger, would live that long. Cohen then pressed him to say when he thought the dawning of the age would come. Incapable of stating a precise figure, Rosenzweig again mumbled, "Perhaps in a hundred years." Cohen then took his student's hand, and exclaimed, "Oh, please, make it fifty."

From an Ethical God to a Personal God

Cohen was raised in a lovingly traditional Jewish home, where God's involvement with each individual was taken for granted. After finishing elementary school in Coswig, he attended high school in nearby Dessau, Mendelssohn's birthplace. During these high school years his father, a cantor and teacher, traveled from Coswig to Dessau every Sunday to continue training his son in Talmud. Although Cohen's father had hoped his son would become a rabbi, Cohen dropped out of rabbinical school to pursue a career in philosophy.

Despite his traditional upbringing, during much of Cohen's life God was an *idea* rather than a living presence. In fact, God is the central idea steadily holding together his system of thought. Nevertheless, his speculation about God did evolve, and toward the end of his career he began to move away from an abstract God of ethics, concerned with humanity as a whole but not with individuals, toward a God more directly concerned with each individual.

The God of Ethics.   Cohen saw the task of ethics as never ending and to be advanced only in this world. But he was faced with scientific work claiming that nature is a continuous process of decay. In such a world, which science tells us is on the road to eventual extinction, what keeps people involved in the task of ethics? Why do they continue to strive for a better future? Cohen felt that only the idea of God can resolve the contradiction between the world of science and the world of ethics.

God's purpose, Cohen explained, is to guarantee that there will always be a world in which moral ideals can be advanced. "God means that nature has its duration guaranteed as surely as morality is eternal." He pointed out the connection between this "God-idea" and the biblical God, who, following the flood, established a covenant with humanity never to wipe out creation. In this system, God is clearly an entity constructed by human reason, not a loving and judging actual presence in human lives.

Franz Rosenzweig tells another story about Cohen that sheds some light on the tension Cohen may have felt between attachment to the personal God of his boyhood and the "God-idea" of much of his professional career. While a professor at the University of Marburg, Cohen took some time to explain God's role in his system of thought to an elderly Jew, who paid close attention to the explanation and followed it easily. But when Cohen had finished, the old man turned to him and asked, "But where is the Creator of the Universe?" The question, pointing out the gap between Cohen's "God-idea" and the personal God of traditional Judaism, must have struck a chord somewhere deep inside Cohen. Struck dumb by the question, he could not control the tears streaming down his face.

The God of Religion.   Whether this incident helped bring about the change in Cohen's religious thought we do not know. But his move in 1912, at the age of 70, from the German university in Marburg to Berlin's famous academy for Jewish studies was accompanied by a shift in emphasis. In Cohen's Marburg system, God is the creation of human reason. In his later system, developed in his monumental work *Religion of Reason from the Sources of Judaism*, Cohen interpreted the biblical concept that humanity was created in God's image to mean that human reason is God's creation. To support this new perspective, he pointed to the prophet Zechariah's words, "God forms the spirit of man within him" (12:1) and to the statement in the Book of Job describing the human spirit as "the portion of God from above and the inheritance of the Almighty from on high."

A staunch monotheist if there ever was one, Cohen was not yielding to polytheism by distinguishing between "the God of ethics" and "the God of religion." He was showing that there is more to religion than ethics and that each person's religious relationship with God is different, and more personal, than the strictly ethical relationship.

In addition to changing his approach to God, Cohen also modified his attitude to religion in general. While holding firm to the belief that religion must never violate ethical standards, he now began to argue that ethics is concerned with humanity as a whole, not with individual human beings. The God of all humankind is the God of ethics. However, the individual human being sometimes feels isolated from society or not worthy of being part of it. This individual needs the God of religion, concerned with each individual and not merely with humanity in its entirety, to relate to personally.

During the time Cohen viewed religion and ethics as more or less the same thing, he felt particularly attached to the earlier prophets. Later, when he began to focus on the relationship between the individual and God, he drew closer to the prophet Ezekiel. The earlier prophets had grounded religion in ethics, but Ezekiel was the first to pay attention to the individual's relationship with God.

The earlier prophets had focused on social sins, the misdeeds of society with respect to the downtrodden. But Ezekiel turned his attention to the individual's sin against God. In doing so, Ezekiel established the worth of each individual for God.

It is interesting to note that Hermann Cohen's Hebrew name was Ezekiel. It would seem that beyond rediscovering his Hebrew name and the meaning of the work of his namesake, in drawing closer to a more traditional perspective late in his career, Cohen also discovered the possibility of a personal relationship with the God of his boyhood.

Sin and Atonement in Judaism and Christianity

Cohen's rediscovery of the personal God of religion who deals with individual sin is connected with another major change in his thought. At the beginning of his career he insisted that there was no significant difference between Judaism and Christianity, and he never specifically retracted this view. But as he developed his speculation about the nature of sin and atonement in Judaism, he began to focus on two areas in which Judaism and Christianity differ sharply: sin and atonement.

The Basic Similarities.   At the age of 31 Cohen was interviewed for his position at the University of Marburg. The philosopher who was to become his department chairman asked him, "Is there any serious difference between us in regard to Christianity?" Cohen answered, "No, because what you call Christianity, I call prophetic Judaism." Focusing as he then was on ethics, Cohen felt that the essential matter was the two religions' shared emphasis on ethical behavior, not the specific practical differences between them.

Seven years later, in 1880, Cohen followed in the footsteps of many earlier Jewish thinkers by publishing a defense against an anti-Semitic attack. The defense was unusual, however, for it contained the statement that "I dare to confess that I cannot possibly see any difference in the scientific concept of religion between Israelite monotheism and Protestant Christianity." Cohen explained that Judaism and Lutheran Christianity share a belief in individual moral responsibility. And in a book about the historical development of the Sabbath, written while he was still in his late twenties, he claimed that modern Judaism was part of Christian culture.

Judaism's Approach to Sin and Atonement.
By the time Cohen was in his late sixties, however, his position on the relationship between Christianity and Judaism had changed. In 1910 he was asked to be one of two Jewish representatives to the World Congress for Religious Progress. Cohen's paper to the congress on "The Importance of Judaism for the Religious Progress of Mankind" identified six characteristics of Judaism. Two of these characteristics sharply distinguished between Judaism and Christianity: First, Judaism rejects the idea of "original sin" and stresses that people are all responsible for their own actions. Second, it rejects the idea that individuals are incapable of communicating with God on their own. Cohen here stressed that Judaism is a religion of individual moral responsibility to a much greater extent than is Christianity.

According to the Christian doctrine of original sin, each person is born with the tendency toward evil, transmitted from Adam to the entire human race because of his sin of disobedience to God. Only through baptism—that is, only through the grace of Christ—can a person be cleansed of original sin. Cohen emphasized Judaism's rejection of this idea. In Judaism no one is born sinful or basically evil. The choice of how to behave is up to each individual.

According to Christian theology, Jesus was the *Christ*, the Greek word for "Messiah," who came to earth to bear the sins of mankind. Cohen rejected any linkage of this belief to the prophets' view of the Messiah, underscoring that Judaism does not permit anyone but the sinner to shoulder responsibility for a sin.

In Judaism, each person communicates with God; no mediator or go-between is needed. Judaism recognizes the need only for teachers, not for mediators. Cohen felt strongly that Christianity deprives the individual of personal responsibility, while Judaism stresses individual moral authority. In Christianity, he said, Christ's intervention can magically wipe away sin, while in Judaism the sinner is responsible for turning back to God. The individual alone must truly repent without divine intervention. At every moment, each person can start afresh by making a firm commitment to live a better life.

Even though it is up to the individual to repent, God does play a role in repentance. Just as parents cannot live their children's lives for them but can guide and reassure them, God's role is not to do the sinner's job of repentance but rather to assure the sinner that the job can be done. In other words, God will grant forgiveness to the repenting sinner.

Cohen quoted Ezekiel to show that there is a true partnership between the repentant person and God. In one verse, Ezekiel says, "Cast away from you all transgressions, whereby you have transgressed, and make you a new heart and a new spirit." In a related verse, the prophet says in God's name, "A new heart also will I give you, and a new spirit will I put within you." According to Cohen, the two verses represent the two sides of the coin of repentance. The sinner must take the initiative and turn back in repentance, but God assures the sinner that repentance is not in vain because forgiveness will be granted.

Cohen stressed that by taking over the job of repentance, God would be robbing the sinner of human dignity. The Christian sinner has less moral responsibility because God plays a major role in the process of atonement. Furthermore, Judaism alone has a special day on its religious calendar devoted to the processes of personal repentance and atonement, namely, Yom Kippur. The purpose of Yom Kippur is not for God to free us magically from sin. Rather, it involves accepting full responsibility for our own actions. If we resolve to do better in the future, God will overlook our past actions and make it possible for us to begin the new year with a clean slate.

In Cohen's view, Judaism emphasizes individual moral authority and responsibility. He believed that God created the world as a place where humanity can exercise its moral powers for improvement, and where individuals act in partnership with God in seeking that improvement. The world, he said, provides unlimited opportunity for improvement and growth, and therefore the task of ethical perfection is eternal and never-ending.

Oil spill cleanup, California

CONFRONTING CONTROVERSY AS JUDAISM'S SPOKESMAN

Activist in Public Debate

Cohen was involved in Jewish life from his student days on. He believed that the messianic era could be brought about only if people modeled themselves on Moses' brother Aaron, who, according to the rabbis, "loved peace and pursued peace" and busied himself with reconciling adversaries. Ironically, however, Cohen found himself involved in many controversies affecting the Jewish community.

Cohen used public platforms to explore his philosophy and to ensure that his thinking had an effect on the world around him. At times he played the role of public defender, at times that of public prosecutor, and at other times that of public advocate. However, unlike the case with Mendelssohn—another, earlier German-Jewish thinker who used his prominence to speak out on behalf of Jewish causes—Cohen's defense of various aspects of Judaism often angered the mainstream Jewish community.

Public Defender of Judaism

Cohen was not a trained defense attorney, but on several occasions he found himself assuming that position on behalf of Jewish interests. Still, his arguments were not necessarily acceptable to the larger Jewish community, as became apparent in two cases in which he defended liberal Jewish thought and German Jewry. In a third case, where he was actually called in by an official German court to defend the Talmud, the public Jewish response was much more positive.

In Defense of Liberal Thought. When Cohen was eighteen years old and still a student in rabbinical school, a major dispute broke out between two distinguished Jewish leaders. The dispute was to lead to the creation of Conservative Judaism.

The issue was the significance of the traditional term *Halakhah l'Moshe mi'Sinai.* Literally meaning "a law given to Moses at Sinai," the term refers to many laws not found in the Torah. Traditionally, Jews believed that God gave these unwritten laws to Moses at Mount Sinai along with the Torah. But in the nineteenth century, a group of Jewish scholars challenged this belief, claiming that centuries after Moses, rabbis had formulated the laws and associated them with Moses to enhance the laws' authority.

One of these nontraditional Jewish scholars was Zacharias Frankel, considered a founder of the Conservative Movement. Frankel was one of Cohen's teachers at rabbinical school. When Frankel published his position on *Halakhah l'Moshe mi'Sinai*, he was attacked in print by the leader of the Modern Orthodox Movement in Germany, Samson Raphael Hirsch. In his article, Hirsch not only accused Frankel of heresy but also attacked his students for studying under a heretic.

Determined not to accept such insults passively, a group of Frankel's students called a meeting at which they read the draft of a response to Hirsch. Cohen, in the audience, was appalled by the harsh language being heaped on Hirsch and felt obliged to register his lack of support for the response's tone and tenor.

Aware that an ongoing dispute of this sort could only tarnish the Jewish public image, Cohen then decided to write his own personal letter to Hirsch, telling the great Orthodox leader that he was wrong about Frankel, who was in fact a strictly observant Jew.

But the reaction to this effort at civility was not what Cohen would have hoped for. Instead of answering the letter in private, Hirsch published it and his reply without Cohen's knowledge. In his response, Hirsch—continuing his attack on Frankel—insisted that Frankel's publicly printed words proved more than his private behavior.

At this point Cohen backed off from the dispute. While his first try at being a public defender was not very successful, it did result in a first, albeit unintentional, publication.

In Defense of Judaism.   In 1879 an attack on Judaism by a famous German historian took Cohen by surprise. The historian was Heinrich von Treitschke, and his anti-Semitic article was published in *Prussian Yearbooks*, a leading German journal. In the article, "A Word on Our Jewry," Treitschke claimed that Judaism was nothing more than "the national religion of an alien tribe," with nothing to offer the German Christian. Cohen, by now a well-established professor, was deeply dismayed that a scholar would use the prestige of his position to dignify such prejudice.

Whereas some twenty years earlier Cohen had to endure finding a personal letter published openly in a journal, he now experienced an equally disagreeable but opposite experience: Treitschke refused to publish two open letters Cohen sent him. His only acknowledgment of Cohen's letters was indirect: in an article in the next issue of the journal, he dismissed Cohen's criticism by branding him a mere teacher at a "second-rate" German university. Therefore, in 1880 Cohen himself published a response to Treitschke, "A Public Declaration on the Jewish Question." In it, he insisted that one could be both a good German and a good Jew.

Although Cohen later claimed that his renewed commitment to Jewish life began with the Treitschke attack, his pamphlet is in fact more a defense of assimilation than of Judaism. In it, Cohen looked forward to the day when Jews would not appear physically different from other Germans. However, unlike other assimilationists of the time, he insisted that German Jews must value their religion because, despite Treitschke's remarks to the contrary, the Jewish religion had much to offer German Christians. "Respect your Israelite monotheism, learn to understand it, preserve it in your mind, and make it your guide to a religious life." The German-Jewish authorities were not pleased at all by Cohen's "defense" of Judaism. They unanimously rejected the pamphlet's assimilationist message.

In Defense of the Talmud.
Cohen served as Jewish public defender in a second anti-Semitic incident in 1888. By this time his reputation as a philosopher had spread; the so-called Marburg School of philosophy that he helped found was one of the most important German philosophical currents in the period before World War I. Thus, instead of entering the fray on his own initiative, Cohen was now called in by the Royal Provincial Court in Marburg. A public school teacher there had publicly attacked the Jews in general and the Talmud in particular, claiming that the Talmud taught Jews to respect only the rights of other Jews and encouraged them to deal unethically with Christians.

In answer, the Marburg Jewish community brought a suit against the teacher for slandering Judaism. The Royal Court brought in two experts—a well-known anti-Semitic scholar and Hermann Cohen. In this so-called Talmud Trial of Marburg, the Jewish community won its case. The teacher was sentenced to a short jail sentence and had to pay all the costs of the proceedings.

Following the trial, the anti-Semitic scholar published his unsuccessful testimony. Cohen thereupon published his own, under the title *The Love of Fellow-man in the Talmud*. Before presenting his arguments, he justified his role as an expert witness. Although a greater specialist in Talmud might have been found, he felt perfectly competent to testify. Not only had he learned Talmud rigorously in his youth, but as a philosopher his task had always been "to ascertain the truth, especially the historical truth, in the realm of morality."

Turning to the matter at hand, Cohen claimed that the problem stemmed from a professor's faulty translation of a Hebrew word in the famous biblical verse "Love your neighbor as yourself." Are only other Jews included in this commandment, or all people? Cohen quoted from both the Bible and the Talmud to prove that Judaism considers not only Jews as neighbors, but also all other human beings. He emphasized that the Jewish idea of the fellow-man is a logical consequence of monotheism: since there is only one God who has created all human beings, all are alike. Whatever ethical responsibility one has for a Jew, one has for a non-Jew as well.

Cohen's testimony in the Marburg Trial has earned him a place among the distinguished defenders of Judaism. He is a much more controversial figure, however, in two other public roles: that of outspoken critic of the Zionist cause, and that of outspoken advocate of "Germanism."

Public Prosecutor of Zionism

Cohen's deep belief in messianism resulted in strong anti-Zionist views, for messianism meant, among other things, a time in the future when national differences would disappear, when all nations would join together as one to worship the one true God.

Because of this attitude, Cohen felt that certain past disasters befalling the Jewish people, such as their expulsion from their homeland and the destruction of their Temple, were only necessary steps toward the messianic goal. Having lost their national ties, the Jews could now serve the cause of humanity as a whole by spreading the ideals of ethical monotheism. He felt that Zionism, by promoting national interests above international welfare, would set back the clock.

In an open letter to Cohen in 1916, the German-Jewish thinker Martin Buber (Chapter 12) argued that Cohen misunderstood the Zionist goal, which could only bring the world closer to the messianic ideal. The Zionists wanted Palestine not as a small, inward-looking Jewish enclave but rather as a universal symbol of how life should be lived.

In response to Buber, Cohen published a booklet arguing that Zionism contradicts Jewish destiny in addition to the messianic goal. According to Cohen, the prophet Isaiah's descriptions of the sufferings of the Messiah (50:4–11; 52:13–53:12) symbolize the suffering of the Jewish people. As long as the Jewish ethical, monotheistic mission has not been completed, the Jewish people must suffer. In addition, Jewish homelessness symbolizes the "final goal of world history," when all people will give up their connections with a particular nation and live together without such distinctions.

Cohen also argued that the Jews have a nationality but should not aspire to nationhood, that nationality constitutes a fact of history and biology, but nationhood involves political will. United by their messianic role in history, the Jews have a nationality. But, he argued, seeking nationhood "is incompatible with the messianic concept and with Israel's mission."

Cohen died thirty years before the founding of the Jewish state. Despite his unrelenting anti-Zionism, a street in Tel Aviv is named after him.

Controversial Public Advocate: Cohen's Pro-German Stance

It is easy to understand why many of Cohen's students disagreed with his extreme pro-German views. Cohen felt not only that all German Jews were duty-bound to respect and honor Germany, but that all European Jews were likewise in Germany's debt. Germany, he argued, was the home of modern Judaism, so Jews everywhere should honor it as "the native country of their soul, as far as their religion is their soul." In addition, he insisted that all Yiddish-speakers should honor Germany for its contributions to their language. Cohen could not have known that Germany's death machine would in the years to come murder countless Yiddish-speakers.

Cohen's fervent German patriotism was so widely known that upon the outbreak of World War I the German government wanted him to serve as an official public advocate. The 72-year-old professor was ready when he received official orders to travel to the United States to win sympathy for the German cause. Although the German government did not follow through with its planned mission, in 1915 Cohen published an article in a New York City German-language newspaper in which he urged American Jews to support Germany, which from the days of Mendelssohn had been the setting for the development of Judaism. A year later he also delivered a speech called "Germanism and Judaism," in which he reverted to the position he had taken in his assimilationist defense of Judaism in 1880. He said that because German culture and Judaism were identical, Jews were obliged to support the German cause.

World War I was not World War II, of course, and many other German Jews were also caught up in the patriotism that wars often stir up. But although he did not live to see the rise of the Nazis to power in his beloved Germany, his wife and many of his students did. His wife, Martha, was one of the millions of Jews swept away without a trace during the Holocaust.

Had Cohen lived to experience the Holocaust, one wonders how his beliefs would have been changed. He believed, after all, that humanity was making continual progress toward the messianic goal. But in these days, when the teachings of ethical monotheism seem to be disregarded all over the world, Cohen's philosophy offers an important basis for ethical behavior and for understanding what different religions share.

> " *Just as the banishment from Paradise constitutes humanity's entrance into civilization, so does our banishment from our country usher in our global pursuit of the idea of the One God. . . . The establishment of a state of our own is incompatible with the messianic concept and with Israel's mission.* "
>
> 1907 address, trans. Eva Jospe

11. FRANZ ROSENZWEIG

1886 – 1929

Franz Rosenzweig's theory of Judaism was strikingly different from that of his contemporaries. Like Herzl, he came from an assimilated background. But while Herzl emphasized modern Judaism as a nationality, Rosenzweig's work allowed many assimilated German Jews to accept it as a religion. Rosenzweig emphasized religion more than did Zionism, the performance of *mitzvot* more than did the Reform Movement, and the personal choice of which *mitzvot* to perform more than did the Orthodox.

A Dramatic Life Cut Short

On the Verge of Conversion

Judaism was not important in the life of young Franz Rosenzweig. Although he underwent the bar mitzvah ceremony, family observance was very limited—he did not know of *Erev Shabbat* until he enrolled in university. At eighteen, he wrote to a friend that God to him was nothing more than a "weather maker."

While working on his doctoral thesis, on the German Idealist philosopher Hegel, Rosenzweig became critical of Hegel's thought, which placed little emphasis on the individual human being. Rosenzweig felt it failed to consider the suffering and longings of real people and was thus inadequate to people's lives. Some of Rosenzweig's friends and relatives had similar views and concluded that they could find the answer to their own personal longing by converting to Christianity.

When one of his cousins converted, Rosenzweig's parents were horrified. But Rosenzweig wrote them that in fact he had encouraged the conversion. In all external things, he wrote, Jews like himself, his parents, and his cousins already lived fully Christian lives. As he saw it, modern Jews who felt some spiritual gap had only two choices: to become Zionists and express their Judaism politically, or to convert to Christianity.

While at university, Rosenzweig took a course in medieval law from Professor Eugen Rosenstock, who had himself converted from Judaism to Christianity. Rosenstock felt conversion had been the right step, and he shared his views with Rosenzweig. The two met on a daily basis. Apparently these meetings convinced Rosenzweig that if he could not justify remaining a Jew, then he too would have to convert.

The conversations between Rosenstock and Rosenzweig reached a climax in July 1913. Unable to convince either himself or Rosenstock that his reasons for remaining Jewish were valid, Rosenzweig agreed to convert. He made only one provision: like the original Christians after the time of Jesus, he would become Christian as a Jew.

With this resolve, he attended Rosh HaShanah services in the synagogue in Kassel to which his family belonged. These services did not move him, just as they had failed to do while he was growing up. While at home during the days between Rosh HaShanah and Yom Kippur, he confided in his mother that although he intended to convert, he would still attend services on Yom Kippur, again at his family's synagogue. His mother's harsh reaction created a turning point in Rosenzweig's spiritual development. Instead of reasoning with him,

> " *The Jewish people has already reached the goal toward which the nations are still moving. It has that inner unity of faith and life which . . . is still no more than a dream to the nations within the church. But just because it has that unity, the Jewish people is bound to be outside the world that does not yet have it.* "
>
> *The Star of Redemption*, trans. Nahum N. Glatzer

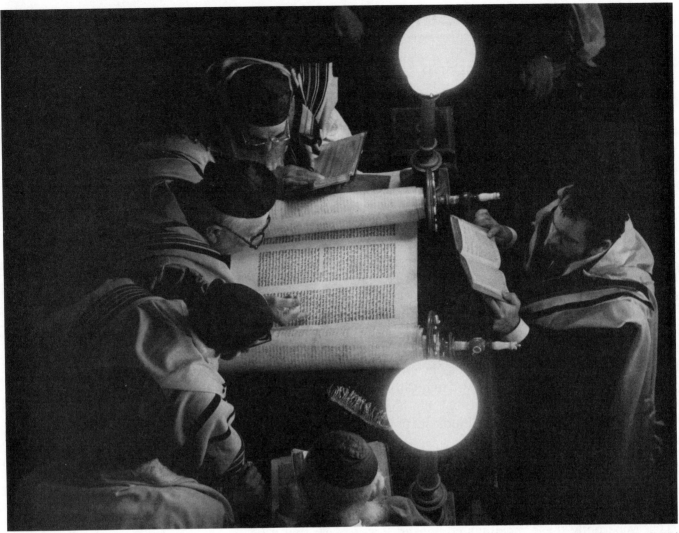

Yom Kippur, Leningrad

In 1913 Rosenzweig decided to convert to Protestantism. But before he did so, he wanted to attend one last Yom Kippur service as a Jew. His mother, feeling him lost, asked him not to appear at the family congregation, so instead he went to a small synagogue in Berlin. There he had a mystical, spiritual experience that persuaded him to remain Jewish and to study Judaism for the remainder of his life. He never revealed the nature of that experience.

she told her son that she would notify the synagogue leaders of his plans and ask them to turn him away. "In our synagogue," she said, "there is no room for one who abandons his faith."

Having been banished from home as well as from the family synagogue, Rosenzweig went to Berlin for Yom Kippur. There, in a small Orthodox synagogue, he underwent a religious experience. Although he never revealed exactly what happened to him, he did allude to sensing a profound power in the Yom Kippur prayers; later, he would suggest that during the prayers a person is "as close to God as possible." His original intention had been to leave the synagogue on Yom Kippur night prepared to enter Christianity. Instead, he left as a Jew who would spend the rest of his life studying, teaching, and practicing Judaism.

Rosenzweig wanted to be certain that this intensely emotional experience would hold up to the test of time. He spent the next year in Berlin studying Jewish religious texts. The outbreak of World War I ended this chapter of his life, and he joined the German army in 1914. Even in the trenches, though, he continued to study Judaism and both Hebrew and Aramaic, the languages of the Bible and the Talmud.

According to a letter he wrote to one of his Christian cousins, his near conversion and return to Judaism had been such powerful experiences that the war itself paled by contrast. "In 1913 I had experienced so much that 1914 would have had to produce the world's collapse to make any impression on me."

A Soldier-Philosopher

Rosenzweig had much time for study and writing during his military service on the Balkan front. Convinced that his own weak Jewish education had led to his earlier confusion, he began what would become a lifelong interest in reforming German–Jewish education. In an open letter in 1917, he presented his ideas for introducing young people to the classical texts of Jewish tradition. He suggested that teaching them "about Judaism" in watered-down summaries meant spoon-feeding them someone else's opinions instead of letting them form their own. He also proposed a new type of teacher-scholar who would combine scholarly research in a not-as-yet-formed Jewish academy with part-time teaching of Jewish students in local high schools.

Over a six-month period beginning in August 1918, Rosenzweig wrote what was to be his major philosophical work, *The Star of Redemption.* Much of its over 500 pages was written in trenches, army barracks, and military hospitals. A truly unique contribution to Jewish thought, these sections were written on army postcards, which Rosenzweig sent home. When he was discharged from the army in December 1918, he completed the work and patched the pieces together.

Rosenzweig began his book by criticizing traditional philosophy. From earliest times on, philosophers have tried to discover one principle from which everything else can be derived. For Hegel—the subject of Rosenzweig's doctoral thesis—that single principle was what he called the Infinite Intelligence or the Universal Spirit. According to Hegel, this Intelligence or Spirit contains all things and never dies. Rosenzweig rejected Hegel's premise. He insisted that human individuality is separate from the Infinite Intelligence. Otherwise, why would people fear death? If people were part of a Universal Spirit, death would be comforting, being a continuation as part of this eternal entity.

According to Rosenzweig, human experience shows that there are three separate aspects of life: God, the world, and people. These three aspects interact. God interacts with the world through the process of *creation*, which is an ongoing event. God interacts with people through *revelation*, thereby demonstrating love for individuals. People respond to God's love by loving those around them. Loving acts begin the process of *redemption*. The process of redemption will be completed when the Messiah comes, and only when the process is complete will the three separate aspects of life combine in the single aspect of God.

The "star" in the title of Rosenzweig's book is really two intersecting triangles, which clarify his system of thought. In the top triangle, Rosenzweig shows the three separate aspects of life: God, World, People. The bottom triangle shows how they interact in the processes of Creation, Revelation, and Redemption.

Much of what Rosenzweig argued in his book is very difficult, and much is also controversial. Two aspects in particular remain disturbing to some Jews. Perhaps as the result of his early attraction to Christianity, Rosenzweig wanted to work out for himself exactly how the two religions were related. In *The Star*, he stated that Judaism and Christianity are equally valid, each having a role to play in world history. Each is an aspect of truth, but neither is the whole truth, which will be revealed only when redemption is completed at the end of history. He compared Judaism, which is not interested in converting the world and is satisfied with its own knowledge of God, to the fire burning at the core of the Star of Redemption. He compared Christianity, a missionary religion, to the outstretching rays of the Star.

Although Rosenzweig insisted that Christianity is no less true a religion than Judaism, he denied that it can offer Jews anything they cannot find within their faith. On the contrary, while a Jew is born into a relationship with God—into the *brit*, or covenant, between God and the Jewish people—no one is born a Christian. The ritual of baptism alone brings a person into the Christian church, but it would be superfluous for a Jew.

The second controversial aspect of Rosenzweig's thought is his concept of Israel's exile. According to him, the Jews became a people not in *Eretz Yisrael* but in Canaan and Egypt. The Jew's true homeland is not a piece of territory, but is within each Jew. Just as Jewish life does not depend on *Eretz Yisrael*, Jewish history is not connected with the history of the rest of the world. Not surprisingly, this position did not sit well with many Zionists.

German-Jewish troops during World War I

Performing Service Through Education

Rosenzweig regarded his book merely as an overture to what really matters, namely, leading a religious life. Shortly after finishing *The Star of Redemption*, he called the book an "episode" in his life, later referring to it as the "armor" protecting him until he learned how to get along without it. He felt strongly that a Jew relates to God primarily through deeds, not ideas. In a letter, he indicated that "I see my future only in life, not any more in writing."

Life to him now meant not scholarship but serving other Jews. One of Rosenzweig's professors offered him a university lectureship, but he turned down the offer. Defending his decision, he wrote the

Like many German Jews, Rosenzweig served in the German army during World War I. He wrote much of his *Star of Redemption* in trenches, barracks, and military hospitals.

professor that he no longer saw knowledge as an end in itself. "The questions asked by human beings have become increasingly important to me." The questions he proposed to answer were posed by assimilated German-Jewish adults looking for some dignified way to return to Judaism.

Rosenzweig had been disappointed when his wartime plan to establish a Jewish academy for teacher-scholars was not realized. An academy was in fact opened, but it was to be purely a research institute. Feeling as strongly as ever that Jewish education needed renewal, he was appointed head of the Frankfurt Independent House of Jewish Learning, the so-called Lehrhaus, in August 1920. Rosenzweig hoped here to turn his energies to the goal of developing full "Jewish human beings" not suffering from a split between their Judaism and the rest of their lives.

What was extraordinary about the Lehrhaus was that the teachers as well as the students came from many different professions. Few of the teachers were rabbis. Like their students, they were seeking ways to be authentic modern Jews. In many classes, which were really discussions, students and teachers together struggled with the meaning of Jewish texts. And instead of being pressed to accept particular interpretations of the readings, the students were encouraged to come to personal terms with the text.

Paralysis of Body but Not of Spirit

Tragically, Rosenzweig was able to function as the school's director for only three years. Toward the end of 1921 he noticed that he was not fully in control of his body and seemed to fall for no reason. In early 1922, a few months before the birth of his only child, the serious nature of his problem was confirmed; he was suffering from a rare and incurable nerve disease leading to complete paralysis. Doctors did not expect him to outlive the year.

At first the disease progressed rapidly. During the summer of 1922 he retired to his apartment, which he never left again. By the end of the year he was no longer able to write on his own, but he continued to dictate his work. By the following spring he was no longer able to speak, and by fall he was completely paralyzed. He continued to live in this condition for another six years, exercising whatever control was possible over his life. He pursued his professional work and hobbies, maintained his friendships, and lived a Jewish life as best he could. And through it all he managed to maintain a sense of humor.

Although Rosenzweig had not wanted to focus his professional life on writing, the disease forced him to change his goals. When he could no longer dictate, he helped design a special typewriter, which the General Electric Company manufactured for him. Eventually he was no longer able to use the typewriter either, and he would communicate by indicating the letters of the words he wanted to use. His wife, Edith, was so in tune with him that she could usually figure out the intended words after only one or two letters. With her help, Rosenzweig was able to work on a second edition of *The Star of Redemption*, translate a group of Yehudah HaLevi's poems and furnish them with a commentary, write several important essays, and collaborate with Martin Buber (Chapter 12) on a new German translation of the Bible.

Rosenzweig had always loved music, and he kept this love alive during his illness. He had both a phonograph and a radio. During the two years before his death he wrote reviews of new records for a newspaper in his hometown, Kassel. Like the philosophical work he produced at this time, his reviews in no way reveal that their author was mortally ill.

During this period, Rosenzweig received visits from many friends and colleagues with whom he was corresponding; his wife spoke on his behalf, since she was often able to guess his words. The visitors also held a regular *minyan* in Rosenzweig's room. On holidays, children came to the house to play with their son, Rafael. His father's condition seemed quite natural to him, since by the time he was born Rosenzweig was already ill. In 1923 the German rabbi Leo Baeck (Chapter 13) conferred the rabbinical title *morenu*—our teacher—on Rosenzweig. This was a source of great satisfaction to him, but because of his modesty the honor was not made public until after his death.

Although Rosenzweig's life makes for moving and dramatic reading, he is much more than a heroic figure. Several aspects of his thought, including his contribution to theories of modern Jewish education and religious practice, stand on their own merit and are still highly relevant today.

On Being a Full Jewish Human Being

Emancipation and the Need for A New Type of Jewish Learning

According to Rosenzweig, Jewish education was an unintended victim of the emancipation. Before then, Jews often came into contact with Gentiles, but at night they would return to the ghetto and have time for Jewish study. Once the ghetto walls crumbled, many Jews felt they could satisfy their thirst for knowledge with secular subjects, often abandoning Jewish learning even if they continued to identify themselves as Jews. In Rosenzweig's words, "The *mezuzah* may have still greeted one at the door, but the bookcase had, at best, a single Jewish corner."

Rosenzweig saw a diminished Judaism among German Jews. Before emancipation, there had been three interconnected pillars supporting Jewish life: the law, the synagogue, and the home. Jewish education and learning were a natural part of the support system. But afterward the pillars began to separate and weaken. Whereas observing Jewish law had once set Jew apart from Gentile, now it merely tended to distinguish the Orthodox Jews from the many who were less observant. Where formerly the home had been the center of Jewish life, every household member was now deeply involved with the outside, non-Jewish world. And while Jews continued to go to synagogue to celebrate weddings or bar mitzvahs or to say Kaddish on a parent's *yahrzeit*, religious worship was no longer a part of the regular life of many Jews.

Rosenzweig's own family history confirmed that the trends in Jewish education, beginning with Mendelssohn, sometimes had unexpected results. The intention of educators like Mendelssohn and Rosenzweig's great-grandfather, Samuel Meir Ehrenberg, had not been to drive Jews to conversion, but that was often the outcome. Ehrenberg had been first a teacher and then the director of a school that gradually replaced traditional Jewish learning with secular learning. The theory behind this educational shift was that when Jews had the same cultural background as their neighbors, they would be accepted as equals. In fact, Ehrenberg's other two great-grandsons, both close friends of Rosezweig, had converted to Christianity.

Rosenzweig did not feel that Jews who converted to Christianity deserved blame. Instead, he saw how the emancipation movement had sometimes led to the undoing of Jewish education, and he proposed a new approach to help solve the crisis. Traditionally, Jews had started with the Torah as the center of their lives and moved out from it to the rest of the world. Now the process had to be reversed. Without abandoning any of the gains of emancipation, Jews needed to bring all their outside knowledge to bear on the study of the Torah and other Jewish texts. In other words, an emancipated Jew need not give up anything, but instead should try to "lead everything back to Judaism."

Instead of being part-time Jews in an otherwise Christian world, said Rosenzweig, assimilated Jews could transform themselves into fully Jewish human beings by studying. Only Jews who themselves studied major Jewish texts could become whole. Corresponding to the philosophy of the Lehrhaus, this did not mean slavishly adhering to what great authorities had to say about the texts but, rather, approaching them with open minds. It meant striving to find in ancient narratives and commentaries meaning that could affect Jewish lives in the present.

Living the *Mitzvot*

For Rosenzweig, a second key to becoming an integrated Jewish human being was to observe as much Jewish law as possible. Just as he felt that every Jew is free to draw independent conclusions from Jewish texts, he felt that each is responsible for choosing the *mitzvot* whose observance would be most meaningful.

Significantly, Jewish laws and *mitzvot* are not exactly the same thing. Laws are for an entire society, but *mitzvot* speak to the individual, and revelation resulted in *mitzvot*, not in laws. In other words, when Jews feel God's love, they may feel a personal commandment by God to perform a given *mitzvah*. In his own life, Rosenzweig felt he could perform only those Jewish laws that seemed to be *mitzvot*, addressed to him as an individual. But he also felt that Jews should not be satisfied with practicing a small number of *mitzvot*; it is much better to find ways of making impersonal laws into personally addressed commandments.

Rosenzweig tried continually to increase his repertoire of *mitzvot*. When someone asked him if he wore *tefillin*, or phylacteries, he answered, "Not yet." He did not rule out the possibility that the day would come when the law of *tefillin* would seem personally addressed to him.

Despite his attitude about the importance of observance in Jewish life, Rosenzweig was very tolerant of the nonobservant. If a Jew was aware of the law but could not in good faith carry it out, so be it. Human choice and human dignity were more important than blindly carrying out acts without meaning. As Rosenzweig wrote, "Judaism is not Law. It creates Law, but is not it. Judaism is to be a Jew." Through his thought and through the example of his life, Rosenzweig inspired many Jews to be Jews—to transform themselves into fully Jewish human beings.

> **"** *Even when God is terribly near, man can turn away his eyes. . . . And even at a very great distance, the burning gaze of God and man can fuse in such a way that the coldest abstractions grow warm in the mouth of Maimonides or Hermann Cohen. . . .* **"**
>
> From a note on a poem by Yehudah HaLevi, trans. Nahum N. Glatzer

12 MARTIN BUBER

1878 – 1965

Martin Buber may be the best known Jewish thinker since the time of Maimonides. He spent the first 60 years of his life in Europe. In 1938 he left Nazi Germany for *Eretz Yisrael*, and he died in the state of Israel in his eighties. With a beard that made him look like many people's idea of a prophet or saint, he was a legend in his own time, influencing both Jewish and non-Jewish thought.

I and Thou: A Philosophy of Dialogue

The Meaning of "Thou": A Problem in Translation

The most famous of Buber's works is a short book published in German in 1923. The English translation of the title is *I and Thou*. English-speakers are often confused about the true meaning of the word "Thou": it seems stiff and archaic, appearing in old literature and in earlier translations of the Bible and of prayers. But in fact, "thou" is simply a translation of the singular, informal form of the German word for "you." While today's English uses the simple form "you" for addressing both one person or many, formally or informally, German has retained these distinctions. For this reason, in German the singular form of "you" is used only for children and for people with whom one is very friendly. German speakers would never use "thou" to address adults they were just meeting or adults with whom they had a formal relationship.

Buber's translator thus used the word "Thou" to suggest a special friendliness or closeness, not formality. The book's title may be misleading to those who do not understand the importance of the distinction in language.

Dialogue and Conversation: Two Types of Relationships

Buber claimed that people deal with the world in two ways: through "I–It" relations and through "I–Thou" relations. Most daily life involves the "I–It" sort, whereby we understand things through objective facts and analysis rather than through emotional involvement.

Sometimes even personal relationships are of the "I–It" type. Even ideally, to a doctor an ill patient is in many ways an "it," and the distance this attitude suggests allows the doctor to decide on an effective treatment. Under other circumstances, though, people resent being treated as an "it." No one, for example, wants to marry someone whose only interest in a future spouse is financial.

The other relationship, "I–Thou," is a close one characterized by openness and trust. Buber called it a type of dialogue.

> " *That you need God more than anything else, you know at all times in your heart. But know also that God needs you—in the fullness of His eternity. . . . You need God in order to be, and God needs you—for that which is the meaning of your life.* "
>
> *I and Thou*, trans. Walter Kaufmann

Dialogue Is Not Conversation

The dialogue of an "I–Thou" relationship is not like a conversation. It needs no words at all. In fact, Buber claimed that individuals can have such relationships not only with other people, but with nature, music, and art as well. With other people, a sympathetic look or a hand placed firmly on a friend's shoulder can also be forms of dialogue.

Conversely, even a conversation may not be dialogue as Buber defined it. Sometimes people are distracted; at other times they are not interested in truly communicating with each other. Buber called these kinds of conversation "monologue," even though two people are talking.

For example, men and women involved in romantic relationships sometimes merely "play" at being in love. A man may tell a woman what he thinks she wants to hear, or vice versa. The listener may think, "This is terrific! I can't wait to tell my friends about it." In such cases, the relationship is not dialogue, but at most only monologue. The words being bandied about may be affectionate on the surface, but they are not genuine. Both partners' deepest concern is not with the other person at all, but with how they themselves feel.

Dialogue with God, the "Eternal Thou"

According to Buber, we can never really understand God's true nature. All attempts to do so make God into an It; only by approaching God as a Thou can we hope to have a relationship with the divine. But there is no magic recipe to follow for entering into an I–Thou relationship, either with a person or with God. Any set of instructions would belong to the world of I–It.

Nevertheless, certain ways of searching for divine dialogue may prove more fruitful than others. Buber explained that there are three ways to have an I–Thou relationship with God: by relating to God's creations, by developing talents, and by reading the Bible.

True dialogue with a person, with nature, or with a work of art requires openness. Buber suggested that we can relate to God only if we are prepared to let God into our lives. We must see how God "speaks" to us through the world and all of creation. Buber rejected the idea of looking for holiness by abandoning the world. Isolating oneself and thinking mystical thoughts will not bring one closer to it. On the contrary, holiness is everywhere in the world, and for that reason we can find it by entering into I–Thou relationships with God's creations. Buber called God "the Eternal Thou" in whom all our other I–Thou relationships intersect.

In his most famous work, *I and Thou,* Buber wrote that people can establish a dialogue with God, and thereby experience God's influence. Buber believed in the power of dialogue. Dialogue, he said, can be carried out only when there is commitment on both sides, as in the historic 1977 meeting between Egyptian President Anwar Sadat and Israeli Prime Minister Menachem Begin.

Since God is everywhere, Buber expressed deep concern about many aspects of modern religious life. Like the Hasidim, he argued that life should not be separated into places or times that are holy and others that are everyday. Buber felt that everything in life can be made holy.

This Hasidic emphasis on sanctifying all of creation points to the second way people can begin a dialogue with God. Buber followed an old Jewish tradition according to which everyone is God's partner in creation. Each person has a specific task to perform in life; by developing our own talents, we meet God in the creation process, together furthering the development of the world.

If these two forms of the I–Thou relationship with God seem vague, it is because they depend so heavily on the capabilities and desires of each individual. The third form, reading the Bible, is more concrete. Buber stressed that the Bible offers a record of ancient meetings between God and the Jewish people; by reading with an open mind, we can meet God today as our ancestors did long ago.

The Eclipse of God

Buber acknowledged that God is not always present for every person. In all I–Thou relationships there are times when one party may not be there for the other. Each person has to be free to make choices. Similarly, God is free to ignore prayers or requests.

Buber used the phrase "the eclipse of God" to explain God's seeming absence. Though the sun is always in the daytime sky, its light is eclipsed when the moon blocks it from reaching the earth. In the same way, God is always there but may not always be available. In a true I–Thou relationship, during the low times each person has faith that the positive side of the relationship will eventually prevail; despite temporary disappointments, everyone should preserve the same faith regarding God. To fail to do so would close out holiness. As Buber put it, "The eclipse of the light of God is not extinction; even tomorrow that which has stepped in between may give way."

God Speaks, But People May Misinterpret

Although we are continually in dialogue with God, we must be careful not to misinterpret divine words. Just as people often misinterpret one another, they also may fail to understand God's message, even when they are open to the dialogue. Buber told a story about himself to demonstrate the point:

From the time he was a boy, he was troubled by a passage in the Bible that suggests God is vengeful and violent. It is the passage in which the prophet Samuel explains to King Saul why God wishes to dethrone him. Saul has conquered the Amalekites and killed them all, except for their prince, Agag, whose life he has spared.

These Amalekites were descendants of the people who had attacked the Israelites from the rear during their forty-year march through the wilderness, killing as many as they could. In response, Moses declared that Israel and Amalek would forever be enemies, instructing his people to take future opportunities to wipe out the name of Amalek (Deut. 25:17–19).

In the Book of Samuel (I Samuel 15) the prophet hears God's voice expressing disappointment that Saul has not fulfilled the commandment to wipe out Amalek. After a sleepless night, he goes to Saul for the last time, informing him of God's displeasure. Then Samuel calls Prince Agag over and hacks the prince to pieces "before God."

As a grown man, on one of his trips Buber met an observant Jew. Somehow their discussion turned to this passage, and Buber admitted to his traveling companion that he had never been able to believe

Samuel's action was the will of God. At first the other man seemed furious with Buber for making such a claim, challenging him to explain what he did in fact believe. Buber's immediate response was that he believed Samuel had misunderstood God. As Buber tells the story, something wonderful then happened. A gentle look replaced the anger on the man's face, as he agreed that Samuel must have misunderstood.

Looking back on the conversation, Buber clarified to himself what he had been trying to tell the man. His idea, of course, went beyond the single passage in the Book of Samuel. He meant that people are at a disadvantage in their dialogue with God. If we are open to the dialogue, God may speak to us, but human beings do not always understand the real message.

A Religious Anarchist, Jewish in Spirit and Deed

Freedom of Observance

Buber's concept of dialogue, however interesting it may be, is not specifically Jewish. Buber himself acknowledged that fact. He once said of himself to his colleague Abraham Heschel (Chapter 15)—a thinker whose thought is clearly Jewish—"I am not a Jewish philosopher. I am a universal philosopher."

Indeed, Buber's thought often distanced him from many of his people. Because he believed that each person is capable of dialogue with God, he rejected the notion that such dialogue might be governed by fixed rules of behavior; he felt that Jews need to observe only those laws they believe God has addressed to them personally, and that insisting on a fixed body of law such as the Jewish *halakhah* only undermines the personal relationship. Buber's position with respect to law and religion is similar to the political theory of anarchism, which rejects all forms of government because they interfere unjustly with personal freedom. As a result, Buber is sometimes called a religious anarchist.

Like many teenagers, Buber rebelled against his religious upbringing. At the age of fourteen he stopped wearing *tefillin*. For many years he preferred reading secular works to Jewish ones. But at the age of twenty, he found his way back to Judaism through Zionism, and from that time on he lived a life intensely involved with Judaism—although one not always approved of by many fellow Jews.

As a result, no one could think of writing a book about Jewish thinkers or Jewish thought without including Buber. Not only did his philosophy emerge from a deep connection to the Bible and to Hasidism, but it also led him into further Jewish studies. His concept of dialogue also enabled Buber to serve as a spiritual leader to German Jewry during the rise of Nazism, and to strive to repair German–Jewish relations after the war. In addition, surely as a reflection of his belief in dialogue, Buber never gave up hope of improving Israeli–Arab relations.

Restoring the Spiritual Past

Translating the Bible.   Buber's philosophy of dialogue led to a massive undertaking: translating the Bible into German. He believed that the Bible was meant not to be read but to be listened to—that only by hearing its voice as first spoken could each individual enter into dialogue with it. When truly listening to the Bible's words, he said, one can hear the living speech of God—the Eternal Thou. "The Bible stems from living recitation and is destined to living recitation." Its written form is "only the form of its preservation."

Buber began the job together with his friend Franz Rosenzweig; the first translated books appeared in 1925. After Rosenzweig's death in 1929, Buber continued the effort on his own. The final volumes appeared in 1961, four years before his own death.

We recall that in the eighteenth century, Moses Mendelssohn had also offered a German translation of the Bible. But Mendelssohn's aim was almost the exact opposite of Buber and Rosenzweig's; he wanted to teach the unenlightened ghetto Jews of Germany how to speak proper German. Buber and Rosenzweig, on the other hand, wanted their readers to learn Hebrew. Their audience, unlike Mendelssohn's, was well educated in secular studies but woefully unprepared to study its Jewish heritage. Buber and Rosenzweig wanted their version to be the most authentic German recreation of the ancient spoken Hebrew, an approach that endowed it with a sometimes strange and haunting aura. To preserve the Bible's spoken quality, they did not try to smooth out the text where it is rough. Passages that are difficult to understand in the original remain so in their translation.

Still, every translation reveals the mind of the translator, who must decide just what words to use. For example, the Hebrew word *kadosh* is usually translated as "holy." Buber and Rosenzweig rendered it as "hallowing," which means "making holy." As a result, in their version the Israelites are not a holy people but a people who hallow, who make things holy—an idea connected to the basic Hasidic ideas underlying much of Buber's thought.

Buber was aware of the terrible responsibility incurred by anyone daring to convey the meaning of God's words to others. "Always when I have to translate or to interpret a biblical text, I do so with fear and trembling, in an inescapable tension between the word of God and the words of man."

Bringing Hasidic Thought to a Wide Audience. Buber not only offered German Jews and other readers of German a new perspective on the Bible, but his collections of Hasidic tales also made this Jewish movement a part of world literature. Between 1906 and 1960 his books on Hasidic themes appeared in German, Hebrew, and English.

For Buber, the theories of the early Hasidic leaders were less important than the way they lived their lives. In one of his tales, aptly titled "To Say Torah and to Be Torah," a follower of the maggid of Mezritch, one of the great Hasidic leaders, explains his devotion not in terms of wishing to hear the master's commentaries on religious texts but, rather, of wishing to watch the way he laced and unlaced his boots. The leader's most casual acts were able to teach others the proper way to live.

But according to Buber, the Hasidic masters did not intend that others merely copy them. Rather, they taught that each of us has specific capabilities, and our task is to develop them as fully and authentically as possible. Buber once summarized Hasidism's basic message as "You yourself must begin." He went on to explain what he meant: "Everything is waiting to be hallowed by you. . . . For the sake of this your beginning, God created the world. He has drawn it out of Himself so that you may bring it closer to Him. Meet the world with the fullness of your being and you shall meet Him."

Resisting the Nazis

In his mid-forties, Buber began to teach Jewish religion and ethics at the University of Frankfurt. In October 1933, after the Nazis' rise to power, Buber did not wait to be officially dismissed from his professorship, but resigned of his own accord.

Up until then, Buber's influence on the Jews of Germany had not been great. But in 1933 he became one of their spiritual leaders. As one of the opening steps in their campaign against the Jews, the Nazis fired all Jewish professors and prohibited Jewish students from attending German universities and schools. The Jewish community responded as best it could to this and similar measures. Frankfurt's Jews reopened the Independent House of Jewish Learning, formerly directed by Franz

Rosenzweig, with Buber as its head. To coordinate Jewish adult education throughout Germany, a Central Office for Jewish Adult Education was set up, and Buber was named director.

Buber organized small groups of teachers and students into communities that lived and worked together. His goals were to strengthen the Jewishness of these people and to keep them from despair, and also to prepare them for resettlement in *Eretz Yisrael*.

Buber spread his message of encouragement and hope to Jews throughout Germany. The Nazis, having become aware of the effectiveness of his message of spiritual resistance, in 1935 ordered him to stop lecturing at Jewish gatherings. After German Quakers began to invite him to speak at their meetings, the Nazis put a stop to his appearances there as well.

Despite the wickedness he was confronting, Buber's exemplary behavior has made its mark on history. One of his German-Jewish colleagues, later to join him on the faculty of the Hebrew University in Jerusalem, said of his activities during this period, "Anyone who did not see Buber then has not seen true civil courage."

Overcoming Conflict Through Dialogue

Buber's philosophy of dialogue also made him into a man of peace—an authentic Jewish role. He believed that dialogue could help heal the wounds between Germans and Jews after the war. He also believed that only dialogue would enable Arabs and Jews to live together in *Eretz Yisrael*. Ironically, his efforts to overcome these conflicts through dialogue and social action brought him into conflict with many Jews.

Repairing German–Jewish Relations.   Even before the war, Buber was involved in bettering relations between German Christians and Jews. In 1924 he founded the first serious journal edited jointly by a Protestant, a Catholic, and a Jew. After the journal stopped publishing in 1929, he continued to speak and write about ways to deepen the Christian–Jewish dialogue, but the Nazis put a stop to all such activities in the early 1930s.

In 1951, thirteen years after leaving Nazi Germany for *Eretz Yisrael*, Buber learned he had been awarded the University of Hamburg's Goethe Prize. The award recognized both his scholarly achievements and his efforts to promote deeper understanding among people. Buber was invited to come to Germany to receive the prize and to lecture at the university. He knew that many Jews in Israel and throughout the world would object to his accepting the German prize—after all, the German death camps had been liberated only five years before. But

Buber decided to accept the award, to show that new relationships could arise "out of the antihuman chaos of our time."

Buber did not make his trip to Germany until 1953, two years later. By then, he had also accepted a second German award, the Peace Prize of the German Book Trade. He donated the money from both awards to an organization that was encouraging dialogue between Arabs and Israelis.

In accepting the second prize, Buber said:

> I believe, despite all, that the peoples in this hour can enter into dialogue, into a genuine dialogue with one another. In a genuine dialogue each of the partners, even when he stands in opposition to the other, heeds, affirms, and confirms his opponent as an existing other. Only so is it possible for conflict, though not to be eliminated from the world, yet to be subject to human arbitration, and so led to the point where it is overcome.

While Buber was being honored in Germany, many Jews throughout the world were horrified by his actions. In 1960, German students were asked to name the greatest spiritual figures of their time, and Martin Buber was third on their list. By contrast, in 1954 a Jewish youth movement threatened to assassinate the editors of an Israeli weekly if they published an interview with Buber.

Buber, however, did not accept German awards mindlessly. In 1960 he learned of a decision to place a commemorative plaque on the house in Heppenheim, Germany, where he and his family had lived before fleeing the country. The Society for Christian–Jewish Cooperation asked him if he would like to speak on the occasion. Buber responded:

> I believe I have served the cause of the reconciliation of peoples to the best of my abilities. But that is a cause which can only thrive under the sign of truth. It would not do justice to the truth, in my opinion, if a plaque were erected on the house in which my family and I lived during the years 1916–1938 which only commemorated the fact of this dwelling but left unmentioned the fact that it was plundering and expropriation which marked the end of our connection with this dwelling. A commemorative plaque such as you plan would, to be sure, mean a high honor for my person, but it would not thereby show the honor due the historical truth which should serve the coming generations as admonition and warning.

Buber's house in Heppenheim is now the headquarters of the International Council of Christians and Jews.

Promoting Arab–Israeli Dialogue.   Buber was among the early Zionist leaders who felt that settlers in *Eretz Yisrael* could not simply ignore the fact that Arabs already lived there. In an address to

Buber was a strong advocate of dialogue between peoples in conflict. He advocated increased contact between Jews and Germans after the Holocaust, as a way of healing wounds. He called for increased contact and cooperation between Jews and Arabs in *Eretz Yisrael*. Here Ibrahim Abu Rebiya, the first Bedouin admitted to Hebrew University in Jerusalem, talks with Dean Aryeh Olitzki.

the Zionist Congress of 1921, he proposed that the movement proclaim "its desire to live in peace and brotherhood with the Arab people and to develop the common homeland into a republic in which both peoples will have the possibility of free development."

The Bubers arrived in *Eretz Yisrael* during a period of intense Arab terrorist activity against Jewish settlers. But he warned those who responded with counterterrorism that peaceful coexistence with the Arabs was a necessity. In 1942 he helped establish a movement calling for a binational state, to be run equally by Jewish settlers and the Arabs already there. Toward this end, the movement hoped to foster social, economic, cultural, and political cooperation between Arabs and Jews.

When Israel became a state in May 1948, Buber expressed mixed feelings: "Today my heart is torn ... my heart trembles today like the heart of every Jew." But he worried that a Jewish state surrounded by hostile neighbors would have to "devote its best forces to military instead of social and cultural values."

After May 1948 Buber put to rest his hopes for a binational state, but he never gave up his wish to see improved cooperation between Jews and Arabs. His views about Israeli nationalism made him unpopular in many quarters, including among students at Hebrew University, where he taught social philosophy until his retirement in 1951.

Still, Buber had his supporters as well as his detractors. In the years just before his death he counseled a group of kibbutz members who came to him with their problems. Shortly after the Six Day War they published a book presenting Buber's thoughts on Arab–Jewish affairs and on general issues of war and peace. Another testimonial to Buber came at his funeral in Jerusalem: A group from the Arab Students' Organization placed a wreath on the grave of the man who worked so hard to achieve peace between Israelis and Arabs.

Buber's influence continues. In the late 1960s the Hebrew University opened the Martin Buber Institute for Adult Education, its purpose being to further dialogue between Israelis and Palestinians. Immediately after the Six Day War the institute began to offer Hebrew courses to Palestinians. As of January 1990—a full two years after the beginning of the Palestinian uprising in December 1987—about 9,000 students had studied Hebrew there.

Buber once described a philosopher as someone who "sees what will happen in the future." He never despaired of a future in which people might work out their differences by talking to one another with open minds and hearts. For many people, Buber's commitment to dialogue thus represents hope, even when the situation in the Middle East seems very bleak. Buber once said, "In real meeting we can reach the soil of salvation after the tragedy has been completed."

> " *Israel is chosen to enable it to ascend from the biological law of power, which the nations glorify in their wishful thinking, to the sphere of truth and righteousness. . . . Israel was chosen to become a true people, and that means God's people.* "
>
> "Hebrew Humanism"

On sabbatical leave from Hebrew University of Jerusalem, in 1948 Buber was a visiting scholar at the University of Judaism in Los Angeles.

13 LEO BAECK

1873 – 1956

Leo Baeck was the only major Jewish thinker to survive a Nazi concentration camp. He is considered the last representative of German Jewry, and the Leo Baeck Institute for the study of the Jews of German-speaking countries was set up in his honor in 1954. His dramatic life teaches as much about his thought as do his two major books, *The Essence of Judaism* (1905) and *This People Israel: The Meaning of Jewish Existence* (1955). Baeck stressed that Judaism is dynamic but that one aspect does not change: each person's moral responsibility to behave ethically.

THE LAST REPRESENTATIVE OF GERMAN JEWRY

Baeck's Leadership Qualities Emerge

Leo Baeck came from a rabbinical family, a fact that made him proud. But he also taught that what gives our life its worth is what we make of ourselves, not which family we are born into. From the beginning of his career as a rabbi and thinker, Baeck showed that he had the makings of a great leader. He was skillful at reconciling opposing points of view, was not afraid to speak his own mind in the face of opposition, and saw the need for Judaism to enhance the rights of its second-class citizens.

The Conciliator.   Fresh out of rabbinical school in his early twenties, Baeck became the rabbi in a small German town. Raised in a traditional Jewish home but drawn to many aspects of the new liberal Judaism (what we now call Reform Judaism), Baeck was able to show from the outset that these two perspectives need not be in opposition.

In the late 1890s many German–Jewish communities were debating whether and how to modernize their synagogue services. The arguments between the traditional and the more liberal Jews could become quite heated. Baeck himself continued to say morning prayers wearing *tefillin*, in Orthodox fashion, but realizing that many members of his congregation did not understand Hebrew, much less share his commitment to tradition, he incorporated some German into the service. While more traditional congregation members occasionally grumbled at this innovation, they took heart in the fact that their young rabbi himself shared their practices. Those who felt that the service was still too traditional were reassured by two of Baeck's other innovations: the introduction of a mixed choir and the installation of an organ.

Courage and Personal Independence of Thought.   Baeck became a rabbi just months before Herzl presided over the First Zionist Congress in Basel, Switzerland, in 1897. The following year, at a meeting of the German Rabbinical Association, the leaders wanted the association to condemn Zionism. After all, German Jews had a homeland in Germany. Why should they need another?

After offering an anti-Zionist resolution, the leaders of the association cut off debate without allowing the Zionists to present their side. When the vote was taken, Leo Baeck was one of only three rabbis willing to risk his career by voting against the resolution. Although not

> " *The characteristic feature of Judaism is thus the relation of man to God. Essential to it is the consciousness of being created. . . .* "
>
> The Essence of Judaism, rendition by Irving Howe, based on translation of Victor Grubenwieser and Leonard Pearl

a Zionist himself, he was offended by what he considered the unfair tactics of its sponsors, who were calling all Zionists bad Jews. Baeck felt that Judaism had always flourished by incorporating, rather than suppressing, opposing points of view.

Supporting Enhanced Rights for Women in Judaism. Baeck was among the prominent German–Jewish figures who believed that women were being treated as second-class citizens within the Jewish community. He began to address the problem by promoting a good Jewish education for Jewish girls; he also showed his concern by officiating as rabbi at confirmation ceremonies for girls in the city of Duesseldorf. Later, as a professor at Berlin's Hochschule, the major liberal German–Jewish institution of higher learning, he worked hard to encourage women students in their hopes of serving the community and being actively involved in its public life.

A Leader in the Developing Storm

When World War I broke out in 1914, Baeck was 41 years old, with a wife and a teenage daughter. Nonetheless, he was one of the first to volunteer as an army chaplain. Like other German Jews, he supported his country's war effort; nearly all German–Jewish men of fighting age served in the army, 12,000 of them losing their lives in the war. All the same, upon Germany's defeat in 1918 some Germans blamed German Jews, claiming they had sabotaged the war effort in order to help Jews in other countries.

By the end of January 1933, Adolf Hitler was chancellor of Germany. At that time, between 500,000 and 600,000 Jews lived in Germany, less than one percent of the total population of 65 million. There was a strong Jewish presence in the major cities, however, especially Berlin, where fully one-third of all German Jews lived. Berlin was also where Baeck had been serving as a rabbi since 1912. He began to understand that the Nazis had in mind nothing less than the destruction of German Jewry.

Saving the Young and Encouraging the Old. In March 1933 Baeck told the leaders of an association of assimilated German Jews that "the end of German Judaism has arrived." He warned them that the Nazi regime would not end soon. However, no one, including Baeck, could have known the full scope of the horrors lying in store for German Jewry.

Baeck proposed a two-part plan: young Jews should be encouraged to leave Germany and helped to start new lives in safer lands; at the same time, the cultural and spiritual life of those Jews remaining in Germany should be strengthened. Although Baeck himself was offered positions in England and the United States, he rejected these offers. More than once he said that he would leave only when he was the last Jew left in Germany.

Baeck knew that it would not be easy for young people to leave their families and friends and move to new countries with strange languages. In order to make things a little easier for them, he wrote letter upon letter of introduction, searched far and wide for pulpits and other positions for young German rabbis, and urged older men to use their connections abroad to help younger people.

On the night of November 9–10, 1938, the Nazis organized the burning and destruction of synagogues and other Jewish concerns. Before *Kristallnacht*—as this "Night of Broken Glass" came to be known—many Jews had been reluctant to abandon Germany, where they thought they still had a future. Nevertheless, Baeck and other leaders succeeded in helping one-third of them escape before this turning point in German history.

After *Kristallnacht*, it was no longer necessary to persuade Jews to take this drastic step; rather, it was now a matter of getting as many people out as possible. In the next ten months, before World War II officially began in September 1939, another third of the German-Jewish population managed to escape. Just before the war broke out, Baeck accompanied a group of German-Jewish children to safety in England, but he himself returned, feeling that the Jews left behind were his responsibility, not to be abandoned.

In order to oversee the twofold plan of emigration and cultural strengthening, as well as to supervise Jewish education and welfare, the Jews of Germany had organized a representative committee in 1933, with Leo Baeck at its head. After *Kristallnacht*, the Nazis broke up the committee, but soon realized that they needed such a group. In February 1939 the Nazis reorganized it, changing its name and the source of its authority. Before, it had been an autonomous Jewish organization, one chosen by and answerable to the community. Now it was answerable to the Nazis.

Leo Baeck stayed on as head of the new organization, and some after-the-fact analysts have criticized him for this decision, on the grounds that the committee simply did the Nazis' work for them. However, the intention of its leaders was to continue serving their fellow Jews, not the Nazis, and to remain a center of resistance to Nazi rule.

Facing the Gestapo.

It is hard to see how anyone could question Baeck's will to defy the Nazis. More than once he showed great personal courage in dealing with the Gestapo.

The Leo Baeck Institute, founded in New York City in 1955, is dedicated to preserving the history and culture of German-speaking Jewry. It contains a library and research center. Among its activities are lectures, exhibits, and seminars.

In September 1935, the Nazis enacted the so-called Nuremberg laws to keep "German blood and honor" pure of Jewish contamination. In an act of defiance, Baeck wrote a prayer of Jewish pride and dignity to be read in synagogues throughout Germany during the upcoming High Holidays. In part, the prayer read: "With the same fervor with which we confess our sins, . . . we . . . express our contempt for the lies concerning us and the defamation of our religion and its testimonies. . . . We look upon each other and know who we are; we look up to our God and know what shall abide." In the last phrase, Baeck was suggesting that justice would ultimately conquer Hitler.

Upon learning of the prayer, the Nazis threatened to arrest any rabbi found reading it. Many rabbis defied the threat, but only one was arrested: Baeck himself. He was held for 24 hours and released. Apparently, the Germans still cared enough about world opinion to be embarrassed by a long report of the incident in *The Times* of London.

Baeck was arrested for a second time in 1937, when the Gestapo closed the German branch of B'nai B'rith—the same Jewish service organization still runs youth organizations and the Anti-Defamation League in the United States today, along with the Hillel Foundation on college campuses. As president of Germany's B'nai B'rith, Baeck was ordered to sign a statement agreeing to turn over all the organization's substantial property to the Nazi government. He refused.

Although declining to leave Germany himself, he saw to it that his daughter, son-in-law, and granddaughter left for London. He accompanied them as far as Hamburg. There, he again defied the Nazis, who had demanded that Jews turn over all their silver, including religious objects. Rather than enrich an evil regime with the Baeck family pieces, some of which had belonged to his deceased wife's family, Baeck took them to Hamburg, rented a rowboat, and dumped the silver in the Elbe River. The spot was carefully chosen: the tides, Baeck felt certain, would carry the silver far out into the channel, never to surface again.

Baeck was also bold enough to scorn the Nazis openly. Gestapo officials summoned him to their headquarters one Sabbath, but Baeck simply refused to go. "I'm not in the habit of showing up in an office on Saturday," he told them. "On the Sabbath, I go to services."

"The Commandment of God Is to Live." Baeck was a strong believer in passive resistance to Nazi rule. The idea of passive resistance—opposing a government by refusing to follow orders or by nonviolent acts such as public demonstrations—is often associated with the name of the Hindu nationalist leader Mohandas Gandhi, who helped free India from British rule by encouraging his followers to carry out such acts.

While Baeck agreed with Gandhi's response to injustice, he did not follow all the Indian leader's recommendations. In November 1938 the Baron von Veltheim, one of Baeck's non-Jewish German friends, met with Gandhi in India and asked him if he had any advice for Baeck. Gandhi's advice was that at a prearranged moment, all the Jews of Germany should commit suicide. Such a gesture, Gandhi argued, would awaken the world to the Nazi threat the way nothing else could.

The baron passed on Gandhi's advice, but Leo Baeck did not think it was appropriate guidance for Jews. "We Jews know that the commandment of God is to live," he said.

The Teacher of Theresienstadt

Baeck was able to stay in his Berlin apartment from the start of the war in September 1939 until late January 1943. (His wife had died in 1937.) More and more Jews were taken to concentration camps as the war progressed, and Baeck sensed that the time was not far off when he too would be taken away. If world opinion had protected him in the 1930s, the Nazis were now at war with most of the world and were no longer as concerned with its opinion. In addition, the organization he headed had been useful to the Nazis in taking care of Jewish needs, but with the decline of the Jewish population, it was of less importance.

Baeck was deported to a camp near Prague, the capital of Czechoslovakia. Theresienstadt (or Terezin, as the Czechs called it) had been set up by the Nazis in 1941 as a "model" camp they could show to visiting officials of the International Red Cross. It thus became a ghetto for "privileged" Jews, including those, like Baeck, with international connections. Though Theresienstadt was not designed to be a death camp like Auschwitz or Bergen-Belsen, of the 140,000 Jews sent there fewer than 9,000 survived the war. Many died of illness or starvation even in this "model" camp, and many others were sent from Theresienstadt to Auschwitz.

By the time Baeck arrived at the camp, a Jewish Council of Elders had already been formed to run its daily life. He volunteered for the task of overseeing the camp's welfare program, visiting the sick and comforting the elderly in this capacity. Like all other new deportees, he was forced to join a labor crew. For several weeks after arriving at Theresienstadt, Baeck, a few months shy of his seventieth birthday, could be seen pulling a garbage wagon through the ghetto's streets. Upon his birthday, according to standard policy he no longer had to do physical labor. He was thus free for another task: keeping the spark of humanity alive in his fellow inmates by teaching them philosophy and history.

> " *In all of the declines of history in which humanity apparently destroys itself or seems to refute itself, one thing surely endured and experienced renewal. That which was searched out and formed by the spirit arose out of ruins and beyond ruins. . . . That which spirit has fashioned is indestructible.* "
>
> *This People Israel*, trans. Albert H. Friedlander

Ever since Theresienstadt's opening, the inmates had been aware that mere physical survival was not enough. Determined to keep their spirit as strong as possible, they lovingly arranged theatrical and musical performances, religious services, and programs to educate the camp's children. After the war, many of the camp's survivors cited the heartening effect of the lecture series arranged by Baeck and other scholar-inmates. The Nazis did not understand the importance of the camp's cultural programs, particularly the lectures, and they allowed these activities to continue. By simply listening to the lectures, the inmates confirmed their status as human beings rather than numbers. In this way, attending a lecture became an act of rebellion.

Just as Baeck had felt a general responsibility for the Jews of Germany, refusing to abandon them for safety elsewhere, he had a strong sense of loyalty toward Theresienstadt's inmates. More than once, he refused to leave. Hearing that Baeck had been deported, a German Zionist living in Jerusalem approached an official of the city's Catholic Church in 1943. He proposed that the Church help find some well-known German who was being held prisoner-of-war in an allied country and work out a trade for Leo Baeck. The Church official responded, "Your mission is in vain; if the man is such as you have described him, he will never desert his flock."

The official was right. In early 1945 the Nazis released 1,200 Jews from Theresienstadt. Leo Baeck refused to join the group. In the spring, as the war's end drew closer, Jewish leaders in England and the United States began to fear that Baeck might be accidentally killed during the camp's liberation, and they arranged to have an American officer rescue him. When the officer showed up, Baeck insisted on staying for two months, until a severe epidemic of typhus—an acutely infectious disease transmitted by the lice that riddled Theresienstadt—was under control. Also, wishing to make sure no Jew left the camp without identity papers of some sort, he spent much time writing letters on behalf of those who had none. His signature on a letter of introduction would assure otherwise unknown refugees a welcome by Jews throughout the world.

At the war's end Baeck was proud of the restraint shown by the inmates of Theresienstadt. Aware that the Russian army was advancing to liberate the camp, all the Nazis fled. The last to leave was the commandant. The man who had had life-and-death power over the Jewish inmates for years rode through Theresienstadt on his bicycle, unarmed, locking doors. The Jewish inmates watched him silently. Baeck commented to a young friend: "Look at it. This can only happen with Jews. Of all the people here, not one has lifted a stone against him. They could have strangled him if they wanted."

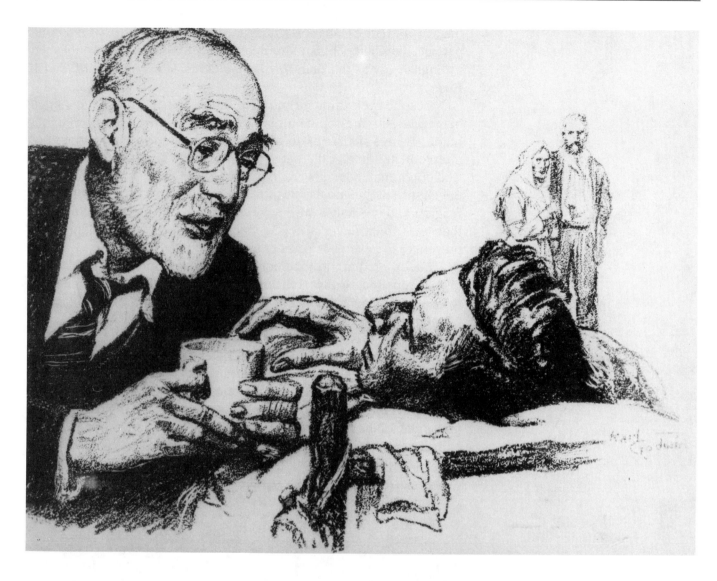

The Survivor's Spiritual Strength

Baeck lived for more than eleven years after the war's end. He made his home with his daughter's family in London, resuming a career of teaching and lecturing around the world. For five years he was a visiting professor at Hebrew Union College in Cincinnati, and he was a guest professor at the Hebrew University in Jerusalem. He also completed a book begun before his deportation. Fearing that the manuscript would not make it through the war, Baeck had entrusted it to Baron von Veltheim—the same man who had asked Gandhi if he had any advice for Baeck. Both the baron and the manuscript survived

Baeck was a leader in the German-Jewish community. When the Nazis came to power he refused to leave Germany, and in 1944, just prior to his seventieth birthday, he was sent to the Theresiendstadt concentration camp. There he became a spiritual leader of the inmates. In 1945 he had an opportunity to leave Theresienstadt, but once again refused.

the war, and Baeck was able to correct the proofs for the book's second part just days before his sudden death in 1956. The book was published in English under the title *This People Israel: The Meaning of Jewish Existence.*

Despite everything he had lived through, Baeck had not changed his earlier thinking about human beings and God. He still believed that human beings are free to do good or evil, and that when God does not intervene in human affairs it is out of deference to that freedom. Not God but human beings were to blame for the horrors of World War II. Baeck still felt that Judaism was at one and the same time an optimistic religion and one fully aware of how evil humanity can be. He insisted that Jews must never accept evil, even just by staying silent in its presence, and even if it is easier to do so.

Baeck felt that the bond between Jews and Germans could never be fully repaired. He also felt, however, that a new connection needed to be made. Toward this end, he was one of the first well-known German Jews to return to Germany in the years after the war, continuing to visit the country in an effort to restore communication between Germans and Jews. In Baeck's eyes, the optimistic strand in Judaism means that a Jew must maintain faith in all human beings. Just as every Jew is created in God's image, so is every other person, including every German. Just as all Jews can dedicate themselves to a godly way of life, no matter what they may have done in the past, so can all Germans.

Like Martin Buber, who wanted to promote dialogue as a way of resolving differences, Leo Baeck tried to restore trust between Germans and Jews by visiting Germany in the early postwar years.

THE CHALLENGE OF MORAL BEHAVIOR

Defining Judaism

Baeck believed that, above all, Judaism is a religion demanding moral behavior from every individual. He often would illustrate this belief by developing comparisons between different themes and concepts.

Faith and Deed. Baeck's *The Essence of Judaism* contrasts Christianity as a religion of faith with Judaism, which Baeck defined as a religion of deed. *The Essence of Judaism* was Baeck's response to a book by Adolf von Harnack, a Christian thinker who asserted that Judaism was a dead religion, superseded by Christianity. Von Harnack defined "faith" in a way Baeck found unacceptable: that "in the end God will do justice. If He does not do it here, He will do it in the Beyond, and that is the main point." Baeck insisted that waiting for the "Beyond" is an abdication of responsibility. A Jew must act now, in this world, to see to it that God's justice is brought about. In fact, for Baeck, to be a Jew means to take action.

Romantic and Classical Religion. In one of Baeck's most famous essays, he offered a similar contrast between Judaism and Christianity but used different terms. He calls Christianity a "romantic" religion, meaning that believers allow their emotions to sweep over them; he called Judaism a "classical" religion, described as one concerned with deeds, not feelings.

Baeck wrote this essay as the democratic government of Germany showed signs of crumbling after World War I. In it, he tried to show that romantic religion can keep people from trying to overcome evil in the world. The Nazis evidently found Baeck's message threatening; in 1938 they destroyed all but ten copies of a new collection of his essays, including this one.

Mystery and Commandment. Baeck also contrasted "mystery," the sense we have that God exists, with "commandment," our moral obligation to perform godly deeds. The sense of God's existence is what creates each individual's drive to act in a moral way.

According to Baeck, Judaism insists on a *union* between the two notions. If we allow the sense of mystery to overwhelm us, we end up with a romantic religion focusing on feelings rather than on moral behavior. The most appropriate way to acknowledge our consciousness of God is to perform moral deeds.

Challenges to Every Jew

The Judaism that Baeck described is a dynamic, involved religion. It demands that each of us take an active role in understanding Judaism, in choosing to devote ourselves to God, in forming our own identities, and in showing the meaning of Judaism to the world.

The Challenge to Interpret. Baeck pointed out that while Christianity may be focused on a single individual, Jesus, and his teaching, in Judaism there is an endless succession of teachers: the rabbis. While it is important for Jews to learn the teachings of the past, it is equally important for each new generation to use its creativity in giving them new meaning.

Baeck taught that each generation must make the Torah its own. The Bible of the age of Maimonides is different from the Bible of the age of Mendelssohn, which, in turn, is different from the Bible of Buber and Rosenzweig. In the same way, each generation must work out its own relationship with tradition and its own interpretation of Jewish law. "Judaism never became a completed entity; no period of its development could become its totality. The old revelation ever becomes a new revelation; Judaism experiences a continuous renaissance."

The Challenge to Become "Chosen." Like Mendelssohn more than a century before him, Baeck did not believe that God played favorites with the peoples of the world—that the Jews were a "chosen people" in the sense that God had bestowed a special religious consciousness on them. Instead, what makes the Jews "chosen" is the active choice or decision to devote themselves to God—a commitment to a life devoted to moral behavior. Each of us is challenged to make this the central commitment of our own lives.

The Challenge to Create Ourselves. According to Baeck, one of the greatest challenges Judaism presents us with is to make something of ourselves. In the first chapter of *The Essence of Judaism* he says: "Our life is fulfilled by what we become, not by what we are at birth. Endowment and heritage mean much . . . and then again nothing; the essential thing is what we make of them."

This challenge is connected to the sense we have of being God's creatures—"the consciousness of being created"—and this reflects the relationship Baeck sees between mystery and commandment. Because we have the sense that God has created us, we also feel that our Creator demands we do something with the raw material we are at birth. All Jews must thus first acknowledge themselves as God's creatures. We must next realize that God created us so that we may create our own lives. "To be both created and yet creator is the heart of Jewish religious consciousness."

The paradox that the creature is expected to be a creator is what truly defines human beings. By demanding that we "give shape" to our own lives, God challenges us to take what we have been given and keep on developing it.

The Challenge to Testify.   A final challenge that Baeck's Judaism presents to every Jew is one he continued to meet throughout his long life: that the lives of Jews demonstrate to the world what Judaism is.

In *The Essence of Judaism* Baeck puts the challenge in clear terms:

> Every Jew is called upon to manifest the meaning of his religion by the conduct of his life. He should live and act so that all men may see what his religion is and of what it is capable—how it sanctifies man, educating and exalting him to be a member of the 'holy nation.' That is the meaning of the commandment of mission, which is imposed on everyone; and so long as he does not do justice to it, no Jew has fulfilled his obligation to the community.

One Sabbath, while living at Hebrew Union College in Cincinnati, Baeck noticed some students playing soccer in full public view and urged them to stop. "But according to Jewish law," protested the students, "it is permissible to play, since we are in a private domain." "Strictly speaking, you are right," said Baeck, "but you are Reform Jews and thus must be stricter."

Leo Baeck's greatest contribution to Judaism is not so much a system of thought as a model of how to live. He once said: "A sermon is not to be delivered. It is the person who must deliver himself. . . . The greatest message one can preach is one's life."

14 ABRAHAM ISAAC KOOK

1865 – 1935

Abraham Isaac HaKohen Kook was born in a Jewish village in Latvia and died in Jerusalem. Often referred to as Rav or Rabbi Kook, he was the first Ashkenazic chief rabbi of *Eretz Yisrael* under the British mandate. His name, which is pronounced like the word "cook," is sometimes spelled Kuk, perhaps to avoid confusion with the English word "kook." Far from being an eccentric, Rav Kook was one of the truly original creators of modern Zionist thought.

A MYSTICAL NATIONALIST

Kook the Mystic

Kook was a modern mystic who brought his mystical views to Zionism. Other Orthodox rabbis of his day were concerned that Zionism would encourage nationalism and that nationalism would displace the Torah from its rightful place at the center of Judaism. Kook, however, believed that nationalism was part of God's plan for the Jewish people and therefore holy, and that nationalism and the Torah were part of a whole. Also, other Orthodox rabbis maintained their fidelity to Yiddish, believing that Hebrew, "the language of the Torah," should be spoken only in the course of study or prayer. But Kook began to use Hebrew instead of Yiddish in everyday conversation when he was still a student.

Although trained along traditional lines as a Talmudic scholar, Kook was convinced that religious leaders must make Jewish tradition relevant to the problems of the modern world, and thus he read widely in secular fields such as science, philosophy, and literature. Because he was at home in both the world of tradition and the modern world, Kook was able to bridge the gap between those Orthodox settlers in *Eretz Yisrael* interested in religious practice but not statehood, and the many Jewish pioneers interested only in a homeland. He thus became a symbol of Jewish unity.

Kook wrote a great deal, because he felt an inner compulsion to do so. His work ranged widely, from mystical verses to closely reasoned essays, and he also wrote many "responsa"—letters and answers to questions about Jewish law.

While mystics are often thought of as people who cut themselves off from the rest of the world to concentrate on drawing near God, Kook did not fit that description. He was different in three respects: he believed in deep involvement with the rest of the world, he was very concerned with communicating his mystical revelations to others, and he acknowledged the importance of human reason in developing an understanding of the world.

Kook maintained that many of the world's problems exist because mystics are often wrapped up in otherworldly concerns. Their failure to involve themselves in the real world enables those unconcerned with holiness to control world affairs. To prevent this from happening, he said that mystics should use their spiritual insight to increase their involvement in all aspects of the world.

> " *Human reason, even at its most sublime, cannot begin to understand the unique holiness of* Eretz Yisrael. . . . *What* Eretz Yisrael *means to the Jew can be felt only through the spirit of the Lord which is in our people as a whole, through the spiritual cast of the Jewish soul, which radiates its characteristic influence to every healthy emotion.* "
>
> The Land of Israel, trans. Arthur Hertzberg

Involvement with the World.   Even Kook's mystical poetry reveals him as a man involved with other people:

> I am not one of God's elected heroes,
> That found all worlds within them
> And did not care if others
> Their riches knew or not. . . .
> But I am to this world enchained.
> The living, they are my friends.
> My soul with them is intertwined.

Revelation and Communication.   How are mystics able to reveal the wonders of the spiritual world to others? Kook was troubled by this problem; he felt that language is not capable of expressing what the mystic knows. "And life is so joyous, so sacred, so filled with the majesty of the Name of the Lord. You long to express His name, to interpret the exalted light. You are filled with an intense thirst, pleasing in the extreme, to fill your mouth with the praise of the God of gods. And out of the abundance of pure fear, the intensity of holy trembling, you return to silence." He lamented in verse the fact that language cannot fully express the mystical experience:

> How, then, illumination share. . . ?
> For all that I relate
> Doth only hide my radiance,
> Becloud my inner light.
> Thus, great is my pain and anguish.

Reason.   Kook shared the views of many other mystics on human reason, believing that it alone is incapable of truly grasping the essence of existence. He thereby set himself apart from Saadia, Maimonides, and Hermann Cohen. In one poem, he wrote:

> I'm filled with love to God . . .
> I cannot sate my soul
> With love that comes from logic's bonds,
> From worldly search and research
> In light of existence,
> To human eyes revealed.

And in another:

> Expanses, expanses
> Expanses divine, my soul doth crave.
> Enclose me not in cages,
> Of matter or mind. . . .
> I thirst for truth, not concepts of truth.

Comparing what we can learn through mystical perception with what we can know through traditional reason and research, Kook said:

"There is no limit to one's power in the inner world; there is no freedom in the outer, physical world." What we perceive as reasoned facts are "in truth nothing but refractions of God's being, sparks of divinity. . . . This truth far transcends the limited findings of the scholarly disciplines that humanity has designed to illumine and clarify the world."

But defying the commonly held notion of a mystic, Kook did not disparage reason. He saw it and the traditional pursuit of knowledge as good approaches to understanding God. A person who cannot achieve mystical divine union should seek to discover God's presence in the world through thought, observation, reason, and scholarship:

How shall one obtain a conception of the majesty of the Divine. . . ? Through the expansion of one's scientific faculties; through the liberation of one's imagination and the enjoyments of bold flights of thought; through the disciplined study of the world and of life; through the cultivation of a rich, multifarious sensitivity to every phase of being. All these desiderata require obviously the study of all the branches of wisdom, all the philosophies of life, all the ways of the diverse civilizations and the doctrines of ethics and religion in every nation and tongue.

In discussing the requirements for effective prayer, Kook also claimed that intellect is actually more important than feeling: "If the natural feelings are accompanied by an intelligent original thought, then only can one pray with holy feelings."

Unlike many religious people even today, Kook thus did not see science and religion as antagonists. If modern research challenges a traditional belief, Kook felt that rather than ignore the research, the belief ought to be reinterpreted.

Darwin's theory of evolution, for example, did not trouble Kook, even though it called into question the biblical account of creation. He argued that the creation chapters in Genesis cannot be taken literally and need mystical interpretation—and also that Darwin's theory of how species evolve from lower to higher forms fits in well with Jewish mystical views, which see the world developing toward perfection. And he believed that the basic lesson from the story of Adam remains unchallenged: people can lose everything by misguided acts, and their mistakes can harm not only themselves but also future generations.

In fact, Kook believed it wrong to compartmentalize religion in one category and science in another. For him, any distinction between religious and everyday matters is false, the whole world being a single organism and all things interconnected. Anything of value to human life has the potential to be holy, "for there is in truth nothing in the universe that is absolutely secular." Holiness, he said, is built on a foundation of the everyday; sometimes even vulgar-seeming things produce spiritual beauty. "And if it were not for the leaven and manure in the spirit of humanity, the ripe fruit, which delights God and human beings, would not have grown."

Not only does holiness spring from worldly things, but in circular fashion it supports worldly activities. Kook claimed that the worship and mystical experiences of holy people give off creative energy, making advances possible in other fields, from science to art to human welfare. This idea, like many of Kook's, are modern variations of themes put forth by Isaac Luria nearly four hundred years earlier.

Kook the Nationalist

As the inclusion of the word *HaKohen* in his name indicates, Kook was descended from the priestly class. While still studying at the famous Eastern European Talmud academy in Volozhin, he confided to a fellow student that he felt an intense personal love for the Land of Israel because of his lineage, and he longed to serve as a priest in Jerusalem's rebuilt Temple.

As Kook matured, he developed a philosophy of Jewish nationalism that went beyond this youthful, personal longing. In 1901, at the age of 36, he published a long essay called "The Mission of Israel and Its Nationhood." Here he argued that Jewish nationalism was not a modern invention but, instead, had been part of God's plan for the Jewish people from their beginning; even those Zionists claiming to be free from the Torah's laws were doing God's work by reviving the nationalist spirit.

Kook asserted that God has stamped the heart of each Jew with the feeling of national loyalty. With the passage of time, the memory of the divine revelation at Sinai will grow dimmer and dimmer, but as it dims, God wishes the sense of loyalty to grow stronger and stronger. Whenever the Jewish people begin to doubt that God has really given them the Torah, this powerful national consciousness will keep them faithful. In a mystical fashion, God has thus permanently united the Jewish people, the nationalist spirit, and the Torah.

Kook argued that since Zionism has always been part of God's plan, its Orthodox opponents must be wrong. Far from being something new and uncharacteristic, it is "the foundation and essence of Judaism."

Kook moved to *Eretz Yisrael* in 1904 to become rabbi of Jaffa, where he further developed such ideas. In an article called "On the Development of Ideas in Israel," he claimed that divine inspiration was responsible for love of Zion. While God intended the sense of nationhood to cement Jewish loyalty, exile had submerged its spirit, making Judaism seem only a religion and leaving it weaker and less creative—less involved with life in the world. Only a restored nationalist spirit could bring Judaism back to the strength and creativity it enjoyed before exile.

For Kook, the Jewish attachment to *Eretz Yisrael* had mystical dimensions. He felt that even nonreligious Jewish nationalists were unknowingly moved by a mystical connection to the land:

> Deep in the heart of every Jew, in its purest and holiest recesses, there blazes the fire of Israel. . . . Hidden away in the deepest recesses of their souls, it exists even among the backsliders and sinners. . . . This is the meaning of the Jew's undying love for *Eretz Yisrael*—the Land of Holiness, the Land of God—in which all of the Divine commandments are realized in their perfect form. This urge to unfold to the world the nature of God, to raise one's head in His Name in order to proclaim His greatness in its real dimension, affects all souls, for all desire to become as one with Him and to partake of the bliss of His life. . . .

Kook was convinced that this subconscious mystical effect on nonreligious settlers would make them return to God and Judaism. Ultimately, he felt, they would regain a sense of being "immersed and rooted in the life of God and bathed in the radiant sanctity that comes from above."

Kook knew that others would disagree about the effect Zionist activities would have on such pioneers:

> An outsider may wonder: How can seeming unbelievers be moved by this life force, not merely to nearness to the universal God, but even toward authentic Jewish life. . . ? But this is no mystery to anyone whose heart is deeply at one with the soul of the Jewish people and who knows its marvelous nature. The source of this Power is in the Power of God, in the everlasting glory of life.

For Kook, religion and nationalism belong together, and true Judaism is their union. While Orthodox Jews needed to recognize that the secular pioneers had full Jewish status, the pioneers likewise had to learn to respect the Torah:

> It is a grave error to be insensitive to the distinctive unity of the Jewish spirit. . . . This error is the source of the attempt to sever the national from the religious element of Judaism. Such a division would falsify both our nationalism and our religion, for every element of thought, emotion, and idealism that is present in the Jewish people belongs to an indivisible entity, and all together make up its

> " . . . *a Jewish nationalist, no matter how secularist his intention may be, must, despite himself, affirm the Divine. An individual can sever the tie that binds him to life eternal, but the House of Israel as a whole cannot. All of its most cherished national possessions—its land, language, history, and customs—are vessels of the spirit of the Lord.*"
>
> *Lights for Rebirth,* trans. Arthur Hertzberg

specific character.... Nationalism, or religion, or any other element of the spirit of Israel, can realize itself only in the context of a
Jewish life that is full, stirring, and entirely true to every shade of its
essence.

Kook's writings contain many variations on the theme that
"Jewish original creativity ... is impossible except in *Eretz Yisrael*.... A
Jew cannot be as devoted to his own ideas, sentiments, and imagination in the Diaspora.... Because reason and imagination are inter-
woven and interact with each other, even reason cannot shine in its
truest glory outside the Holy Land."

Zionism, however, was not an end in itself; the revival of the
Jewish nationalist spirit, and the development of Jewish creativity,
were meant to benefit humanity as a whole. Kook felt that in their own
land the Jewish people would find the social, economic, and political
conditions enabling them to develop fully their ideals of justice and
righteousness. Since the world as a whole would ultimately benefit
from those ideals, Jewish nationalism would help the entire world
progress toward perfection.

WORKING WITH PEOPLE TO SANCTIFY LIFE

Tolerant Bridge to the Pioneers

Kook's philosophy of the profound unity of all creation gave him a
broad view—he could be flexible and adaptable in applying Jewish law
without compromising his basic principles. This continual emphasis
on larger, more general truths at the expense of narrow issues contrasted with what Kook viewed as the rigid approach of many other
Jewish leaders. Equating their approach with a failure to take a long-
term view of the impact of Jewish law on individual human beings,
Kook was often willing to modify the letter of the law to achieve a
greater good. As he put it, "It is our duty to work with the living and for
the living in order to sanctify life."

This readiness to adapt and modify Jewish law was foreshadowed
by an incident in Kook's young manhood. When he was about twenty
and already a rabbi, a plague ravaged his Latvian hometown. Despite
the fact that, according to Jewish tradition, preserving life is the most
important *mitzvah* of all, he knew that when Yom Kippur came, few

Jews would be willing to forgo the traditional fast. Alarmed at this prospect, he decided to set an example. On the Day of Atonement, he boldly stood at the *bimah* with food in his hand, said a blessing, and ate. He then urged the worshipers to break their fast this one time, explaining that the Torah teaches we should live—not die—by fulfilling the *mitzvot*.

Shemittah.

Such religious courage stood Kook in good stead in *Eretz Yisrael.* The first big issue he faced was the question of *Shemittah*, the so-called "Sabbath of the land," meaning that every seventh year no agricultural work might be performed in the Holy Land. Jews had not farmed in *Eretz Yisrael* for centuries, and *Shemittah* observance did not become an issue until the first agricultural colonies were formed in the 1880s.

Kook believed that part of the Jewish heritage is a bond to the land of Israel. As chief rabbi, Kook demonstrated great flexibility in adapting Jewish law to to the needs of agricultural pioneers who wanted to observe the commandments in different ways. However, he defended the rights of those who wished to be more traditionally observant against pressure to change their ways.

Dinner in the fields of Palestine

According to calculations made centuries earlier by Maimonides, 1888 was to be a *Shemittah* year. If the Jewish colonists refrained from farming the whole year, and every seventh year afterward, the economic effect would be catastrophic.

Three great pro-Zionist rabbis determined that *Shemittah* did not have to be observed if the land were sold—in name only—to a non-Jew. This sort of activity was not unknown; each year observant Jews similarly "sell" their *chametz* before Passover. But many rabbis protested, noting the traditional belief that failure to observe *Shemittah* was one cause of the original Jewish exile. Many religious settlers chose to ignore the three rabbis' decision, and the question remained unresolved.

It arose again several *Shemittah* cycles later, in 1909. By this time, Rav Kook was the rabbi of Jaffa and the nearby Jewish settlements, and it was up to him to make a final decision. After considerable reflection, he ruled that colonists could continue farming, but at the same time he instituted some changes in the method of harvesting, to keep farmers aware that it was a special year.

The decision had an unexpected effect: representatives of Baron de Rothschild, the philanthropist and supporter of several colonies, tried to pressure Orthodox colonists into farming during *Shemittah* even though their conscience would not allow it. Learning of such effort, Kook promptly declared that any colonist desiring to observe the custom in its strictest sense was free to do so, despite his own more lenient interpretation of the law.

Support for the Nonreligious Pioneers.
Kook was flexible not only in his interpretation and application of the law, but also in his attitude toward those who failed to observe it. His acceptance of *Eretz Yisrael*'s nonreligious settlers aroused as much opposition from some Orthodox leaders as did his legal decisions.

In this respect, Kook had several answers to his critics. In one case, he referred to the Holy Temple's inner sanctuary—the Holy of Holies, housing the Ark of the Covenant in the first Temple and the so-called Foundation Stone in the second. The Holy of Holies was the most sacred spot of ancient Israel. Only the high priest was permitted to enter, and only once a year, on Yom Kippur. Before entering, the high priest had to undergo a complicated ritual purification. Nevertheless, if repairs had to be made during the year, common workmen were permitted into the Holy of Holies without any preparation at all. In a similar way, Kook argued, the Holy Land itself was now in need of repair, and with it the labor of such working people.

On another occasion, Kook referred to the law of the donkey's firstborn. Although a donkey lacks all the traits the Torah uses to distinguish "clean" from "unclean" beasts, the Torah singles out the animal's firstborn progeny for sanctification. The ancient rabbis explained this honor in terms of the help the donkey offered in carrying the Israelites' baggage in their flight from Egyptian bondage. Kook argued that the labor of nonreligious pioneers was just as important in preparing the way for the Jewish people out of exile back to the Holy Land. Religious Jews should try to draw them back to Judaism through love and respect. The truly righteous, he claimed, do not complain about others' lack of faith—rather, they increase faith by setting a good example.

A third analogy Kook offered to defend his tolerance was based on Jewish history. More than a century after the destruction of the first Temple, Ezra and Nehemiah helped a group of Jews return from Babylonia to the Holy Land. Those Jews willing to leave the comfort of Babylonia to struggle in rebuilding the land were not the most pious, but as a result of their efforts, the second Temple was built, and Torah was once more spread throughout Israel. Kook felt sure that the efforts of the modern-day pioneers would be at least as positive.

He also felt that Jewish religious leaders were to blame if many young pioneers had turned their backs on religion. The young people, he argued, observed that the leaders were more concerned with fine points of Talmudic argument than with social justice. Small wonder that they concluded Judaism lacked such concerns and took it on themselves to repair social problems.

Kook received many despairing letters from Orthodox parents seeking advice on how to react to their children's rejection of Jewish law. He responded by suggesting that they stress how closely religion and nationalism are tied together in Jewish practice. For example, both during the Passover seder and at the end of Yom Kippur, "Next year in Jerusalem" is chanted. Similarly, the grace after meals asks God to rebuild quickly the holy city. And three of the seven blessings recited at traditional Jewish weddings ask God to comfort Zion, bring happiness to the married couple, and make joy complete by restoring Jerusalem. In this manner, perhaps parents could make their children less antagonistic toward their faith.

Kook also encouraged these parents to be patient. He was convinced that it was only a matter of time before their children found within Judaism the ideals they sought elsewhere.

Kook's Firmness: Upholding Principles in a Time of Crisis

Despite his adaptability, Kook remained faithful to the basic tenets of Orthodox Judaism. Although he developed friendships with secular pioneers, he continued to stress that they must respect the

Torah; he recognized that the tension between them and the Orthodox had been caused by both groups. In particular, the pioneers sometimes provoked Orthodox leaders by showing open disrespect for Jewish law. If there was to be peace between the religious and the secular, each side had to be willing to compromise.

Upholding Zionist Ideals.   Although Kook was extremely sympathetic to the pioneers and he himself pioneered in speaking Hebrew as an everyday language, he could not support one particular project of Eliezer Ben Yehudah, the father of the revival of the Hebrew language. Within a year of Kook's arrival in Jaffa, he found himself at loggerheads with Ben Yehudah, who had settled in *Eretz Yisrael* in 1881.

Ben Yehudah was among those nationalists supporting Herzl's proposal to encourage Jewish settlement in East Africa. In part, he favored the project because the British seemed willing to allow Jewish emigration there, while the Turkish masters of *Eretz Yisrael* remained hostile. He felt that only an unreasonable attachment to a mythic past was keeping Jews tied to *Eretz Yisrael*. Ben Yehudah relished the idea that religion seemed to be on the decline among Jewish settlers, seeing the trend as a sign of the younger generation's growing maturity.

Rav Kook vehemently opposed Ben Yehudah. In an open letter, he wrote that a people cut off from its past could have no future; the Jewish people, their land, and their Torah were a single organism not to be permanently torn apart. And, Kook continued, Ben Yehudah seemed to be trying to outdo the anti-Semites in insulting the Jewish people's ancestors.

The East Africa scheme came to nothing. About fifteen years later, however, Kook once again had the opportunity to uphold his Zionist convictions in a political arena. Just before World War I broke out, he left Jaffa to attend a conference of non-Zionist Orthodox German Jews, hoping to persuade them to take up the Zionist cause. Unable to secure passage back to Palestine when the war broke out, and after spending some time in Switzerland, he was invited to serve as rabbi in a London congregation. His presence in England made it possible to help pave the way for the issuing of the Balfour Declaration, the first major recognition of the Jewish claim to *Eretz Yisrael*.

But a group of influential British Jews did not want the Declaration issued. They published a letter in *The Times* of London in May 1917, insisting that the Jews were a religious group and not a political nation, that they were not connected to any one land in particular, and that the world owed them only religious tolerance, nothing more. The authors were so influential that the withholding of the Declaration became a real possibility.

In response, Rav Kook wrote "A Manifesto Concerning the Act of National Treachery," which was read in all the Orthodox synagogues of London. In it, he insisted that Judaism is both a religion and a nationality: "A bitter mockery is this dispute, as to whether our national or religious assets constitute the content of our life. The wholeness of 'Thou art One and Thy Name is One, and who is like unto Thy people Israel, one nation in the earth' cannot be separated or broken up."

Kook's manifesto drew attention both in the Jewish world and outside of it. London synagogues adopted resolutions stressing the

In 1917 Britain's foreign secretary, Arthur Balfour, issued the Balfour Declaration, endorsing the idea of a Jewish state in Palestine. When Lord Balfour dedicated Hebrew University in 1925, Rav Kook was the chief rabbi of Palestine and was one of the speakers at the ceremonies. He is seated at the far left of the dais.

close bonds between Zionist goals and Jewish religious tradition. Kook's argument was even referred to in the British House of Commons.

Upholding Ideals of "Truth in Its Purity."

Kook's unwillingness to compromise his passion for truth and justice involved him in bitter controversy during his final years. The roots of this controversy lay in a split among the Zionists.

Kook's affection for the settlers had won him many friends in the Jewish labor organization, the Histadrut, but his rejection of militant nationalism had alienated the Revisionists. This party, founded in 1925, was dissatisfied with the pace at which other Zionist groups were moving toward attaining their goals and argued that force was the only way to make rapid progress. Kook disagreed strongly. "This is not what God wants. Israel will not complete its historic journey in a storm."

With tension growing over what means should be used to achieve the Zionist goal, Kook tried to make peace between the warring factions. In one open letter after the next, addressed to both groups, he tried to convince them that they were members of the same family and urgently needed to "join hands for one sacred goal, the salvation of the whole nation, its security and its honor."

Kook tried to remain impartial in the dispute between the Histadrut and the Revisionists. Despite his rejection of the Revisionist program, especially its advocacy of force, he found himself supporting the Revisionists in the most bitter conflict between the two organizations, which was centered around the assassination of the Histadrut leader, Hayyim Arlosoroff.

Arlosoroff had been murdered while walking with his wife along the Tel Aviv beach, and his wife identified two members of the Revisionist party as the assassins. The police charged a Revisionist leader with plotting the murder, but all three men denied involvement in the crime. Two of the accused were acquitted in district court. The third, Abraham Stavsky, was convicted.

Despite the fact that most of the Jews of *Eretz Yisrael* were ready to believe Stavsky was the murderer, Kook was not convinced by the evidence. He considered the trial a mockery of justice and was unwilling to stand by silently. In one letter he wrote: "Only truth in its purity . . . leads me to attempt to save him who was condemned to death, with no grounds whatsoever for . . . accusation. I am completely permeated with the conviction that the accused is innocent and just and entirely pure of the slightest taint or suspicion of murder." Finally, in 1934, the Supreme Court acquitted Stavsky for lack of supporting evidence. Only in the aftermath of the Stavsky trial did people begin to agree that Kook had been right.

Kook died of cancer the following year. On his deathbed, he is reported to have said, "Nothing justifies and permits division in Israel."

We are left to wonder how the presence of a figure like Kook on the current Israeli scene might change the course of the Jewish state, of the Middle East, and of the world. Kook once said, "We are a great people, and our mistakes are equally great." Perhaps the kind of wisdom he showed in settling the *Shemittah* question and in supporting Stavsky could help resolve some of the many problems confronting the state today, for Kook was able to see beyond the "woes" suffered by Jews to "the consolations that follow them," with assurance that the woes and the consolations "are both on a grand scale."

15 ABRAHAM HESCHEL

1907 - 1972

Abraham Joshua Heschel was born into the world of Hasidic scholarship in Warsaw, Poland, and died in New York City. He bridged not only the traditions of Hasidic Eastern Europe and the modern academic world but also the worlds of study and action. His scholarly work on the prophets led him to promote social action in a religious context. Heschel also sought to awaken in modern Jews the sense of wonder underlying early religious responses. He has been called "the most productive and by far the best theological mind in modern and contemporary Judaism."

Nature, God, and Humanity

Radical Amazement

According to Heschel, modern life has deadened the inborn sense each person has of a divine presence in the world. But all we have to do to regain it is look around: a rainbow in the sky or the sight of autumn leaves is testimony to God's existence. Even the objective knowledge that a rainbow forms because water drops reflect and refract light, and that leaves turn beautiful in the autumn because of the breakdown of chlorophyll, offers such testimony. Human reason and scientific advances that explain nature will never eliminate this sense of wonder.

Heschel used the term "radical amazement" to describe this sense of wonder and awe. When we allow ourselves to be overcome by radical amazement, we are aware that "what is intelligible to our minds is but a thin surface of the profoundly undisclosed." In other words, human understanding can only scratch the surface of the mysteries of the world.

Every child is born with a sense of this mystery, but with age many people close themselves off to it. Thinking it old-fashioned and unsophisticated to believe in God, they try to reduce the world to formulas and equations. In fact, however, each new scientific development opens up vast new areas of human ignorance, and scientific discoveries should therefore strengthen rather than undercut the world's wonder. As Heschel said, "Wonder . . . does not come to an end when knowledge is acquired; it is an attitude that never ceases. There is no answer in the world to . . . radical amazement."

To Heschel, if we truly open ourselves up, once again, to the wonder that we felt as children, the divine influence on the universe will become obvious. It is only lack of sensitivity to nature and the world that allows people to ignore the divine presence. For Heschel, this lack of sensitivity is the root cause of all human shortcomings.

Heschel explained the Jewish system of blessings as a traditional way to prevent people from losing their sense of radical amazement. Before drinking a simple glass of water, eating a slice of bread, or sniffing a flower, an observant Jew says a blessing thanking God. Likewise, many ordinary events, from observing a rainbow to meeting a scholar, should be occasions for blessings. Take nothing for granted, said Heschel; every experience is a gift of God and should be acknowledged.

Although as a young man Heschel gave up the Hasidic life of his ancestors for university studies in the secular world, many Hasidic

> " *We must continue to ask: What is man that God should care for him? And we must continue to remember that it is precisely God's care for man that constitutes the greatness of man. To be is to stand for, and what man stands for is the great mystery of being His partner. God is in need of man.* "
>
> *Between God and Man: An Interpretation of Judaism*

traits stayed with him. "I have one talent and that is the capacity to be tremendously surprised, surprised at life, at ideas. This is to me the supreme Hasidic imperative."

Heschel wrote that every child is born with a sense of the wonder of even the most ordinary things in the world. He called it "radical amazement." As they get older, he said, people lose this sense of radical amazement by trying to explain the world through rational analysis.

God and Humanity

Radical amazement is not a synonym for religion; it is only the foundation. It sensitizes people to the possibilities of God's existence. How they react to these possibilities is what makes them religious people. According to Heschel, the appropriate reaction is a sense of being addressed by God—a sense that God requires something from each individual.

God Pursues Us.   Heschel's interpretation of the relationship between God and human beings takes many commonly accepted attitudes and stands them on their heads. For example, many people assume that human beings must take the initiative in order to have a meaningful relationship with God. Not so, says Heschel. In one of his best-known books, called *God in Search of Man: A Philosophy of Judaism*, he maintains that it is God who has always taken the first step in the relationship. "God is not a being . . . to be sought after, but a power that seeks, pursues, and calls upon" us. Whenever we find ourselves thinking about such questions as "Why am I here?" or "Is there a God?" we are actually reacting to the presence of God pursuing us and demanding something of us.

Heschel insisted that biblical history is a drama in which God turns toward human beings while they in turn flee. He pointed to the fact that none of the biblical prophets sought God out; each felt overcome by God's presence. Many prophets sought to avoid the demands God made of them. Jeremiah's response is typical: "Ah, Lord God! Behold, I cannot speak; for I am a child" (1:6).

Revelation and Prophecy.

Heschel's view of revelation—the way God and God's demands are disclosed—is also unique. He argued that revelation is "a voice in the world that pleads with us in the name of God."

In the tradition of Maimonides, Heschel claimed that many people take biblical vocabulary too literally and thus misunderstand revelation. He described this misinterpretation with a sense of humor, as imagining "that God spoke to the prophet on a long-distance telephone." When the Bible talks of God addressing the prophets, we must not imagine instructions being dictated to unthinking individuals. As Heschel said, when we read "And God said: Let there be light," we know it is not equivalent to "And Smith said: Let us turn on the light."

Heschel suggested several other reasons why people find it hard to come to terms with the concept of revelation. Some feel too intelligent and capable to need divine help. Others feel too insignificant for God to bother helping. Still others find that the idea of revelation goes against human reason.

But, said Heschel, we should let radical amazement overcome our doubts about what might have happened in biblical times. Just as a blade of grass can absorb the sun's energy, might not certain individuals have absorbed God's spirit? Even if the idea of revelation seems unlikely, can anyone prove it impossible? Furthermore, can we really argue that the prophets were simply mad, overcome with the illusion of having been approached by God? Doesn't the timeless importance of their message—that we must do justice and be kind to one another—support their claim to speak "God's word"?

God Needs Humanity.

Traditionally, religious thinkers have stressed the need that people have for God, but Heschel stressed the reverse: that God needs humanity. In doing so, he developed concepts put forth by the Talmudic rabbis on one hand, and by Jewish mystics on the other.

Heschel carefully distinguished God's need for people from what earlier civilizations felt their gods needed from them. For example, whereas the ancient Phoenicians and Ammonites believed their god Moloch had demanded that children be burned as offerings, Heschel said that what God needs of us is a partner in developing and helping to redeem this world.

> " *As civilization advances, the sense of wonder declines. Such decline is an alarming symptom of our state of mind. Mankind will not perish for want of information, but only for want of appreciation. The beginning of our happiness lies in the understanding that life without wonder is not worth living. What we lack is not a will to believe but a will to wonder.* "
>
> God in Search of Man

According to the Talmudic rabbis, from the moment of creation God intended human beings to be such partners in creation, making wheat but not bread, clay but not bricks. Heschel developed this ancient idea of human responsibility as one of "active assistance."

Heschel also developed an idea from Lurianic Kabbalah and later Hasidic thought that each person is God's partner in the redemption of the world. "The meaning of redemption is to reveal the holy that is concealed, to disclose the divine that is suppressed. Every man is called upon to be a redeemer, and redemption takes place every moment, every day."

Heschel summarized these two strands of Jewish thought by saying that God "is in need of the work of man for the fulfillment of His ends in the world."

God's Demands of Humanity.

Whereas thinkers have often stressed that faith in God can console us, Heschel insisted that the essence of faith is to make demands of us. Heschel went so far as to define human beings as beings "of whom demands may be made." The most important discovery each of us can make in life is that "a question . . . follows me wherever I turn. What is expected of me? What is demanded of me?" But realizing that the question has been asked, that the expectation has been made, is only the first step.

How are we to respond to God's demands? Through our deeds, said Heschel. In fact, since there is no foolproof way to prove God's existence, holy acts serve as witnesses. "God is hiding in the world and our task is to let the divine emerge from our deeds." When we perform such deeds, said Heschel, we are truly partners with God. We identify ourselves with the divine will and truly become God's partners. "No one is lonely when doing a *mitzvah*, for a *mitzvah* is where God and man meet."

At a time when the existentialist philosopher Kierkegaard's phrase "leap of faith" had become popular in American religious thought, to describe how a doubter could achieve belief in God, Heschel coined the phrase "leap of action." Often, he insisted, the very act of performing the *mitzvot* can lead a Jew to such belief. "By living as Jews we may attain our faith as Jews. We do not have faith because of deeds; we may attain faith through sacred deeds." This statement by no means implies, however, that we should go through the motions of the *mitzvot* without any conviction; their point is to transform us, to make us elevate God's wishes above our own desires.

Theomorphism and Theotropism.

According to Heschel, the God of the biblical prophets is above all a God with feelings. The God who pursues us, needs us, and makes demands of us feels the pain of the mistreated and the unfortunate.

Earlier thinkers, including Maimonides (whose biography Heschel wrote while still a young scholar in Europe), tried to explain away such anthropomorphisms. They insisted that when the Bible talks of God's feelings, it does not mean literally God has them, but is only using language people can understand. In typical fashion, Heschel turned the issue on its head, rejecting the belief (which Maimonides accepted) that a God without feelings is superior to a God with feelings.

Furthermore, asked Heschel, who can claim that the description of God as having overriding concern for the poor and downtrodden is basically the description of a human trait? As we know from our own experience, the few people whose lives are guided by such a trait are often called "saints," suggesting that the behavior is more godlike than human. Biblical adjectives describing God's passion for social justice are thus not really anthropomorphic—based on comparing the divine to human beings. Rather, the response to suffering that the prophets demand of us is truly "theomorphic"—that is, it presents a model for human behavior based on a comparison to God. "God's unconditional concern for justice," said Heschel, "is not an anthropomorphism. Rather man's concern for justice is a theomorphism."

In another reversal of the expected, Heschel claimed that the Bible represents not our theology—the human study of God—but divine anthropology—God's study of (and expectations for) human beings. In his view, the Bible has more to tell us about what God expects of us than about what our ancestors thought about God.

Heschel made another use of the prefixes *anthropo-*, which comes from the Greek word for "human being," and *theo-*, which comes from the Greek word for "God." The tendency of a plant or animal to turn in response to some external stimulus is called a "tropism." For example, a sunflower turns toward light. Since the Greek word for sun is *helios*, we say a sunflower displays a positive heliotropism. In a similar fashion, Heschel calls God's behavior in the Bible "anthropotropism," because God is turning toward human beings. "Theotropism," or our turning toward God, can be either positive or negative. Much of biblical history reflects negative theotropism: the attempt of people to evade God's call.

Heschel and the Holocaust

Any summary of Heschel's views on the relationship between human beings and God must consider his response to the Nazis' destruction of six million Jews. He suffered terrible personal loss as a result of the Holocaust, his mother and sisters being among the millions murdered. Heschel was lucky enough to escape. In 1938 he was expelled from Germany, where he had been studying and teaching for more than a decade, and forced to return to Poland along with all other Polish-born Jewish residents of Germany. But a few weeks before the Germans invaded Poland, a teaching invitation brought him to America. Later he referred to himself as "a brand"—or burning stick— "plucked from the fire on which my people was burned to death . . . and on which so much else was consumed," including many people's faith in a God of compassion and justice.

Heschel wrote a book, *The Earth Is the Lord's*, that has been called the epitaph of the Eastern European victims of the Holocaust. Still, his references to philosophical problems raised by the Holocaust, such as evil, human guilt, and God's absence, tend to be indirect. Often, they appear in the context of other issues, such as the relationship of Christianity to Judaism.

Essentially, Heschel suggested that it was the failure of human beings to *react* that made the Holocaust possible. He distinguished between guilt and responsibility, and argued that while guilt for the Holocaust may fall only on those who committed crimes, those who did nothing to prevent them were responsible. He contrasted *evil* with the *evil of indifference*, saying: "There is an evil which most of us condone and are even guilty of: indifference to evil. We remain neutral, impartial, and not easily moved by the wrongs done to other people. Indifference to evil is more insidious than evil itself. . . . A silent justification, it makes possible an evil erupting as an exception becoming the rule. . . ." The prophets were the first to discover the evil of indifference, to point out that "one may be decent and sinister, pious and sinful."

Not God, but the all-too-human evil of indifference thus caused the Holocaust, according to Heschel. In an image calling up the smell of Jewish bodies burning in concentration camp ovens, Heschel wrote, "The decay of conscience fills the air with a pungent smell. Good and evil, which were once as distinguishable as day and night, have become a blurred mist. But that mist is man-made. God is not silent. He has been silenced."

Elsewhere, Heschel again blamed the world's evils on people. "The will of God is to be here, manifest and near. . . . God did not depart of His own volition. He was expelled. God is in exile."

Heschel stressed that once we acknowledge God's demands on us, it is our responsibility to fulfill them. Putting off the divine call could lead to disaster, as in the case of the Holocaust. In another connection, he recalled bursting into tears at the age of seven when reading, with his teacher, the biblical story of the near sacrifice of Isaac. Knowing that his pupil was familiar with the story's ending—that an angel would stop Abraham from slaying his son—the man tried to comfort him. But the boy responded, "Suppose the angel had come a second too late?" The rabbi again reassured him, saying, "An angel cannot come late." Years later Heschel insisted that while an angel may always be on time, human beings can sometimes be too late. For that reason, he urged people to follow the dictates of their conscience before time ran out.

Heschel had no doubt about who was to blame for the horrors of the Holocaust. "The question about Auschwitz to be asked is not, 'Where was God?' but rather 'Where was man?'"

Heschel emphasized that actions are an important part of Jewish observance, and that the demands of observance and conscience must be fulfilled promptly. If delayed, they may be too late. As a boy, Heschel heard the story of the binding of Isaac, in which Abraham is prevented by an angel from slaying his own son, and asked his teacher what would have happened if the angel had arrived only a moment later.

The Sabbath and Heschel's Philosophy of Time

In addition to his unique interpretation of the relationship between God and human beings, Heschel is also well known for his study of the importance of time in Judaism. He presented his philosophy of time in *The Sabbath: Its Meaning for Modern Man.*

According to Heschel, before there was such a thing as a holy person or a holy place, there was holiness in time. The first biblical use of the Hebrew word *kadosh*, or "holy," is at the end of the story of creation in Genesis: "God blessed the seventh day and made it holy." Only later, at Mount Sinai, does God tell the Israelites, "You shall be unto me a holy people." Similarly, the significance of the Sabbath is to remind us of the holiness of time. During the work week we concentrate on the world of space—on being God's partners in the ongoing work of creation. On the Sabbath "we are called upon to share in what is eternal in time." By turning away from our daily work, we shift focus "from the results of creation to the mystery of creation; from the world of creation to the creation of the world." (Elsewhere, he added that by learning restraint and how to give up certain activities, we also enhance our sense of dignity and self-respect.)

Heschel's emphasis on the primacy of time over space in Judaism has been questioned. If space is less holy, why do Jews feel so strongly about Israel and about Jerusalem? Such criticism notwithstanding, there is lasting meaning to Heschel's thoughts on the Sabbath day. His work suggests that from early on Judaism recognized the human need to structure time. The weekly Sabbath built a structure of time into Jewish existence.

ICONOCLAST AND ACTIVIST

A Prophet for Our Own Time

Reinhold Niebuhr, one of the most influential Protestant thinkers of this century and a close personal friend of Heschel, called him "the most authentic prophet of religious life in our culture." Heschel's attitude to life was certainly reminiscent of the description of the biblical prophet as "a man who feels fiercely. . . . God is raging in the prophet's voice," and as "a person who suffers the harm done unto others. Wherever a crime is committed, it is as if the prophet were the victim and the prey." Like such figures, Heschel felt called upon to speak out whenever he saw injustice. Just as the prophets were often hated for what they said, Heschel's views tended to make him unpopular. But he sought justice, not popularity.

It is unlikely that Heschel himself would have felt comfortable with this comparison. He accepted Jewish traditional teaching, including the idea that prophecy ended in biblical times. Perhaps, however, he would not have minded being compared to a pair of other heroes from Jewish history: our forefather Abraham and the great thinker Maimonides.

Like Abraham, a Smasher of Idols

According to tradition, Abraham was the first to understand the idea of one God. The Midrash recounts that, left one day to mind the idols in his father's showroom, he smashed them all. He did so despite the fact that his father made a living from selling them and that idol-worship was the basis of his society, rejecting the practice because it was based on superstition.

From the Greek words for "image" and "break," we get the word "iconoclast" in English. An iconoclast challenges behavior or institutions that seem misguided, no matter how socially accepted they may be. Heschel, himself both named "Abraham" and possessing an iconoclastic personality, felt that religion must instill in people what he called the "Abraham complex" and should not merely provide personal satisfaction. "Religion is critique of satisfaction. Its end is joy, but its beginning is discontent, detesting boasts, smashing idols."

In this vein, Heschel directly challenged the organized religious institutions of Jews, Protestants, and Catholics, asserting strongly that all the major religions made far too few demands on their followers.

Taking on the Jewish Religious Establishment.
Heschel criticized Jewish leaders in Israel and the United States alike. After the death of Rav Kook, religious leaders in Israel insisted on strict conformity to Orthodox law, even though large numbers of Israeli citizens lived completely secular lives. Heschel observed that subsequent Orthodox leaders, instead of trying to reach out to the nonobservant, as Kook had, were "ready to surrender the multitudes of Israel." Quite to the contrary, he said, it was their responsibility to advise each person to "observe as much as you are able to, and a little more than you are able to."

American Jews were also targets of Heschel's criticism. Jewish charities seemed to him to measure religious commitment in dollars and cents. He reminded Jewish leaders that, according to tradition, the world stands on three pillars: learning, worship, and charity. "We are not going to invite a friend to sit on a tripod, a stool designed to have three legs, when two legs are missing." He cautioned Reform leaders to "beware lest we reduce the Bible to literature, Jewish observance to good manners, the Talmud to Emily Post." And he criticized Conservative rabbis for leading lifeless religious services that lacked all sense of "spiritual adventure."

Taking on the Christian Religious Establishment.
When Heschel was asked to contribute to a journal devoted to the question, "Is Protestantism reformable?" he focused on two sensitive issues—the Church's rejection of its Jewish roots, and scholarly treatment of the Bible as if it were "any other book." He concluded his article by saying that "the greater problem today is not how to preserve the Church but how to preserve humanity." Heschel also pointed out how inappropriate it was for Church leaders during the war to give communion to officers of death camps after they had killed thousands of people each day.

> " *To perform deeds of holiness is to absorb the holiness of deeds.* "
>
> *Between God and Man*

Like Maimonides, from Scholar
To Champion of the Suffering

One of Heschel's first publications was a biography of Maimonides. Heschel was the first scholar to detect a change the great philosopher experienced during the final years of his life, in the process unwittingly predicting a crucial change in his own life. What Heschel termed "Maimonides' metamorphosis" involved a shift from his books to his patients: "from metaphysics to medicine, from contemplation to practice, from speculation to the imitation of God. . . . Preoccupation with the concrete man and the effort to aid him in his suffering is now the form of religious devotion." Similarly, in his old age Heschel once remarked during a television interview that "early in my life, my great love was for learning, studying. And the place where I preferred to live was my study. . . . [Now] I've learned from the prophets that I have to be involved in the affairs of . . . suffering man."

Heschel was not a physician like Maimonides. Instead of saving individual lives, he became active in various movements working to transform society. Among these were the interfaith movement, the movements for civil rights and against the war in Vietnam, and the movement to overcome anti-Semitism in the Soviet Union.

Interfaith Affairs.   Perhaps more than any other Jew in the course of history, Heschel influenced official Catholic attitudes toward the Jews, helping to revise the Church's longstanding position that its ultimate hope was to see Jews convert. When he saw a draft of a new document asserting that "the Church expects in unshakable faith and with ardent desire . . . the union of the Jewish people with the Church," Heschel worked behind the scenes to have it changed. He wrote to the Catholic officials responsible for the document that "I am ready to go to Auschwitz any time, if faced with the alternative of conversion or death." The final draft of the document no longer called for conversion, thanks in large part to Heschel's efforts.

Civil Rights.   In 1963 Heschel delivered the keynote address to the National Conference on Religion and Race. The conference led to the involvement of many clergymen in the August 1963 march on Washington, aimed at convincing the federal government of the need to eliminate discrimination in public places. In 1965 he walked alongside the great black civil rights leader Martin Luther King, Jr., in the famous protest march to secure voting rights for blacks in Selma, Alabama.

In the years following King's assassination in 1968, relations between blacks and Jews began to deteriorate. It is noteworthy that a 1983 conference meant to help repair them was based on the personalities of Heschel and King, the conference brochure speaking of the two men as "spiritual leaders, whose thoughts, teachings, and deeds inspired Americans of all faiths to join together to work for racial and social justice."

Peace. Heschel opposed the war in Vietnam and felt that American involvement there showed both moral insensitivity and groundless self-righteousness. According to Heschel, war was too serious a matter to be left to "a few individuals in Washington." He insisted that to hand over "our conscience to a few diplomats and generals" is "a very, very grave sin." As national cochairman of a group called Clergy and Laity Concerned about Vietnam, he strongly advised people of all religions that "to speak about God and remain silent on Vietnam is blasphemous," and he urged the country to dedicate itself to peace rather than victory.

In a letter to *The New York Times* before the 1972 presidential elections, Heschel spoke openly of corruption in the American government, asking how the prophets of old would have reacted. Heschel's open antiwar stance made him unpopular with many Jewish leaders, who feared the U.S. government would react by hardening its policy toward Israel. Heschel, however, felt he had to put conscience above friendship.

Saving Soviet Jewry. Heschel was one of the first to bring to the world's attention the policy of the Soviet Union's Communist government to discriminate against the country's Jews. In one of his first speeches on the subject, he compared the Soviet Jews to the ten tribes of Israel in ancient times. Why, he asked, were the tribes' members finally "lost" after being carried away into exile? Because, he answered, of the remaining two tribes' failure to concern themselves with their fate. "Russian Jewry is the last remnant of a people destroyed in extermination camps." Heschel urged his listeners not to participate in this community's demise by failing to become involved with their fate. Heschel himself was among those who picketed Soviet diplomats because of the treatment of Russian Jews. He would surely be delighted to know that some of the Jews who were able to leave the Soviet Union for the United States are learning about Judaism at schools named in his honor.

Heschel once said that "what we need more than anything else is not *textbooks* but *textpeople.* It is the personality of the teacher which is the text that the pupils read; the text that they will never forget." Heschel was such a teacher. He not only wrote important works about Torah but himself was what Hasidic Jews call a "living Torah," inspiring others by his actions. His daughter Susannah, one of America's Jewish feminist thinkers today, is only one example of the many young people whom he inspired.

16 MORDECAI KAPLAN

1881 – 1983

Mordecai Kaplan was born near Vilnius, Lithuania. As a child he moved to New York City, where he died at the age of 102. The first English-speaking Orthodox rabbi in the United States, Kaplan was a professor for over 50 years at the Conservative Movement's Jewish Theological Seminary, as well as the founder of Reconstructionism. Although the Reconstructionist Movement remains small, Kaplan's thought has had enormous influence on the other branches of liberal Judaism and on the way American Jews think about Judaism and themselves.

FOUNDING RECONSTRUCTIONISM

How a Movement Got Its Name

The Reconstructionist Movement emerged from Kaplan's conviction that Judaism needed to be rebuilt from its foundation up. Kaplan felt that modern educated Jews could no longer believe three fundamentals that had always been taken for granted: that God was a supernatural being; that the Torah was a supernatural document—an exact record of God's words to Moses; and that as God's chosen people the people of Israel themselves had supernatural prestige. For Kaplan, modern scientific studies had completely and permanently undermined such beliefs. No wonder Judaism in the United States was in such disarray, he said, with many Jews only halfheartedly identifying themselves as Jewish, if at all.

The Shaping of Kaplan's Thought

Like many other Jewish thinkers, Kaplan developed his ideas from a combination of Jewish and non-Jewish influences. He concluded that Judaism represented an entire civilization, but that none of the existing movements within it were able to respond to the problems of modern Jewish life.

A Broad Range of Influences. Like Heschel, Kaplan was born to Orthodox parents in Eastern Europe and received his early education exclusively in Jewish religious studies. Unlike Heschel, he was still a young boy when he arrived in the United States. It was actually in his parents' New York City apartment that he began to question traditional beliefs.

Kaplan's father, Israel, was a rabbi himself, with a reputation for extensive Talmudic scholarship and a background in modern Hebrew literature. For over a decade, from the time Mordecai Kaplan was preparing for his bar mitzvah, his father was regularly consulted by a Bible scholar, Arnold B. Ehrlich, on the Talmud's use of important biblical words.

Ehrlich was unwelcome in many Orthodox homes. He had helped a German missionary translate the New Testament into Hebrew, and his own biblical scholarship challenged accepted ideas about the Torah. He argued that many biblical passages made sense only if it was noted that some material had been accidentally left out or repeated, or that some letters had been mistaken for other, similarly shaped letters.

> **"** *The Jewish woman became aware that she was accorded a more dignified status outside Jewish life. This explains why many talented Jewish women not only began to lose interest in Jewish life, but actually turned against it. . . . If we do not want our talented women to follow their example, we must find in Judaism a place for their powers. This cannot come about unless all taint of inferiority will be removed from the status of Jewish women.* **"**
>
> *Judaism as a Civilization*

The Torah, he concluded, was a human document, not a God-given one at all. Ehrlich left manuscripts of his work for Kaplan's father to read, and from the time the boy was thirteen he would spend half an hour each day poring over the material while still wrapped in the *tallit* and *tefillin* he wore for morning prayers.

For many years Kaplan found no way to reconcile his conviction that the Torah was a human document with his strong belief in its incalculable worth. The author who enabled him to make this accommodation was the nineteenth-century English critic and poet Matthew Arnold, who, although not a Jew, had a deep appreciation of the Bible and of Hebrew culture.

Reading widely in the new disciplines of sociology, anthropology, and psychology in college and graduate school, Kaplan became convinced that social groups are critically important to a religion's development. He concluded that society must develop before religion forms, that all societies are fundamentally religious, that all religions develop along similar lines, and that no single religion is exclusively the true one.

Outside of school, Kaplan read the work of Ahad HaAm. He was especially struck by Ahad HaAm's likening of the Jewish people to an organism that has developed over time but has kept its essential identity—here because of devotion to the Hebrew language and the spirit of the biblical prophets.

Judaism Is a Civilization.

Kaplan's studies led him to believe that every religion, including Judaism, is only part of a larger culture. Therefore, he said, Judaism is more than a religion; it is an entire civilization. Not merely religious texts but also language, literature, and even arts and crafts are a part of it. This line of thought resulted in the publication in 1934 of Kaplan's first and most famous book, *Judaism as a Civilization: Toward the Reconstruction of American Jewish Life.*

Kaplan felt that this new culture-oriented perspective could help relieve the crisis in American Jewry. American Jews would be more attracted to an ever-growing, changing culture, even with its strong ties to the past, than to a set of changeless beliefs and rituals.

Dissatisfaction with Organized Jewish Life in America.

Kaplan did not expect his new conception of what it meant to be Jewish to be advanced by any of the organized American Jewish groups. While pleased that a sector of the Orthodox Movement had begun to supplement religious studies with secular learning, he believed that the Orthodox insistence on the supernatural nature of God, the Torah, and the people of Israel would continue to alienate many educated Jews.

Kaplan applauded the Reform Movement for enabling many who might otherwise have abandoned Judaism to continue to identify themselves as Jews. But he disapproved of other aspects of the movement, believing that it often adapted to modern life for the wrong reasons—that instead of making Judaism more intellectually honest, many Reform changes were designed to satisfy the outside world. For example, modifications in synagogue ritual seemed designed to allow Jews to appear more refined and less different in the eyes of Gentiles.

In addition, the Reform Movement still believed that the Jews had been chosen by God to spread ethical monotheism among the world's nations, and to that idea Kaplan objected; he felt that the Jewish idea of God was no more highly developed than that of other cultures. At the same time, the movement was then focusing on Judaism exclusively as a religion, denying the Jews of one country real ties with those in another or in *Eretz Yisrael*. For Kaplan, Jews everywhere were part of the same civilization, centered in the Holy Land.

Even though Kaplan both taught and had been ordained at the Conservative Movement's Jewish Theological Seminary, he did not feel this movement was taking the right steps to rebuild American Jewry either. It was too true to its name; while stressing the scientific study of Judaism's past, it conservatively refrained from using this sort of study to bring about creative change.

Kaplan also faulted organized Zionism. He admired the movement's challenge to the traditional belief that Jews could not return home until the coming of the Messiah. But the Zionists painted an unrealistic picture of life in the Diaspora, insisting that all Jews should plan to move to the Jewish homeland. Kaplan argued that there was a place for Jews both in a Jewish state and in other democratic nations, the two groups working together—and both being needed—to rebuild Judaism.

In short, Kaplan thought that none of the Orthodox, Reform, Conservative, or Zionist movements constituted the ideal manifestation of Judaism. He maintained, however, that there was room for each of them within a reconstructed Judaism.

Rebuilding Judaism's Foundations

Jews have long considered God, Torah, and Israel as the three pillars of their life and thought. For Kaplan, reconstructing Jewish culture meant developing a new understanding of each of these concepts.

Reconstructing Israel.   Kaplan said a change was needed in the traditional ordering of the concepts: the Jewish people—not God—needed to be the focus of a reconstructed Judaism. The Jewish people must not only be at the center of Judaism, said Kaplan, but they must also reject all supernatural conceptions of their peoplehood. He objected to the idea of the Jews as a chosen people, seeing it as intellectually hollow and perhaps even racist and immoral, arguing that God is not a person making choices and that Jews should not claim to be better than others. While every nation feels it has a specific calling, that of the Jews should be to demonstrate how belief in God can lead to a peaceful, just, and humane social order. "The *purpose* of Jewish existence is to be a people in the image of God. The *meaning* of Jewish existence is to foster in ourselves as Jews, and to reawaken in the rest of the world, a sense of moral responsibility in action."

As leader of the Society for the Advancement of Judaism, the first Reconstructionist congregation, Kaplan was able to incorporate this point into the liturgy. For example, he replaced the phrase "who has chosen us from all the peoples" (*asher bahar banu mikol ha-amim*), traditionally included in one of the blessings over the Torah, with the phrase "who has drawn us to his service" (*asher querevanu la-avodato*).

The Reconstructionist concept of Israel also included a new emphasis on Zionism. But Kaplan's was Zionism of a new sort—"Diaspora Zionism." In his vision, while *Eretz Yisrael* will always be important as the cradle of Jewish civilization, a strong Jewish life in the Diaspora is also essential; Zionism should never become its substitute. To guarantee the future of their own Jewish life, American Jews need to practice Judaism, not only support the Jewish state. Israeli Jews also need religion, because without Judaism's ethical teachings, the Jewish state could end up as just another ordinary nation.

Rabbi Mordecai Kaplan affixes the *mezuzah* at the dedication of the Reconstructionist Rabbinical College in October 1968. The college ordains rabbis and serves as the spiritual and intellectual center of the Reconstructionist Movement.

Kaplan noted that land and language are inseparable in every civilization, and he concluded that Zionism goes hand in hand with an emphasis on the Hebrew language. It not only unites the far-flung Jewish people, but also gives Jewish children a sense of connection with the past, present, and future of their culture.

To help make active participation in Jewish culture a part of daily American Jewish life, Kaplan felt that a new type of institution was called for: the Jewish community center. Such centers could help reconstruct American Jewish life in the same way that synagogues helped Jews adjust after the destruction of the Temple. After all, if Judaism was a civilization and not merely a religion, a synagogue alone could not answer all its religious, educational, and recreational needs. Kaplan is considered the father of this now-familiar institution, sometimes popularly described as "a shul with a pool and a school." From 1915 to 1921 he served as rabbi of the first one, New York City's Jewish Center, which still functions today.

Kaplan's reworking of the concept of Israel allowed for a very open and tolerant definition of who is a Jew. "Loyalty to Judaism should be measured by active participation in Jewish life." In language reminiscent of Ahad HaAm's, he asserted that the only belief required of a Jew is "an unqualified acceptance of Jewish survival." Never expecting all Jews to share wholeheartedly his belief in Israel, Torah, and God, he agreed instead that each has a responsibility to work out the nature of his or her own Jewish identity. While willing to offer some alternatives, he declined to dictate standards to which Jews are expected to conform. He acknowledged, in fact, that those who still hold traditional beliefs in a supernatural God, Torah, and Israel will have no reason to accept his reconstructionist ideas.

Reconstructing Torah.

Kaplan rejected the traditional concept of *Torah min haShamayim*, "Torah handed down from heaven," but he still saw a clear connection between the Torah and God. Instead of God having revealed the Torah to the Jewish people, according to Kaplan it is the people who reveal God through the Torah. He derived one of his favorite theological definitions from Matthew Arnold: God is a lasting power encouraging human beings to strive for righteousness and guaranteeing that it can be realized on earth. By calling for people to act righteously in God's name, the Torah reveals God to the world.

Kaplan's understanding of the term *Torah* extended beyond the Five Books of Moses and the Bible as a whole; he believed it should be appreciated in the broadest possible sense, including "whatever knowledge would enable us Jews to retain our individuality as a people, discern our true destiny, and know the means and methods of achieving it." Kaplan himself deepened his attachment to Judaism by studying works by non-Jewish authors along with secular Jewish writings. He felt that the concept of Torah should have room in it for "the wisdom of all peoples, both ancient and modern, acquired by them in the course of their striving for the fulfillment of human destiny."

Reconstructing Torah involves reconstructing the idea of *mitzvah* as well. While the Hebrew term literally means "commandment," Kaplan argued that such supernaturalism needed rethinking. Jews should observe the *mitzvot* not from fear of punishment if they do not observe, or in the hope of reward if they do, but because observance strengthens their ties to the Jewish people. Furthermore, the laws of Jewish civilization were created by human beings and are not God-given, and present-day Jews should therefore feel free to modify them as circumstances create new needs.

Kaplan insisted that many *mitzvot* can be observed traditionally while being interpreted in new ways. For example, according to the Torah, God commanded the *mitzvah* of *kashrut* in order to keep the Jews holy or separate, and in fact for many it is a good way to maintain Jewish identity. But still other Jews believe *kashrut* increases sensitivity to the value of animal life, and they observe the commandment for this reason. Kaplan urged Jews to be creative not only in preserving traditional observances but also in designing new ones to help enhance their Jewishness. The ceremony now observed in many congregations of naming a baby girl in the synagogue is an example of such innovation.

Kaplan also argued that reading the Torah itself must be revitalized, and he urged teachers to focus on three of its aspects: the unfolding story of the Jewish people, to help students grasp the meaning of Jewish unity; references to *Eretz Yisrael*, to increase their understanding of the concept's importance in Judaism's historical development; and the Torah's laws and moral teachings, to make them aware of God's moral purpose.

According to Kaplan, if the Torah explains something in supernatural terms, it means that ancient people of the time interpreted life differently from the way we do today. Although their knowledge of the natural world differed from ours, in other respects the Bible's authors had much in common with us, and their insights thus remain profoundly valuable.

Reconstructing God. Rejecting the traditional idea of God as a supernatural force, Kaplan also felt quite comfortable with the idea that God means different things to different Jews. In various passages in his writings, he himself defined God in different ways: as the sum of everything that renders life worthwhile; as the force in the universe making for goodness, justice, mercy, and truth; as those natural forces making it possible for us to achieve our ideals; as that aspect of the Jewish people giving meaning to its peoplehood. For Kaplan, accepting the sovereignty of God means accepting divine assurance of the worth of human existence.

In a related manner, Kaplan rejected the idea of salvation as a supernatural process. For Kaplan, as in traditional Judaism, salvation does come from God, but this fact does not imply the promise of a reward in a world-to-come. Instead, it means striving for self-fulfillment in this world—for goals such as peace and ethical behavior. It is through such striving that people become worthy of being called the image of God.

Reconstructing the concept of God meant for Kaplan reconstructing Jewish prayer as well. Since he associated God so closely with individual self-fulfillment, for Kaplan prayer is directed to the best parts of ourselves. But he viewed prayer not as an individual communing with God; rather, the group joins together to affirm "a power in nature that responds to human need, if properly approached." Community prayer enables the individual to go beyond purely private concerns.

Convinced that Jewish worshipers should never feel required to pray for things in which they do not believe or in a manner they might possibly consider offensive, and believing that new prayers were needed to reflect modern needs, in 1945 Kaplan and some of his colleagues at the Society for the Advancement of Judaism boldly revised the traditional prayer book. At the time, his actions led an influential group of Orthodox rabbis to ban him and his works. But Kaplan's efforts helped foster the variety of Reform and Conservative prayer books available today.

Many Jews who have otherwise found much to admire in Kaplan's Reconstructionism, and who have incorporated many of his innovations into their lives, take strong exception to his concept of God. Some argue that he equates God only with positive forces; given that there is evil in the world, is there also a divine power of evil? Also, what exactly does Kaplan's insistence on self-fulfillment mean? For example, if Nazis truly felt that self-fulfillment required ridding the world of Jews, should their behavior be considered godly? It is impossible to model ourselves on a God who is so closely linked with self-fulfillment.

Other critics say, in more general terms, that Kaplan's God is only a figment of the human imagination—in effect, that he has created a divinity to serve human needs and by doing so has focused on only one of its aspects. Furthermore, by calling God a power in the universe, Kaplan failed to address the question of how the universe itself was formed. Many critics also object to the absence from Kaplan's theology of the silence and awe we so often feel when contemplating the universe. In this regard, the enormous growth in the Orthodox Movement in recent years, including the Hasidic Movement, testifies to the fact that Kaplan's idea of God leaves many searching Jews unsatisfied.

> " *A magnetic needle, hung on a thread or placed on a pivot, assumes of its own accord a position in which one end of the needle points north and the other south. . . . Likewise, man normally veers in the direction of that which makes for the fulfillment of his destiny as a human being. That fact indicates the functioning of a cosmic Power which influences his behavior. What magnetism is to the magnetic needle, Godhood or God is to man.* "
>
> *Questions Jews Ask*

TEACHER AND INNOVATOR

Intellectual Honesty, Women's Rights, and Family Peace

During Kaplan's long life, enormous change came to the Jews of America, to America as a whole, and to the world. He arrived in the United States as part of the late nineteenth-century wave of Jewish immigrants from Eastern Europe. His early teaching career and leadership of the Jewish Center coincided with America's participation in World War I. In the 65 years between the end of the war and Kaplan's death in 1983, America suffered through the Great Depression, World War II, the Korean War, and the war in Vietnam. Advances were made in civil rights and women's rights. Six million Jews died in the Holocaust. The Zionist dream of a Jewish state in *Eretz Yisrael* was fulfilled.

Kaplan left an indelible mark on American Jewry during this period. By focusing on a few aspects of his career, we can get a sense of the man and his impact.

Kaplan as Teacher. Kaplan began his career as an Orthodox rabbi, but this was not a fulfilling time for him. No longer believing in a supernatural God who bestowed the one true Torah on a chosen people, he felt like an impostor preaching to his congregants. He considered leaving the rabbinate and going into business.

Then, in 1909, he received a call that changed his life—as well as the future of Jewish life in America. Solomon Schechter, the president of the Jewish Theological Seminary, asked him to head the new Teachers Institute there. Kaplan accepted and, soon after, became a professor at the seminary's Rabbinical School as well. In the course of nearly four decades at the Teachers Institute, he introduced future educators to his ideas of Israel, Torah, and God. At the Rabbinical School, where he taught both Midrash (interpretation of biblical texts) and homiletics (the art of giving sermons), he introduced future rabbis to his belief that Torah study should be relevant to modern times.

Many of Kaplan's seminary students have said that only his guidance enabled them to become rabbis. This guidance was more than strictly religious. In the period between the two world wars, many Americans wondered if Communism was the solution to the country's economic and social problems, and Kaplan himself was strongly attracted to the movement's social ideals. Alone among the faculty at the seminary, he helped his students think through their ideological problems, teaching them, as he reminded himself, that a rabbi can do a great deal to promote economic equality by serving as "gadfly and conscience of the people who thrive on the capitalist economy."

Promoting Jewish Feminism.

Fifty years before equality for women in Judaism became a widely discussed issue in America (see the Epilogue), Kaplan was spearheading this cause. His father's influence seems, once again, to have been a factor. While the Kaplan family was still living in Europe, Rabbi Israel Kaplan faced the community's hostility for teaching Hebrew and religious texts to his gifted daughter, Mordecai's sister, Sophie. This incident may well have taught Mordecai both that women are just as capable of learning as men and that being unpopular should not deter us from acting on our beliefs. Kaplan had his first chance to advance women's rights in Judaism at the start of his career as rabbi at the Jewish Center in 1915. To mark the Center's dedication, each member of the congregation—including each woman—participated in the completion of a Sefer Torah ("Torah scroll") by inscribing a letter. On Kaplan's insistence, no *mechitzah* (the traditional curtain or divider separating women from men) was erected, the men being located in a large center section, with the women in full view in smaller sections on either side. Later, in a memorable sermon in the fall of 1918, he cited a line in Genesis (1:26) to stress that women were indeed intended as men's equals; he translated the verse: "Let us make humankind in our image, according to our likeness. Let *them* have dominion over the fish of the sea." Moving from this passage, Kaplan argued that God's original plan was to have men and women share equally in the world's business. Since the con-

Kaplan was a leader in advocating full women's participation in Jewish life and ritual observance. As early as the 1920s his sermons stressed the equality of women under Jewish law. In 1922 he officiated at the first Bat Mitzvah in the United States, that of his eldest daughter, Judith, paving the way for modern-day Bat Mitzvah ceremonies, such as the one shown here.

gregation at the Jewish Center was Orthodox, such early steps toward equality for women are all the more noteworthy.

Kaplan made up his mind to resign from the Jewish Center at the end of 1921. In 1920 he had published an article, "A Program for the Reconstruction of Judaism," in which he stated, "Nothing can be more repugnant to the thinking man of today than the fundamental doctrine of Orthodoxy, which is that tradition is infallible." The traditional members of his Orthodox congregation were outraged. When Kaplan and a group of like-minded members of the Jewish Center left to set up the Society for the Advancement of Judaism, equality for women was among the new congregation's first innovations.

In March 1922, Kaplan held the first bat mitzvah in the United States. The eldest of his four daughters, Judith, was called to the Torah at the Society for the Advancement of Judaism. On an earlier trip to Rome with his wife he had attended what was called a group bat mitzvah and had been disappointed by the young women's lack of involvement. In contrast, Judith Kaplan recited the blessings over the Torah, read the Haftarah, and performed all the other rituals expected of a young man.

Kaplan and Family Peace.
Kaplan was a believer in sh'lom bayit, or "peace within the family"—both the individual family unit and the larger family of American Jewry. An incident recorded in his diary for October 1922 shows his commitment to maintaining his own family's peace.

Each Friday before sundown, Kaplan had the habit of writing a letter to his mother. But one Friday he remembered it only after the Sabbath had already arrived. Traditional Jews do not write on the Sabbath, and Kaplan was still observing many mitzvot despite his break with the Orthodox Movement. But rather than let his observance upset his mother, after dinner he wrote his letter—in the bathroom— so as not to transgress in public.

Kaplan demonstrated his concern with communal sh'lom bayit in another way. For decades, some of his students urged him to break with the Conservative Jewish Theological Seminary and set up a separate Reconstructionist Movement, but Kaplan resisted. There were already too many issues dividing American Jews, and his main goal was to unify them, not to convince others of his wisdom.

But in 1968, five years after Kaplan's resignation from the Seminary at the age of 82, his students finally had their way. The Reconstructionist Rabbinical College opened its doors, and Reconstructionism became a separate American Jewish movement. The movement has flourished in the years since but remains small. Kaplan's impact on American Judaism, however, continues to be great.

The Influence of Reconstructionism on American Judaism

Kaplan has been compared to the Baal Shem Tov, the father of Hasidism, another influential Jewish religious movement. In a unique fashion, Hasidism and Reconstructionism remain bound up with the personalities of their founders. But unlike any other Jewish movement to date, Reconstructionism is purely American in origin.

American Jews tend now to take for granted many of the things Kaplan stood for, forgetting they are relatively new ideas that he introduced to the American Jewish public. Today's Orthodox, Conservative, and Reform Jews, for example, all accept Kaplan's position that religion and culture are intertwined. At Orthodox day schools, children learn not only Torah and commentaries but also modern Hebrew grammar and literature, Jewish history, and Israeli history and geography. From today's vantage point, it is hard to believe how radical Kaplan's suggestions seemed when he first made them.

Kaplan's Reconstructionism made it possible for many Jews to feel that their Jewish lives do not conflict with their lives as secular Americans. He presented a faith that Jews could uphold without having to tuck away their secular knowledge because it seemed to undermine traditional beliefs. Just as important, he showed that not only unpopular but even apparently heretical ideas can come to be warmly accepted over time.

RICHARD RUBENSTEIN

EMIL FACKENHEIM

ELIEZER BERKOVITS

IRVING GREENBERG

JOSEPH SOLOVEITCHIK

EUGENE BOROWITZ

CYNTHIA OZICK

RACHEL ADLER

BLU GREENBERG

JUDITH PLASKOW

EPILOGUE

ISSUES IN CONTEMPORARY JEWISH THOUGHT

Jewish thought continues to evolve. Today, a new generation of Jewish thinkers is addressing the issues and problems posed by our times, focusing on the areas of the Holocaust, the state of Israel, problems of modernity, and the changing role of women in society and in Judaism.

A DEVELOPING FIELD

Each of the preceding chapters has focused on a single individual whose life and work had lasting impact on Jewish thought. But philosophy does not stand still—it evolves, and today the field of Jewish thought continues its growth. In universities, seminaries, and scholarly journals, many men and women are making contributions to the field. We cannot know who ultimately will be considered the most significant, but we can identify several key questions that have engaged the minds of modern Jewish thinkers, and the individuals who have responded most clearly and directly to them. These men and women have defined the dialogue of the late twentieth century.

This epilogue discusses three issues occupying many modern Jewish thinkers. How do the Holocaust and the emergence of the state of Israel affect traditional Jewish belief and activity? How should Jewish obligation and belief reflect the problems of modernity as we enter the twenty-first century? How can Judaism best respond to the changing role of women in society?

In exploring modern thought, we do not know who the key thinkers will be, so we must organize our exploration around *areas* of thought rather than the lives of the *thinkers* themselves. This chapter will move its focus away from presenting a comprehensive view of each thinker's work, away from the biographical details of each thinker, and toward an understanding of the nature of the thought and where it appears to be heading. Which individuals will ultimately prove to make the greatest contributions must await the judgment of history.

HOLOCAUST AND STATE

Wrestling with God in the Aftermath of the Holocaust

The word "holocaust" means "great or complete devastation or destruction." Capitalized, Holocaust refers to the systematic destruction of European Jewry by the Nazis and their collaborators from 1933 to 1945. The Holocaust and the subsequent emergence of the state of Israel demand new ways of thinking about God and the Jewish people. Why did God not stop the Nazis from their brutal course of murder? Does the existence of a powerful Israel show that God is once again taking part in the course of history? And is the idea of God as important in our time as it was in the past? These questions continue to challenge the minds of Jewish thinkers.

Although World War II ended in 1945, over twenty years passed before the Holocaust became a central issue in Jewish religious thought. Several reasons have been suggested for this delay. First, the trauma of the Holocaust left some Jewish thinkers so numb that they could not absorb its meaning until the passage of years began to heal their wounds. Second, guilt over their inability to save their fellow Jews may have prevented others from considering it fully. Third, Jews began to feel strong enough to speak out against anti-Semitism only during the 1960s, when a period of ethnic pride began in the United States with the emergence of the civil rights movement. Fourth, the victory of the state of Israel in the Six Day War of 1967 made Jews feel less like victims of history, and more willing to confront the time when they had been most cruelly victimized.

The writer Elie Wiesel, himself a survivor of the Auschwitz death camp, was the first to open up the issue of the Holocaust. Wiesel concluded that Jews can no longer be satisfied with traditional explanations for God's failure to stop evil, and that the survival of the Jewish people has now become a sacred duty. But most profoundly, he pointed out that the Holocaust was so singularly different from any other human experience that it may be impossible to even formulate the right questions, let alone answer them. Yet this is the very challenge that other thinkers have tried to meet. For expressing the uniqueness of the Holocaust and for exploring the meaning of hate in modern times, Wiesel won the Nobel Peace Prize in 1986.

Following Wiesel's example, other thinkers began to use the name of the death camp Auschwitz as a symbol for all the ghettos and camps. How should a Jew respond to God's seeming absence from Auschwitz? At least four distinct positions, each associated with a different thinker, have emerged. While none of the views can be accepted as final, all four points of view illuminate important issues that need further thought.

Richard Rubenstein: "God Really Died at Auschwitz"

American-born Richard L. Rubenstein asks what responsibility God bears for Auschwitz. In 1961 a German-Protestant clergyman known as Probst Gruber told Rubenstein that the Holocaust "must have been God's will," inscrutable as it may be. Remarkably, Gruber had himself endangered his life by saving many Jews during the war.

This comment led Rubenstein to develop one of the truly important, and radical, modern Jewish theologies.

Rubenstein found Gruber's suggestion unacceptable. What sins could justify God's bringing such punishment on the Jews, or on any people? For Rubenstein, the God of Jewish tradition simply could not have let the Holocaust occur, and he concluded that this God does not exist.

But, surprisingly, Rubenstein found religion all the more important in the face of the death of God, and he developed a new theory of Judaism. Human beings—not God—plan their own lives, protect themselves, and in doing so give meaning to their lives. It is Jewish observance and community that allow this meaning, by ensuring that individuals have others to share their joys with and to assist and support them in times of trouble and distress. Rituals and observances bind people to their community. Jews belong to a tribe or nation that has a duty to preserve itself and protect its members.

Rubenstein argued that the concept of the Jews as a chosen people died with God, that Jews and Judaism occupy no such special status. Survival, not chosenness, should now be the key focus for Judaism. The state of Israel is key to Rubenstein's view of post-Holocaust Judaism, because it ensures Jewish survival and gives meaning to Jewish destiny. Perhaps as a result, he also argued that Israel cannot be held to a higher moral standard than other nations and that although Jews should lead ethical lives, Jewish standards of ethics need be no higher than other people's standards. Rubenstein also noted the importance of the American Jewish community for the survival of the Jewish people and said that American Jews are obligated to maintain a position of strength not only for themselves but also for the sake of Jews everywhere.

Emil Fackenheim: "The 614th Commandment"

Emil L. Fackenheim has a completely different view. Fackenheim spent several months in the Sachsenhausen concentration camp following *Kristallnacht*. He was among the last young liberal rabbis to leave Nazi Germany (in this case, to Canada); his escape was accomplished, in his words, "by sheer and incredible luck."

Fackenheim says that every religion has "root experiences" that profoundly influence all subsequent religious thought and belief. The first Jewish root experience was at the Red Sea, where the Israelites experienced "God's saving presence." The second was at Mount Sinai, where they experienced "God's commanding presence." For Fackenheim, these are two fundamentally different ways in which God can deal with human beings, and they explain the question of God's apparent absence at Auschwitz. There, he says, God's *commanding* presence was at hand, but God's *saving* presence was not.

We know that God gave the Torah with its 613 commandments at Mount Sinai. But Fackenheim says that at Auschwitz God issued a 614th commandment stating that "Jews are forbidden to hand Hitler posthumous victories." Though Hitler is dead, Jews who abandon their faith help carry out Hitler's wish to rid the world of the Jews. For Fackenheim, Jewish survival after Auschwitz is sacred in itself—without need of any higher purpose.

The 614th commandment encompasses one positive command and two negative ones. Jews must "remember the victims of Auschwitz, lest their memory perish." And Jews must never abandon faith in humanity or faith in God. In Fackenheim's words, Jews are forbidden "to despair of man and his world . . . lest they cooperate in delivering the world over to the forces of Auschwitz" or "to despair of the God of Israel, lest Judaism perish."

Fackenheim's insistence on this 614th commandment boldly defies the age-old Jewish tradition that considers the number 613 fixed for all time. But his boldness in itself is proof of the transforming significance of the Holocaust to modern Jewish life and thought.

According to Fackenheim, a Jew need not be religious to fulfill the 614th commandment. He feels that secular Jews are carrying out the commandment simply by remaining Jewish, living lives of "holy secularity." They keep God alive and preserve the memory of the spiritual resisters who perished in the death camps, who for Fackenheim have become the new model for Jewish observance.

The state of Israel is also a survivor of Nazi Germany; its very existence is a clear reminder of the commitment of the Jewish people to life. It too continues the spiritual resistance of the Jews in the death camps. Any threat to Israel recalls the Holocaust and its threat to Jewish survival.

Fackenheim insists that Jews must see the connection between the Holocaust and Israel and must preserve this connection. "The heart of every authentic response to the Holocaust . . . is a commitment to the autonomy and security of the state of Israel." For Fackenheim, one of the most important commandments is to build up Jewish life in Israel. He does not explicitly reject the idea of dying for the sake of God, but he places the highest value on living, and on living as a Jew.

Eliezer Berkovits:
"History Is the Area of Human Responsibility"

A third view comes from European-born Rabbi Eliezer Berkovits, who was able to leave Berlin in 1939. He came to America and served as an Orthodox rabbi and intellectual leader of his community. For Berkovits, Auschwitz is unique only in the magnitude of the evil it represents, not in the problem it presents for religious belief.

For Berkovits, dealing with the Holocaust does not force Jewish life and thought into new or nontraditional directions. The same question should be asked whether one or six million persons are murdered: How could God allow such a thing to happen? He observes that the Book of Lamentations asks a similar question about the destruction of the First Temple: "Look, Lord, and see: who is it whom You have tormented in this way? . . . All those whom I raised were destroyed by my enemies" (2:20, 22). Likewise, Psalm 44 asks, "Though we have not forgotten You, or been false to Your covenant . . . for Your sake we are slain. . . . Why do You hide Your face?"

Berkovits considers Auschwitz a gross injustice "countenanced by God" but caused by human beings with free will. According to Berkovits, God must be absent from history if human beings can be free to choose or to reject moral behavior. God's absence from history is in fact a sign of power: "God is mighty for He shackles His omnipotence and becomes 'powerless' so that history may be possible." Human beings create history, not God. Human beings, not God, are responsible for Auschwitz.

Berkovits does not claim to understand why God permitted "all the suffering of the innocent in history," but he has the traditional Jewish faith that in a realm beyond history, God will "redeem" all suffering. Furthermore, he argues that during the Holocaust many people performed acts of incredible heroism at great personal risk. There are many stories of heroism, ranging from simple families to whole communities, like Le Chambon, France, whose residents banded together to save Jews. Our knowledge of such acts should keep us from focusing exclusively on the Nazis' behavior.

Berkovits believes that viewing all Jewish history through the Holocaust misrepresents that history. The survival of the Jewish people after Auschwitz proves that godliness ultimately triumphs over evil. Berkovits sees the state of Israel as further proof that God continues to redeem human beings.

For Berkovits, Israel is even more important for Jews than was the Temple in Jerusalem 2,000 years ago. After the Romans destroyed it in

70 c.e., the rabbis developed a new Judaism independent of the Temple, which allowed Jews to continue to believe in God and practice Judaism in exile. Berkovits implies that the fate of Judaism today is more closely tied to the fate of Israel than the fate of Judaism of old was to the Temple. "The State of Israel is not the Temple of the Lord. But God can do without His Temple; He cannot do without Israel, the people, nor can He, in this post-Holocaust phase of world history, do without Israel, the State."

Irving Greenberg: The Holocaust Is a Challenge to Morality

American-born Rabbi Irving Greenberg has focused attention on the relationship among the Holocaust, the state of Israel, and American Jewry. Israel, he says, plays a key role in Jewish life, and American Jews play a key role in forging the future of Judaism.

Greenberg emphasizes that Jews are now full-fledged players on the world stage, and he criticizes what he views as earlier emphasis on Jews as victims. Greenberg also sees a commandment arising from the Holocaust, one demanding that Jews not only survive but also recognize the "human dignity and equality" of all people. Auschwitz requires that Jews ensure that they never deny "the absolute and equal dignity of the other."

As a result, Greenberg states, Jews have a special moral challenge. All Jews must be careful not to become indifferent to "the Holocaust of others." Israelis must be careful not to "use Israeli strength indiscriminately."

Greenberg divides Jewish history into three distinct periods. During each of these periods, he says, the covenantal relationship between God and the Jewish people has been fundamentally different. He calls them the Biblical, Rabbinic, and post-Holocaust periods.

The Jewish people was formed during the Biblical era, during which God was available to people through Temple rites and the words of the prophets. After the destruction of the Second Temple came the Rabbinic era, in which the rabbis developed ways for Jews to draw meaning from their powerlessness and exile. The rabbis interpreted the Jews' defeat not as a sign of God's abandonment but as God's calling Jews to a different type of relationship. The synagogue and Torah study replaced the Temple and biblical prophecy as the focal points of religious life.

The third era began with the Holocaust, and the covenant changed once again. Synagogue and Torah study are not enough. To fulfill the new demands of the covenant, says Greenberg, Jews must undertake a "new secular effort to recreate the infinite value of the human being." Jews must also work to build the Jewish state.

Greenberg argues that the existence of the state of Israel signals a profound change from the Jewish condition of powerlessness during the Rabbinic era. Jewish powerlessness is now immoral, since it threatens Jewish survival. No one, he says, should be equipped with less power than is necessary to achieve and maintain survival with dignity.

It is interesting to watch Greenberg wrestle with the implications of the use of Jewish power. In much of his work, Greenberg seems to share Rubenstein's view that Israel must not be judged by higher moral standards than other countries. Critics of Israel's use of power must beware lest their criticism endanger its survival.

But Greenberg also observes that political power complicates the life of the moral person. Jews must use their power, but they must use it appropriately. He insists that Jews never forget their former power-lessness and never become insensitive to the suffering of other people.

In "The Ethics of Jewish Power," Greenberg calls attention to what he calls "the dangerous alternatives" Jews have in reacting to Israel's political power. The alternatives are stark: "undermining Israel or abandoning it through excessive criticism and faulty judgments" on the one hand and "betraying Israel by giving it a moral blank check and uncritical love" on the other. Americans, and in fact Jews of every Diaspora community, must also remain strong, both for themselves and for the sake of the survival of the state of Israel. But all have a responsibility to balance the need for power—as the path to survival—against the obligation to use that power sensitively and appropriately.

THE COMPLICATIONS OF THE MODERN WORLD

Judaism in Modern Technological Society

Many people argue that the Holocaust was a turning point in world history. In earlier times, many people had faith in human per-fectibility—the idea that in each succeeding age human nature im-proves, that the advance of history means progress. For many, the horrors of World War II destroyed that faith. As if the Nazi atrocities were not enough, other political regimes in succeeding years have also inflicted unspeakable horrors on people other than Jews. It seems sometimes that the world is devoid of values and that ethical stan-dards—basic notions of right and wrong—are irrelevant.

Technological developments also trouble many. New technologies have made life safer and easier in many ways, but they can have a destructive side as well. Technology has changed the way people live, sometimes discouraging time–honored family practices. For example, many modern families spend their evenings watching television instead of engaging in the more traditional evening conversation. In households with many television sets, each family member may watch his or her own show, in complete isolation from other family members.

How to find a firm footing in a technological world seemingly without values is a problem that contemporary Jewish thinkers have approached from different perspectives. Joseph B. Soloveitchik has addressed the issue from an Orthodox point of view, while Eugene B. Borowitz views it through a liberal Jewish lens.

Joseph Soloveitchik's Lonely Man of Faith

Joseph B. Soloveitchik asks a simple question: Can a way of life based on *Halakhah*—Jewish law—offer anything to individuals in today's modern world? He says yes. Soloveitchik has been profoundly influential as one of the leaders of Orthodox Judaism. Through his learning, prominence, and writings he has had a significant effect on other branches of Judaism as well.

In his famous essay "The Lonely Man of Faith," Soloveitchik focuses the question more narrowly: Does a technological society have any room in it for the religious person, or is the religious person a useless oddity? Soloveitchik asks, "What can a man of faith like myself, living by a doctrine which has no technical potential, by a law which cannot be tested in the laboratory . . . what can such a man say to a functional utilitarian society. . . ?" In such a world, says Soloveitchik, religious faith "is given little credence as a repository of truth."

Soloveitchik concludes that the person of faith still can contribute. In fact, he argues that even in a technological society the requirements to adhere faithfully to Jewish practice are as strong as ever. He bases his argument on the two versions of the creation story in the Book of Genesis, and he develops a unique interpretation.

The first two chapters of Genesis tell the story of creation twice, but in two different ways, and Soloveitchik rejects the explanation that each was written by a different author. He insists that the two different versions instead reflect the twofold nature of every human being. He uses the names Adam I and Adam II to refer not only to the two different biblical versions but also to these two tendencies of each person.

Soloveitchik says that Adam I was created in God's image at the same time as Eve and was told by God—called *Elohim*—to "subdue" the land. Adam II, formed from dust and without a female partner, was told by God—called both *Adonai* and *Elohim*—to cultivate the earth "and to watch it" as a caretaker.

According to Soloveitchik, Adam I represents the drive to increase human dignity by overcoming natural obstacles and threats. Adam I strives to master nature and refuses to stand helpless in the face of disease, famine, and natural disaster. Adam I is fully at home in the world of technology, and is interested in understanding how the world works. Soloveitchik says that technologically oriented human beings are carrying out God's will that people not be enslaved by their environment.

Adam II represents our dependency on, and our need to seek relationship with, God. Indeed, Soloveitchik's description of Adam II may remind the reader of Heschel's understanding of God in search of man and Buber's focus on developing a relationship with God. But Soloveitchik describes the search in a unique way, saying that Adam II wonders: "Why was the world created...? From the depths of my being, I sense a message and challenge being directed at me. What is it? Who is it who trails me steadily, like a persistent shadow...?"

Where Adam I seeks to master nature, Adam II seeks only to be its caretaker as a privileged servant of God. Adam II is satisfied to limit his activities out of deference to God. The fact that God breathed into Adam II's nostrils "the breath of life" suggests for Soloveitchik just how close the relationship is between God and Adam II. The difference in the two Adams' relationship with God is underscored by the different names of God in the two versions. Soloveitchik says that Adam I is satisfied with acknowledging God as *Elohim*, the name that tradition interprets as "Ruler of All Natural Forces." But Adam II wants a more personal relationship with God and seeks *Adonai*, the name that traditionally represents the God of mercy, of dialogue, of intimacy.

Soloveitchik does not ignore the role of the two Eves in the creation stories. Eve I is created together with Adam I, who never experienced loneliness. As a practical man, he needed a work partner from the beginning. Their relationship, however egalitarian, was one only of convenience. But Adam II went through the experience of loneliness first, and only then gave up part of himself so that Eve II could be formed. Their relationship was deeper than the working partnership between Adam I and Eve I. Together they formed what Soloveitchik calls the first "faith-community," by reaching out to God and to each other.

Soloveitchik calls Adam II "the lonely man of faith" in today's world. Although Adam II might prefer to withdraw from the world,

Halakhah requires that he "become involved in the worldly work community as a creative participant." Soloveitchik suggests two contributions that Adam II can make to technological society. First, Adam II can demonstrate that religion is more than a mere "useful adjunct to life." Technology has *not* made our world spiritually better, and emphasis on the human religious spirit is therefore essential. Adam II can show that religion, whatever its social utility, is truly based in the divine and that "there is more to religion than the pious gesture and the reassuring ceremonial."

Second, Adam II can demonstrate that God underlies human ethical concerns. Adam I's ethical positions "are not anchored in the absolute," which makes it too easy to compromise ethical standards. "Adam II would envelop ethics with Godliness and restrain man's rampaging nature." Both Adam I and Adam II have important contributions to make, says Soloveitchik, and both are indispensable.

Ultimately, Soloveitchik finds no way out of loneliness for the person of faith. No matter how many friends and associates Adam II may have, loneliness is a religious condition from which there is no escape—it is the "historical mission" of Adam II to bring the message of faith to the world. Technological society has not done away with the need for the contribution of faith or for the requirement to adhere faithfully to Jewish practice.

Eugene Borowitz: The Need for Spirituality in Liberal Judaism

Eugene B. Borowitz, a professor at Hebrew Union College–Jewish Institute of Religion, has pondered the same issues for liberal Jews: How do developments in the modern world affect the beliefs and the practices of Jews today? He cautions that liberals, in their emphasis on ethical behavior, may have neglected the spiritual content of Judaism *and* the Jewish content of spirituality. They may have neglected the central role of the covenant that binds each individual Jew to God. By doing so, he says, liberal Jews have moved away from the specifically Jewish nature of the religious quest, creating a modern crisis that demands a threefold response from Jews: increasing the emphasis on traditional Jewish practice and observance; developing a greater sense of connection between Jews and God and among Jews; and building a commitment to the human spirit that transcends human experience.

While modern science and technology have made the physical lives of most people better and easier, Borowitz points to large numbers of people for whom physical well-being is far from enough, who find a purely material existence profoundly hollow. He points to many liberal Jews who formerly described themselves as agnostics, claiming it is impossible to know whether there is a God. But Borowitz believes that in witnessing amoral behavior—of both governments and individuals—many self-styled agnostics have become aware of the horrific consequences of "truly believing in nothing." This awareness has inspired many of these Jews to search for a spiritual foundation to their lives.

Borowitz believes that Judaism can provide a spiritual foundation for life in modern society. He says that in fact there is a "spiritual content implicit in what they thought was non-belief," and that Jewish spiritual fulfillment depends on a belief in "the Transcendent Other," a sense of God that gives meaning to human experience even when people do not consciously think of God. It is the part of human experience that is greater than human beings themselves.

But this transcendent God must be experienced through observance in Jewish contexts, says Borowitz, and with a sense of the Jewish place in the broader world. How can liberal Jews be brought to this awareness? Borowitz emphasizes three existing features of Jewish life: leadership roles, religious practice, and sensitivity to experience.

Jewish Leaders as Spiritual Role Models.

When Borowitz talks of leaders as spiritual role models, it is reminiscent of the Hasidic teaching that the *Tzaddik* should "be Torah" rather than merely teach it. But Borowitz goes even further. He believes that leaders should communicate their religious ideas and personal religious development with others, openly and without self-consciousness, since they are all involved in this search. Leaders must "reach out to the other's spiritual reality which we should learn to regard as seriously as our own."

Religious Practice as a Route to Spirituality.

Borowitz argues that merely performing *mitzvot* does not guarantee a sense of spirituality but that liberal Jews *can* make the *mitzvot* that they perform more meaningful. For example, many Jews welcome *Shabbat* by blessing the candle-lighting, wine, and bread. Borowitz suggests that as they say these and other blessings, liberal Jews should try to see them as ways "to renew our contact and strengthen our relationship with the Transcendent Other." And Borowitz adds that "If I could learn to say more *berachot* ["blessings"] I might be able to expand the place of the Transcendent Other in my daily life."

Borowitz does not designate which practices are most important. Early in his career he recognized the personal ability of every Jew to determine how to practice Judaism and which customs to engage in. Borowitz claimed that while the Jewish relationship to God is based on a commandment to each individual Jew, God "does not deprive" any Jew of the freedom to respond to that commandment individually. The covenant remains, but freedom is retained.

Sensitivity to Powerful Moments. Borowitz's third approach to enhancing the spiritual content of life involves being open to "moments of special spiritual potency which can occur at any time." It is all too easy, he says, to let such moments slip by, but if prepared, one can "say a word, do an act, create a silence, that links the soul to the Transcendent Other."

Borowitz offers no magical road to the spirituality that he believes is essential to finding meaning in modern Jewish life. But he emphasizes the need for personal freedom in each Jew's relationship to God, and he puts the important religious themes into fresh, modern contexts. For example, Borowitz introduced the concept of "reverse *tzimtzum*." Isaac Luria developed the concept of *tzimtzum* to refer to God's self-restraint at the time of creation: God had to draw back to make room for creation in a universe that was totally filled by God. Borowitz brings the idea forward by talking of reverse *tzimtzum*: liberal Jews who have been content to think that people can "do it all" have to withdraw a bit to make room for God in their lives. Borowitz thus underscores the urgency of restoring the spiritual life of the liberal Jew.

THE ROLE OF WOMEN AS JEWISH THINKERS

Jewish Feminist Thought

Many readers of this book will not remember a time when there were no female rabbis, or when women were not counted in a *minyan* or called to the Torah. But all readers may note that this book has thus far discussed no female thinkers. There is a simple reason: for centuries, the highly valued life of study and prayer was reserved for men.

Today in the American Jewish community women serve as rabbis, congregational leaders, and scholars. But Jewish law and the interpretation of biblical and rabbinic texts have historically been formed by Jewish men alone. Feminist thinkers have shown that female experiences have been excluded from texts, from observance, and from prayer. But since the 1970s Jewish women in the United States have been seeking a more active role in the development of future thought and law. A number of modern scholars have sought ways to change the laws to reflect modern practices and to allow women to participate more fully in Jewish intellectual and spiritual life.

A Response to the Holocaust or to Secular Feminism?

Most Jewish feminists associate the development of their movement with the rise of secular feminism in the United States. But for the writer Cynthia Ozick, feminist issues are raised by the Holocaust itself. According to Ozick, who was born in 1928, the Holocaust made clear to women of her generation the effects of "mass loss . . . of those who would have grown into healers, discoverers, poets." She insists that making this connection broadens the meaning of the Holocaust, of "its famously inescapable message: that after the Holocaust *every* Jew will be more a Jew than ever before."

Ozick laments the fact that generations of Jewish women have been prevented from participating fully in Jewish life, have been lost to Judaism as "Jewish ethical thinkers, poets, juridical consciences." She estimates that the loss has exceeded that of a hundred pogroms. More frightening, she says, is that Jews have inflicted this loss on themselves. By silencing the voices of half the community, Jewish authorities have practiced "cultural self-destruction."

Can *Halakhah* Respond to Jewish Feminist Demands?

Jewish feminists disagree whether women can achieve full participation in Jewish life through *Halakhah*—Jewish law. Ozick, a traditional Jew herself, believes that *Halakhah* is flexible enough to respond to the demands of Jewish women. Two other thinkers who have shared that point of view are Rachel Adler and Blu Greenberg.

Adler's essay, "The Jew Who Wasn't There: *Halakhah* and the Jewish Woman," appeared in a special issue of *Davka* magazine in 1971, and has since become a classic text of Jewish feminism. Adler began the essay by asserting that women have been made "peripheral Jews," a category in ancient literature that includes not only women but also children and slaves. Women, children, and slaves are all exempt from fulfilling selected *mitzvot* and are ineligible to provide testimony in a Jewish court of law. But boys can grow up and become men, and slaves can be set free. Only girls, later women, must remain in this category from birth until death.

Adler acknowledged that for centuries Jewish women were better protected under religious laws than were non-Jewish women. But she noted that the last major ruling to improve the condition of Jewish women took place nearly a thousand years ago, when Rabbenu Gershom ben Judah forbade Jews of the Western world to marry more than one wife. She further observed that many of the Jewish laws of marriage and divorce still discriminate against women.

Adler called for the *halakhic* scholars of the day to confront these problems. Marriage and divorce laws needed rethinking. Women must no longer be seen solely as caretakers of their families' physical needs, as "tools with which men do *mitzvot*." Makers of Jewish law must recognize that many Jewish women are "Jewish souls in distress."

Adler concluded that if *halakhic* scholars do not respond to feminist pleas, women themselves must take *Halakhah* in their own hands: "The most learned and halakhically committed among us must make *halakhic* decisions for the rest." But she insisted that such actions should be undertaken only as a last resort. "That is a move to be saved for desperate straits, for even the most learned of us have been barred from acquiring the systematic *halakhic* knowledge which a rabbi has."

Blu Greenberg pushed Adler's thought further, while remaining committed to solutions rooted in *Halakhah*. A poet, writer, and active feminist, Greenberg called for women to become active participants in the *halakhic* process. "Women must be trained to make legal decisions, not only for women, but for the entire Jewish community."

Beyond *Halakhah* into History and Theology

Since the early 1970s women have dramatically expanded their participation within the Jewish community. The Conservative, Reform, and Reconstructionist movements all have welcomed women as rabbis and cantors. There are more women today in Jewish academic life. Changes have occurred in many official settings: the classroom, the synagogue, and the workplace. And as more women become religious and scholarly role models for the Jewish community, we can expect additional growth in the participation of women, even if this growth occurs slowly over a long period of time.

In subsequent years, new thinkers have built upon the work of Ozick, Adler, and Greenberg. One such thinker is Judith Plaskow, who asserts that changes in *Halakhah* alone will never be enough to meet the goals of Jewish feminism. She notes that women had no part in creating *Halakhah* and asks why women should have confidence that it will be their "medium of expression and repair."

For Plaskow, Jewish feminism means more than equal rights for women in a system completely formulated by men; it means "the thoroughgoing transformation of religion and society." Women must be encouraged to go beyond merely moving into men's roles, to a point where they develop unique women's roles and expressions of Jewish life.

Similar fundamental changes in Judaism have occurred in the past, notes Plaskow. She compares the revolution she advocates to the enormous rethinking of Judaism that took place after the destruction of the Second Temple. Rabbinic Judaism "itself was the product of enormous change—a shift from Temple sacrifice as the center of worship, to study and prayer as the dual foci of Judaism." Why, she asks, do we view this major change as "a transition" and not as a break with the Jewish past or even as a revolution? Today's Jewish community can will itself to bring about a fundamental restructuring of Judaism without viewing it as a rupture with the past.

In order to bring about this fundamental restructuring, Plaskow calls for a complete reevaluation of each of the the three basic Jewish categories: Torah, Israel, and God. Mordecai Kaplan also felt that each of these categories needed to be "reconstructed," but the problems he identified were different. From Plaskow's perspective, each of the categories needs to be rethought because each has been shaped almost exclusively by men, and each contributes to the image of women as secondary to men.

Torah. Plaskow's radical Jewish feminism does not seek to do away with Torah but, rather, "to create a Torah that is whole"—a Torah inclusive of women. To do so, she calls on feminists to expand the boundaries of Torah through Midrash, the interpretation of biblical texts. In the past Midrash has enabled the rabbis (always men) to expand concise biblical statements into fully developed *Halakhah*. The technique of Midrash also enabled the rabbis to go beyond the stories in the biblical texts—to develop characters, motives, and deeds far beyond what the text itself actually states.

Plaskow notes that when the Torah deals with women, it does so mainly from a man's point of view. Jewish feminists have already begun expanding the boundaries of Torah by using the techniques of Midrash themselves. Ellen Umansky, for example, has written a Midrash shedding some light on what Sarah might have been feeling during the binding of Isaac. Other feminists can continue to expand the Torah's meaningfulness for all members of the Jewish community.

Israel. The central Jewish category "Israel" is a broad one, encompassing not only the Jewish people but also the Land of Israel and, since 1948, the Jewish state as well. For Plaskow, this category also must be rethought.

Why are the Jews called the people of Israel, after all? Israel is an alternative name of the patriarch Jacob. Jacob had two wives, but the Jews are not called the people of Rachel and Leah. Similarly, the biblical twelve tribes are named for the sons of Jacob. His daughter was not so honored.

Plaskow also highlights social conditions in the state of Israel that are at odds with feminist goals. Many people believe that early Zionists sought a society in which men and women play equal roles, but early pioneer women often washed, cooked, and cleaned for the men, who worked the land. According to Plaskow's controversial view, "Sexual equality never was taken seriously in Israel as an important social goal."

God. Perhaps the Jewish category most resistant to change is the one we call "God." The language we use to speak of God is so firmly ingrained that to many people changing it would be revolutionary, too much a break with the past. And yet, notes Plaskow, if "to speak of God is to speak of what we most value," then every time we talk of God as a father, a king, or a warrior, we are affirming male, but not female, roles. Every time we think of God in masculine terms, we "value the quality and those who have it." By implication, she says, we devalue women, excluding them from "a central attribute of God."

Plaskow points to a few images of God as a mother in the Bible. The prophet Isaiah, for example, speaks of God's crying "like a woman in labor" and offering to comfort the people of Israel "as a mother comforts her son." But she also notes that none of these female images is used in Jewish prayer. She suggests that Jews follow the example of feminists who have already begun to use female language when addressing God. Incorporating women's experiences into our view of God will help bring "the suppressed experience of women into the Jewish fold." Poet Marcia Falk, for example, has composed important prayers that take women's experiences into account.

The goals of Jewish feminism, "while they include *halakhic* restructuring, reach beyond *Halakhah* to transform the bases of Jewish life." Plaskow speculates that to become part of feminist Judaism, *Halakhah* would have to "begin with the assumption of women's equality." Women and men would play an equal role in forming *Halakhah*, "codetermining the questions raised and the answers given."

Plaskow does not rule out the possibility that today's Jewish society will follow the model of the Jewish world after the destruction of the Second Temple and accept a total reshaping of Judaism. But she does not believe it likely. Instead, she foresees a mixture of Jewish feminist responses to *Halakhah*. Some women will "reject *Halakhah* entirely." Others will "quietly promote revolution in their own communities, making real in their lives the Judaism they hope someday to see in the wider Jewish world." In fact, Plaskow contends that "a *halakhic* revolution is already in process" as a result of the fact that more and more women are becoming rabbis and studying *halakhic* sources.

LOOKING TO THE FUTURE

No one can predict what course Jewish thought will take over the next thousand years. What issues will engage the minds of Jewish thinkers? Will there be as many women thinkers as men? From what countries will they come? In what languages will they write? How will their views of Judaism differ from views familiar to Jews today? What attitudes will they have toward the concepts of God, Torah, and Israel?

There are no answers, but it is certain that Jewish thought will continue to grow and thrive. There are some notable signs. In the 1920s Franz Rosenzweig lamented that the Enlightenment had unintentionally impoverished Jewish life by luring many Jews from religious study to secular pursuits. Today Jewish and secular studies enrich each other. The same author may write for a general magazine or for one of the twenty or more journals aimed at primarily Jewish audiences. Jewish-studies programs at hundreds of universities introduce both Jewish and non-Jewish students to the world of Jewish scholarship.

In today's world people can travel and communicate with one another as never before. More people are aware of the interactions among various fields of study and thought. In this expansive and global intellectual change may lie the greatest opportunity for the mutual enrichment of Jews and non-Jews. Jewish thought can now, more than ever before, retain its unique color while participating in the intellectual issues of the broader world.

GLOSSARY

Agnosticism: from the Greek word meaning "not knowing"; the belief that questions about the existence of God cannot be answered.

Amidah: the Hebrew word for "standing"; the central prayer of every Jewish service, which is nearly always said while standing.

Anthropomorphism: from the Greek words for "human" and "form"; attributing human characteristics to a nonhuman being or thing.

Assimilation: the process through which one social and cultural group becomes part of another social and cultural group.

Ayn Sof: the Hebrew words for "Infinite" or "Endless"; according to the Kabbalists, the deepest level of God, which the human mind can never comprehend.

Blood accusation, blood libel: the claim that Jews use the blood of a murdered non-Jew to prepare Passover matzah. Arising in England in the twelfth century, the blood libel was leveled against the Jews in several countries more than forty times in the nineteenth and twentieth centuries, notably in the Damascus Affair in Syria in 1840, and in the Beilis case in Russia in 1911.

Brit: the Hebrew word for "covenant," especially one between God and humanity.

Covenant: from the Latin meaning "to come together," or "to agree"; the agreement binding God and the Jewish people together from biblical to modern times.

Devekut: the Hebrew word for "cleaving" or "clinging"; the state of mind of one who feels constantly in the presence of God, not only during worship but also in all other activities.

Dialogue: the key term in Martin Buber's philosophy, which extends it beyond its everyday meaning of "conversation"; according to Buber, dialogue is an "I-Thou" (as opposed to "I-It") relationship, which need involve no words. Human beings can enter into dialogue not only with one another but also with nature, with art, and with God.

Diaspora: from the Greek word for "dispersion"; Jewish settlement outside Israel.

Diaspora Zionism: the view of Zionism associated with Mordecai Kaplan, that Jewish life in the Diaspora and in Eretz Yisrael are each necessary and should enrich one another.

Emancipation: from the Latin word meaning "to free from control"; in Jewish history, the abolition of laws limiting the freedom of Jews.

Emanations: in Kabbalistic thought, the hidden powers and lights that issue forth from the Ayn Sof. See also Sefirot.

Ethical monotheism: the belief that the unique God sets high ethical standards that encourage humanity to seek a more perfect world. One of the linchpins of the philosophy of Hermann Cohen. See also Messianism and Prophetism.

Ethics: a system of moral principles.

Exilarch: literally, "leader of the exiled"; one of a line of hereditary rulers of the Babylonian Jewish community from about the second century C.E. to the beginning of the eleventh century.

Free will: the doctrine that human behavior results from personal choice and is not simply predetermined by outside forces.

Halakhah: from the Hebrew word meaning "to walk"; the entire body of Jewish law.

Hasid, pl. Hasidim: literally, "pious one"; a member of a sect founded in eighteenth-century Poland by the Baal Shem Tov. See Tsaddik.

Hasidism: the principles and practices of the Hasidim, including an emphasis on mysticism, prayer, religious zeal, and joy.

Haskalah: literally, "enlightenment"; a movement to transform Jewish education and habits to bring them into line with those of the non-Jewish world. The Haskalah movement led to a rebirth of Hebrew language and literature.

Hibbat Zion: literally, "love of Zion"; a nationalist movement that arose among Russian Jews in the 1880s, which sought to establish Jewish settlements in Eretz Yisrael before the creation of the World Zionist Organization.

Histadrut: the General Federation of Labor in Israel, organized in 1920.

Homiletics: the art of preaching sermons.

Kabbalah: literally, "tradition"; Jewish mysticism. *The Zohar* is the basic work of the Kabbalah.

Kabbalist: a student of or expert in the Kabbalah.

Karaite: from the Hebrew word for "Scripture"; a member of a Jewish sect founded in the eighth century, which claimed that the Bible was the only source of Jewish law and practice, and therefore rejected the Talmud and other rabbinic teachings.

Kavannah: literally, "intention" or "concentration"; the ability to act—and especially to pray—with true feeling and understanding.

Lurianic Kabbalah: the system of Kabbalah developed by Isaac Luria. See also Tzimtzum, Shevirat HaKelim, and Tikkun.

Marrano: from the Spanish word for "swine"; a Spanish or Portuguese Jew who was forcibly converted to Christianity, especially one who remained secretly faithful to Judaism.

Messianism: the belief in a better future for all mankind; according to Hermann Cohen, the idea of messianism began with a focus on a single human savior but developed into a belief in an era of history in which the task of ethics would be advanced. See also Ethical Monotheism and Prophetism.

Midrash: literally, "investigation"; a type of rabbinic literature that explains and amplifies the Bible, often through maxims and stories.

Mitzvah: pl. Mitzvot: literally, "commandment." One of the 613 commandments the Torah is traditionally believed to contain. Also, any good deed or act of kindness.

Monotheism: from the Greek words for "one" and "god"; the belief that there is only one God. See Polytheism.

Mysticism: the belief that contemplation or ecstasy can enable the human soul to enter into direct union with God.

Myth: a traditional or legendary story, especially one about a deity that explains some phenomenon.

Political Zionism: movement founded by Theodor Herzl, which held that the "Jewish problem" could be solved only by the establishment of a Jewish state recognized by the great world powers. See Spiritual Zionism.

Polytheism: from the Greek words for "many" and "god"; the belief in many gods.

Prophetism: one of the linchpins of the philosophy of Hermann Cohen, who believed that the teachings of the biblical prophets helped focus Jewish moral awareness. See also Ethical Monotheism and Messianism.

Proselyte: from the Greek "newcomer"; a convert.

Radical amazement: a term used by Abraham Heschel to describe the sense of wonder and awe people feel when they are open to manifestations of God's presence in the world.

Rationalism: the philosophical doctrine that reason alone is the source of knowledge.

Redemption: the idea of salvation, which has meant different things in different eras of Jewish history. In Lurianic Kabbalah redemption is hastened by the performance of mitzvot. In the philosophy of Franz Rosenzweig, redemption is the way people interact with the world—a turning towards other people of a person who has experienced God's love through revelation.

Responsa: from the Latin meaning "replies"; answers in letter form by noted rabbis and Jewish scholars to questions sent to them about Halakhah.

Revelation: God's self-disclosure to human beings. According to Franz Rosenzweig, revelation is the way in which God interacts with human beings, resulting not in laws binding on all but in commandments personally addressed to an individual.

Revisionists: a Zionist party founded in 1925, which called for a more militant approach to realizing Zionist goals than those favored by other Zionist groups.

Sefirot: from the Hebrew meaning "spheres"; in Kabbalistic thought, the ten spheres issuing forth from the Ayn Sof, through which God interacts with the world. See also Ayn Sof and Emanations.

Shemittah: the Hebrew term for "sabbatical year"; according to the Bible, every seventh year, during which the land had to lie fallow and all outstanding debts were cancelled.

Shevirat HaKelim: literally, "the breaking of the vessels"; in Lurianic Kabbalah, a cosmic accident took place at the time of creation, as a result of which some divine sparks of light are scattered, imprisoned in husks of evil.

Spiritual Zionism: form of Zionism advocated by Ahad HaAm in preference to Herzl's Political Zionism. According to Ahad HaAm, before a Jewish state was established, the spiritual survival and development of the Jewish people needed to be assured. The Jewish homeland in Eretz Yisrael should above all be a spiritual center for Jewish communities in the Diaspora.

Theomorphism: from the Greek words for "god" and "shape"; a term associated with the philosophy of Abraham Joshua Heschel. According to Heschel, the prophets' demands on people are theomorphic, because they are models for human behavior based on a comparison to God. See also Anthropomorphism.

Theotropism: from the Greek words for "god" and "turning"; a term associated with the philosophy of Abraham Joshua Heschel. Theotropism is the turning of human beings toward or away from God.

Tikkun: from the Hebrew meaning "repair" or "improvement"; in Lurianic Kabbalah, the process through which human beings can set the world in order, to eliminate the evil unleashed at the time of Shevirat HaKelim.

Tsaddik: literally "righteous one"; in Hasidism, a charismatic leader of Hasidim.

Tzeddakah: from the Hebrew word for "justice." Money for the needy. Also, the act of giving charity.

Tzimtzum: literally "drawing back" or "contraction"; in Lurianic Kabbalah, the contraction of the Ayn Sof at the time of creation, to make room for the universe.

Unifications: in the Kabbalistic system, the responses in heaven to the observance of mitzvot on earth; unifications make it possible for God's mercy to flow down to earth, while failure to observe mitzvot causes heavenly blemishes that prevent unifications.

Zionism: a worldwide Jewish movement that resulted in the establishment of the state of Israel and that continues to promote the development of that state.

Zohar: literally, "splendor"; the basic text of Kabbalah.

INDEX

9R